THE FILMS OF FRANK SINATRA

THE FILMS OF

FRANK SINATRA

GENE RINGGOLD AND CLIFFORD McCARTY

A CITADEL PRESS BOOK   PUBLISHED BY CAROL PUBLISHING GROUP

PHOTO ACKNOWLEDGMENTS

CBS; Columbia Pictures Television; Valerie Douglas and Herb Honis, United Artists; Albert Lord; Metro-Goldwyn-Mayer; Arthur C. Peterson; Gene Ringgold; Frank Rodriguez, 20th Century-Fox; Ric Ross; Showtime; Frank Sinatra; Jerry Vermilye; Warner Bros.-Seven Arts.

For their various courtesies, the authors also thank the American Society of Composers, Authors and Publishers (ASCAP); Ric Ross; Joan Stadman, Time-Life Broadcast Inc.; Mildred Simpson and staff, Library of the Academy of Motion Picture Arts and Sciences.

Special thanks to Alvin H. Marill for updating this latest edition.

CONTENTS

FOREWORD

The facets of Frank Sinatra's career are so many and so varied it will take more than several volumes to capture his professional life completely. His personal life is a matter he may one day share with the world. A volume devoted exclusively to Sinatra recordings is imminent and the man of television and the nightclub circuit deserves recognition. This volume, however, deals only with Sinatra's motion picture career. For it is Sinatra, the actor, who is, in my opinion, always interesting and often versatile.

Some of his films are a monumental tribute to him personally because they are so poor, albeit commercial. One may well wonder why he consented to appear in them. And yet the roles with which he has been most successful, Maggio in *From Here to Eternity* and Frankie Machine in *The Man With the Golden Arm*, are not like the real Sinatra at all. They are genuine characterizations of which any artist can be proud. His musical contributions to films have all been delivered with the same charm and ease Bing Crosby displays and even if he can't dance as well as Fred Astaire or Gene Kelly he can still be a top chorus boy.

A proud, complex, diverse and passionate man, Frank Sinatra is also something else; something wrongly attributed to other show personalities: total talent.

GENE RINGGOLD

At a recording session.

INTRODUCTION

Sinatra, second from left in front row, with a Major Bowes amateur troupe.

Frank Sinatra's legendary career has been so all encompassing it is impossible to chronicle all aspects of it in one book. And although his talent remains as potent as it was during his reign as "The Voice" it seems the ideal time to reflect on his career as a motion picture star now that he has announced his "retirement" plans.

No other show business personality, past or present, has had quite the success, notoriety, or public involvement in his career as the phenomenon known as Frank Sinatra. Other singers of popular songs have been more highly regarded but are certainly less durable. Other actors are more talented and sought after but few of them can match the charm, ease, competence, and professionalism which generates audience interest in all his performances. Other recording stars have sold more records and made much more money at it but none have enjoyed the longevity and high calibre of artistry which almost all Sinatra platters contain. Surely no other superstar has aroused so many mixed feelings about his private as well as his public image.

It's not surprising that he has rightly been named "The Chairman of the Board" of all show business. Who else but a man of his total talent deserves to be so called?

THE "STARLING" YEARS

Francis Albert Sinatra was born in a frame house on Monroe Street in Hoboken, New Jersey, on December 12, 1915, although during his early days as a singing star the year was given as 1917. The birth was a difficult one because he was a large baby and instrument delivery was necessary. During the course of it one of his ears, his neck, and part of his face were injured by an anxious doctor's forceps. In later years, much to the dismay of executives at both RKO and MGM studios, Sinatra disdained their suggestions that he submit to cosmetic surgery to have those birth scars removed.

His father, Martin Anthony Sinatra, and his mother, Natalie Garavanti, both of Italian ancestry, had been married more than six years when Frank, their only child, was born.

Before Frank's birth, his father had been a professional fighter and used the name of Marty O'Brien. For a while Marty owned and operated a local tavern where his wife worked as a barmaid. Another fighter in the family was an uncle, Dominick Garavanti, a flyweight boxer who called himself Babe Sieger.

Natalie Sinatra, known to her friends as Dolly, was never very enthusiastic about working in her husband's tavern, so consequently she became a trained practical nurse. More often than not she was hired and paid by some public works organization to attend the needs of people who could not otherwise afford medical care at home. During the course of her work she became interested and involved in the problems of the working class of Hoboken and got to know the wives and families of the many longshoremen and other dock workers in that thriving seaport. It wasn't too long before her philosophy for settling a worker's complaint against a threatening landlord or an impervious steamship company official of "Let's fight this out at city hall" became well known.

Ultimately Natalie became politically active in the Democratic Party then ruled by the tough and notorious Boss Hague. Every election, she could be counted on to deliver a large bloc of votes from her district for the current Democratic candidate. It has been said that through her connections with Hoboken's mayor, Bernard McFeeley, for whom she had vigorously campaigned, her husband Marty was appointed to the city's fire department. Subsequently he earned a promotion to the rank of captain.

During the years immediately following Frank's birth, Natalie had little time for domesticity, so his care and early upbringing was attended to by his maternal grandmother, Rosa Garavanti, who operated a neighborhood grocery store. Nevertheless Frank was never denied the love and attention of his doting parents. His mother lavished him with an ample allowance of spending money and saw to it that he was the best dressed child in elementary school. His father, and his uncle Dom, stressed the importance of physical training and the need to learn the art of self-defense. By the time Frank was ten other neighborhood boys, two and three years his senior, discovered that the thin and frail looking kid, known by the nickname of Slacksy, because of his penchant for always being well dressed, was more than capable of defending himself whenever the occasion presented itself. Gregarious and generous in sharing his weekly allowance with less fortunate playmates, he had no trouble making friends.

Life, however, was something less than idyllic in the city of Hoboken and the population, a mixture of many races and nationalities, lived in an atmosphere that was always charged with brutal racial tensions. One of Frank's earliest ambitions, reflecting the love and intelligence with which he had been raised, was to fight racial intolerance in whatever way he could whenever the opportunity presented itself. More than once he forced that opportunity, thereby making enemies and headlines.

"I'm not the kind of guy who does a lot of brain work about why or how I happen to get into something," he said. "I get an idea, maybe I get sore about something. And when I get sore enough I do something about it.

"In Hoboken, when I was a kid, I lived in a plenty tough neighborhood. When somebody called me a 'dirty little Guinea' there was only one thing to do—break his head. When I got older I realized you shouldn't do it that way. I realized you've got to do it through education.

"Children are not to blame, it's the parents. How can a child know whether his playmate is an Italian, a Jew or Irish, unless his parents had discussed it in the privacy of their home. They hear their parents talk about the McGintys and the Ginsbergs and they must think there is something wrong with being a Catholic or Jew. They would not have such thoughts in their minds if they hadn't already been planted there."

Years later, in Hollywood, Sinatra discussed his philosophy with producer-director Mervyn LeRoy, a crusader who helped bring about humane changes in Georgia's penal system through his powerful indictment of it in his 1932 film, *I Am a Fugitive From a Chain Gang*. LeRoy suggested they work together and make a film dealing with the subject. In no time at all they interested producer Frank Ross in their project and ultimately their combined efforts resulted in *The House I Live In*, a brilliant short subject dealing realistically with racial intolerance among the young. Mervyn LeRoy directed it and Sinatra starred. RKO donated the necessary studio facilities and paid the costs of printing enough copies of it so that it had the widest possible theatrical circulation. Lewis Allan and Earl Robinson composed lyrics and music for a title song which Sinatra recorded and included in his repertoire for years afterward.

The House I Live In is the harbinger which marked Hollywood's "coming of age" in taking a definite stand on a heretofore taboo subject. Within two years of its release, in 1945, many had forgotten Sinatra's pioneer film and credit the industry's brave and adult assault on racial intolerance to Darryl F. Zanuck and Elia Kazan, for *Gentleman's Agreement*, Dore Schary, for *Crossfire*, and later, Stanley Kramer, for *Home of the Brave*. One of the institutions that neither forgot nor overlooked Sinatra's efforts was the Board of Governors of the Academy of Motion Picture Arts and Sciences which voted him a special Academy Award. This was his first, and by no means last, association with "Oscar."

Frank's first experience with singing in public really began while he was attending Demarest High School. Whenever there was a dance or an occasion for the school to hire a band to play, he was always invited to be the featured vocalist. Long before becoming a teenager he had started collecting records and decorating his bedroom walls with photographs of all the popular singers and, in the early 1930s, when Bing Crosby popularized crooning on radio, he became Frank's idol. His earliest opportunity to imitate the "maestro" was at the many social functions, weddings, and showers, of close relatives. And by the time he was a high school junior, Natalie saw to it that her son was paid "a couple of bucks" every time he sang at a political gathering.

Much to his father's consternation, Frank quit high school before he was eighteen and devoted his time to staying home and singing, on Friday and Saturday nights, at one of the local nightclubs. Marty Sinatra had other ideas about his son's future and got him a job on a newspaper, the *Jersey Journal*, loading delivery trucks. After much browbeating by his parents, he enrolled for some courses at the Stevens Institute of Technology. At the *Journal* he was promoted to copy boy and then to junior sports writer.

"But," he said, years later, "I disappointed Pop again terrifically when I decided to quit that job and make a go of it singing. I went through the toughest period of my life when making that particular break. Because I had actually been doing quite well in the newspaper job."

To prove his sincerity to his father, and also to reinforce his own esteem of his singing capabilities and his potential, he sang at every amateur night contest he could that was held in the various vaudeville and movie houses in Hoboken, Newark, Jersey City and New York. This pursuit eventually got him a spot on the Major Bowes national radio broadcast and the opportunity to tour with the Bowes unit. But, by the time they reached California, late in 1937, Frank had become so disenchanted that he quit and returned to Hoboken.

This turned out to be a smart move on his part because by early 1938 he was singing on eighteen different radio shows for five local stations in New Jersey and New York. None of the networks, except the Mutual Broadcasting System, which gave him a weekly carfare allowance, paid him any salary. Nevertheless he reasoned that

somehow, someone who could do him some good would eventually hear him. This optimism sustained him for just so long. Finally, somewhat in desperation, he gave up the radio circuit to take a job as a headwaiter, master of ceremonies and occasional crooner at an Englewood roadhouse called the Rustic Cabin. His starting salary was a weekly $15.

The apparent force behind his decision to forsake his radio work was his fiancee, Nancy Barbato, the girl with whom he had been in love for several years.

Within a short time his Rustic Cabin salary was increased to $25 a week which, considering the prevailing economic situation in those last depression days, was quite good. Frank and Nancy heeded the theory of all young lovers of the era—that two can live as cheaply as one. On February 4, 1939, they were married in a double ring ceremony at Our Lady of Sorrows Church in Jersey City, where the newlyweds set up housekeeping in a small apartment. It didn't take them very long to explode the young lovers' myth so, to help supplement Frank's modest salary, Nancy took a secretarial job in nearby Elizabeth with the American Type Foundry.

Soon Frank was singing at the Rustic Cabin with a group called Bill Henri's Headliners which did so little to stimulate business that the management gave all of them, including Frank, their notice. Frustrated with the turn his singing career had taken and burdened with the responsibilities of married life, he decided to return to newspaper work as a sportswriter. It was at this low point that his fortunes changed.

A few days before leaving the Rustic Cabin, Harry James, a former trumpet player with Benny Goodman's band, who had heard Sinatra sing and had liked what he heard, offered him a job as featured vocalist with his newly formed band. Frank accepted with alacrity and signed a two year contract with James that guaranteed him $75 a week.

"The first thing I did," Sinatra said, "was to telephone Nancy and tell her the good news. I told her to quit her job. She was going to travel on the road with me and Harry James!"

Songstress Connie Haines, also working with the James band, recalled: "Our first booking after he joined us was the Hippodrome in Baltimore. Frank was so new he wasn't even billed. The fans didn't know his name. But, nevertheless, they were standing at the stage door, screaming and yelling for him. I saw it. I was there."

The band worked a cross-country tour of mostly one night stands which netted them only modest financial recognition but a great deal of experience. In July of 1939, Frank cut his first record with Harry James— "From the Bottom of My Heart" and "Melancholy Mood"—released on the Brunswick label. The following September, after that recording, and two subsequent ones had appeared, George Simon, then writing and reviewing for Metronome magazine, noted that the James band was very good with ballads and that they featured "the very pleasing vocals of Frank Sinatra, whose easy phrasing is especially commendable."

Altogether Frank cut ten sides with the James band, including a song that was to be associated with him throughout his career, "All or Nothing At All."

It was while they were appearing in Los Angeles that Frank learned Nancy was pregnant. He insisted she return to Jersey City and made arrangements for her to stay with his parents whose anticipation of a grandchild was overwhelming. A few years later, when Frank was the idol of the bobby-soxers and earning more than a million dollars a year, Nancy recalled those days on the road as the happiest of her life.

Just before Christmas, while appearing at Chicago's Hotel Sherman, Frank was offered the opportunity to sing with the very popular Tommy Dorsey band. Dorsey had recently parted company with his featured vocalist, Jack Leonard, who suggested Sinatra as his replacement. But it was really a very magnanimous Harry James who made the change possible by telling Frank he would not hold him to his contractual obligations and urging him to accept Dorsey's offer.

"Frank still kids about honoring our deal," James said many years later. "He'll drop in to hear the band and he'll say something like 'Okay, boss'—he still calls me boss—'I'm ready anytime. Just call me and I'll be there on the stand.' "

The success of the Dorsey band was attributed to the unusual musical phrasing of Tommy's horn, and their entire performance was built around his unique "sound." When Frank joined them, late in January of 1940, he was immediately aware of Tommy Dorsey's fabulous musicianship. "I figured if he could do that phrasing with his horn, I could do it with my voice." And his ability to do just that became the secret of his style.

During his Dorsey tenure, which lasted until early in July of 1942, Frank became a popular and easily recognizable recording star. He cut 84 sides with Dorsey. Many are classic performances and have been reissued more than once in albums.

Five months after joining Dorsey, Frank's daughter Nancy was born (on June 8, 1940). Sinatra asked Tommy to be her godfather.

As a child, Nancy, Jr., was immortalized with a song, "Nancy With the Laughing Face," recorded *con amore* by her father. Later, after graduating from University High School in West Los Angeles, she attended the University of Southern California one semester. She got a secretarial job but left that to study drama in New York. She worked for awhile as a salesgirl in a swank Beverly Hills sportswear shop but the urge to get into show busi-

Dining out with Nancy, Frank, Jr., and Nancy, Jr. Christine, then two years old, was too young for the nightclub circuit.

ness could not be ignored. It can justly be reasoned that her first break was on the strength of the Sinatra name but she soon proved she had the talent, the stamina, and the capabilities to make it on her own.

Her career really got underway when she appeared on a television special dedicated to welcoming Elvis Presley home after his tour of army duty in Germany. In September of 1960 she married rock 'n' roll singer Tommy Sands in Las Vegas. They were divorced in 1965. Her popularity as a stylish songstress with a good voice and vast sex appeal kept her busy with nightclub engagements, television appearances and film work (*For Those Who Think Young, Wild Angels, et al.*).

On her father's fifty-fifth birthday, December 12, 1970, she married television choreographer Hugh Lambert in a Roman Catholic ceremony in Cathedral City, California. She had chosen that day because "Daddy likes to give things away on his birthday."

She also said this about her famous father: "He is better than anybody else, or at least they think he is, and he has to live up to it."

A vocal group calling themselves The Pied Pipers also joined Dorsey soon after Frank became a part of the "family." Although never a member of the group, he often vocalized with them. Jo Stafford, the distaff Piper, remembers him with great affection.

"He was very well liked in the band, and he certainly worked hard to fit in," she said. "Most solo singers usually don't fit too well in a group, but Frank never stopped working at it and of course, as you know, he blended beautifully with us. He was meticulous about his phrasing and dynamics. He worked very hard so that his vibrato would match ours. And he was always conscientious about learning his parts."

5

The Tommy Dorsey band became the summer replacement for the Bob Hope Radio Show in June of 1940, and the following October they got their own radio show. That same month the Dorsey band was hired as the feature attraction to open the very glamorous Hollywood Palladium Ballroom. A few months later Frank, vocalizing a chorus of "I'll Never Smile Again" with the Pied Pipers, appeared with Tommy Dorsey and the band in a low budget Paramount musical, *Las Vegas Nights*. While still associated with Dorsey, he also made some minor musical contributions to MGM's *Ship Ahoy*, which had a big budget, the antics of Red Skelton, and some sprightly dancing by Eleanor Powell. Neither film did anything to advance Frank's career. His actual screen debut, if it can be called that, occurred some years earlier when he made a test film under the auspices of the redoubtable Major Bowes.

While still with Dorsey Frank revealed another facet of his talents that was also to become synonymous with the Sinatra name: getting into public brawls. The first one to be noted by the press occurred when three drunks made some slurring remarks in his presence about Tommy Dorsey, the host of the cocktail party they were all attending. Frank retaliated with a few fast punches and thereby achieved a kind of immortality he could very well have done without. Newsmen and columnists made much of the incident although none of them took the trouble to report the motivation behind his action. All that seemed to interest them was the fact that the frail-looking songbird was short on temper and quick with his fists. Consequently, through the years, his altercations, and there have been a few of them, have been as well reported as his performances. All of which has done little to endear many newspaper and magazine writers, and a few nationally syndicated columnists, to Frank.

Less than a month after the Japanese attack on Pearl Harbor, *Metronome* magazine, after conducting a poll of its readers, reported that Frank Sinatra had been voted the best male band singer of the year.

Tommy Dorsey, a musical genius capable of recognizing genuine talent, had done a great deal to advance Frank's career. He soon came to the realization that Frank was now doing much for his band. Dorsey's publicity man Bullets Durgom confirmed to Tommy what he already knew, and added that whenever he tried to push a Dorsey record with the disc jockeys they only wanted to know whether or not Frank was vocalizing on it. "All they wanted to hear about was Frank," Durgom reported.

Other band members were also aware of the Sinatra charisma because wherever they appeared couples stopped dancing and gathered around the bandstand to watch Frank while he sang. He accused drummer Buddy Rich of drumming too loudly while he was singing on several different occasions and that resulted in a great deal of animosity between the vocalist and the musician while lasted the duration of Frank's association with Dorsey. Years later, however, when Buddy Rich formed his own band, Frank was his financial backer.

Although he had job security, a good salary, and an iron-clad contract with Dorsey, Frank decided it was time to try and make it as a solo attraction. Once he made that decision, by no means an easy one, he cut two records, conducted by Axel Stordahl, which had favorable reactions and an offer, from Manie Sacks, of Columbia Records, of a recording contract whenever he severed relations with Tommy Dorsey. That happened in September of 1942.

It wasn't as easy for him to get away from Dorsey as it had been to leave Harry James. In addition to his musical talents, Dorsey was also a shrewd, hard-headed businessman well able to estimate Sinatra's financial potential. Dorsey's deal for giving Frank his freedom was one third of his earnings for the duration of his contract and an additional ten percent for his business manager, Leonard Vannerson.

Despite Dorsey's demands, Frank's decision to leave turned out to be a brilliant maneuver because not long after his departure, James Petrillo, of the American Federation of Musicians, placed his infamous ban on the recordings of the dance bands. That ban would eventually affect the entire music industry. The death knell, announcing that the era of The Big Bands was over, sounded.

The sound that heralded the forthcoming era of the Big Name Singers was a bobby-soxer's swoon.

THE SWOONING YEARS

"There's no teacher like experience," Frank said. "And singing with a band is like lifting weights. You're conditioning yourself."

It's a tribute to how well he had conditioned himself while singing with Dorsey. Because, by the end of 1942, he was well on the way to becoming an American Institution.

His first free-lance effort was to come west to discuss the possibility of taking over as staff singer on NBC's Hollywood-based radio show. He didn't get the job but he did get a spot—singing "Night and Day"—in a Columbia musical *Reveille with Beverly*, starring Ann Miller as a tap dancing disc jockey! Things got much brighter, however, when he returned to New York and Mike Nidorf, vice president of General Amusement Corporation, agreed to represent him and signed him to an exclusive contract. GAC immediately booked him into the Mosque Theatre in Newark and got him a CBS radio show of his own—"Songs by Sinatra"—which sustained him from October through February of 1943.

During a broadcast with Xavier Cugat in 1944.

At a night-time baseball game in the forties. Above, with Groucho Marx and Robert Mitchum. Below, with bat girls Virginia Mayo and Marilyn Maxwell. (*Pictures courtesy of Tom G. Murray.*)

Late in December of 1942, moonlighting from his radio show, he appeared with Benny Goodman and his band at New York's Paramount Theatre, where the feature attraction was the all-star musical *Star Spangled Rhythm*. Among others in its large cast was Bing Crosby, his idol since childhood.

Frank's performance was so tremendous, and his effect so overwhelming, that *swoon*, a word that had been almost obsolete since the Civil War period, became a part of everybody's vocabulary. Teen-aged girls stampeded the theatre, all impatient for Frankie's appearance. And when he came onstage, before singing a note, they screamed, shrieked, shouted, fainted, applauded, wet their panties, and panted. The bedlam lasted through every performance. The first time it occurred, Benny Goodman, recoiling at the wall of noise thundering across the footlights, exclaimed "What the hell was that?"

Amateur psychiatrists, among others, attempted to answer that question. Frankie's effect on bobby-soxers was called a manifestation of wartime degeneracy. Others said he aroused the maternal instinct in all women everytime he burst into song. Bobby-soxers, however, reacting to his misty-eyed magic, and to a style that made each of them feel he was singing only to her, put it in words universally understood: he was "solid" and "in the groove."

While breaking young hearts and shattering old box-office records at the Paramount, he devoted his spare time to taking daily boxing lessons from Tami Mauriello, a top prize fighter, and his late hours appearing at The Riobama, an almost obscure nightclub that automatically became the most popular nitery in town. Much to the delight of the management of The Riobama, Frank proved that as far as he was concerned no generation gap existed among his female followers.

He was suddenly the talk of show business in New York. Frank Sinatra jokes, and imitators, were suddenly standards in almost every nightclub and vaudeville act. By the following February his name was a household word throughout the entire country. This happened after he replaced Barry Wood as the star of the Lucky Strike radio show, "Your Hit Parade," the most popular Saturday night program on the networks. For the next two years Frank appeared, with increasing irregularity, on the Lucky Strike show. Recording dates, motion picture work, road tours, salary disputes and a general dissatisfaction with the program's conservative musical arrangements, kept fans wondering from week to week whether or not he would be on the air to sing his share of the most popular songs of the day. And some of the songs he was required to sing—"Praise the Lord and Pass the Ammunition," "Mairzie Doats," and "Pistol Packin' Mamma"—were the kind of specialty numbers for which he considered himself wholly unsuited.

When he returned to the Paramount in May of 1943, he was already known as "The Voice" and his competitor-idol, Bing Crosby, was known as "The Groaner." And while Humphrey Bogart, John Wayne, and Errol Flynn alternately fought the Japs and the Germans on our motion picture screens, "The Voice" and "The Groaner" competed on radio in the battle of the baritones.

He bought a Cape Cod cottage in Hasbrouck Heights, a small and exclusive residential area in the Passaic Valley. Before too long the address of his new home was well circulated among the bobby-soxers. And like a swarm of locusts they invaded the area seeking souvenirs and autographs. The assault became so acute the local police department was required to patrol the area and discourage Frankie's faithful followers. But even the announcement that Nancy was expecting another baby could not completely dispel the onslaught.

And by the time that Frankie made his third Paramount appearance, in October 1944, his frantic fans had become the concern of Mayor Fiorello LaGuardia. By 4 a.m., on the opening day of his third engagement, bob-

Arriving at Los Angeles airport in 1947 and being greeted by Nancy, Frank, Jr., and Nancy, Jr.

The idol of the bobby-soxers being greeted as he arrives in Pasadena

by-soxers were lined up at the box-office, five hours before it was scheduled to open. A battery of policemen was required to keep them orderly. The question of whether or not they violated a nine o'clock curfew called for tact and diplomacy on the part of Mayor LaGuardia. He finally concluded that the youngsters were early risers and had not broken any curfew regulations.

But the Board of Education's School Commissioner George Chatfield accused Frank of contributing to truancy. He also said, "We don't want this sort of thing to go on! We cannot tolerate young people making a public display of losing control of their emotions." In reporting all this, the ultra-conservative *New York Times* acknowledged Frank's cultural effects.

The seventeen months between those two Paramount Theatre appearances were among the busiest and most eventful of his colorful career. How financially rewarding they were can best be described by the way one fan magazine printed his name: $inatra.

The Music Corporation of America, the largest talent booking agency, originally rejected adding Frank to their roster of artists. After his notable New York appearances, however, MCA became very interested in representing him and investigated his contractual and financial commitments. It was soon discovered he was earning a fortune—for other people. By intricate legal manipulations, MCA was able to buy out Tommy Dorsey's interest in his earnings, settle his contract with GAC and arrange with Manie Sacks of Columbia Records a recording contract for which the $25,000 advance on his royalties was used to help settle some of the obligations.

He also accepted a film offer made by RKO. His triumphant return west was celebrated when 5000 screaming fans, mostly female, met and mobbed him in the Pasadena railroad station. He spent his first Saturday night back in tinsel town singing to a capacity audience at a Hollywood Bowl concert. Bing Crosby invited him to appear on his radio show. Songwriter Jimmy McHugh, who became a close and lifetime friend, was selected by RKO brass to be Frank's official host.

McHugh, and Harry Adamson, composed the songs for his film, *Higher and Higher*. Among them: "I Couldn't Sleep A Wink Last Night," "The Music Stopped," and "A Lovely Way to Spend An Evening." Although he was awarded only co-starring billing on the film's credits, after Michele Morgan and Jack Haley, RKO's publicity department, then headed by one of the great publicity men, Perry Lieber, shrewdly advertised *Higher and Higher* as "The Sinatra Show." Critical acclaim was rather mild but response at the box-office was wild.

Frank's draft board gave him a 1-A classification. Expecting to be called into service at any time, he made a cross-country nightclub and theatre tour backed by Jan Savitt's band. But after taking an army physical, in December 1943, he was reclassified 4-F. The examination revealed he had a punctured eardrum. His disappointment was abject as he had looked forward to army duty. To compensate, he began making USO tours and taking a great deal of ribbing from servicemen all too eager to heckle him.

But he never failed to entertain them with a program of songs and a comedy routine in which he burlesqued all his own foibles. Later he did a six week tour of military bases in Europe and Africa. Returning from that tour, he complained to the press that most of the facilities and personnel staging GI shows were inadequate and most of the entertainment second rate. Among others taking exception to his comments was Marlene Dietrich, no stranger to servicemen overseas.

"What did he expect it to be like," she wondered, "an appearance at the Paramount?"

Years later, La Dietrich's chagrin disspelled, she worked with him in a guest appearance in Mike Todd's spectacular *Around the World in 80 Days*. Henceforth she has always referred to him as "The Mercedes-Benz of men."

Returning to Hollywood he began work on *Step Lively*, a musical remake of *Room Service*, a Broadway comedy success which, when first filmed by RKO in 1938, had been the Marx Brothers first fiasco. Filming was interrupted on January 10, 1944, while Frank swooned after Nancy telephoned him from a New Jersey hospital to tell him he had just become a father again. The following day, via photo-wire, he had his first glimpse of Franklin Wayne Sinatra. Although he was named after President Roosevelt, he has become much better known as Frank Sinatra, Jr.

By the time Frank, Jr. was old enough to attend school, his parents had bought Mary Astor's house and were living in the Toluca Lake community of the San Fernando Valley. He later attended Ralph Waldo Emerson Junior High and University High School in Los Angeles. His senior year was spent at a private school in Idyllwild, California.

Not long after his sister Nancy became involved in show business, he also got the bug. Like Nancy, his first opportunities came as a result of his name. But, again like his sister, he has managed a moderately successful career on his own considerable talents. He learned his name was also something of a hindrance when, on numerous occasions, he was denied a chance to audition his talents because producers and managers felt he was merely attempting to capitalize on his father. One thing of his father's he did capitalize on was heeding the old man's sage observation that overnight success is the culmination of practice, hard work and experience.

Some of his experiences have been unique. He headlined nightclub acts in New York, Las Vegas, and other major cities, including a grueling and successful European concert tour. While he was breaking in his new nightclub at Harrah's Casino, in Lake Tahoe, in 1964, he became an international celebrity. This occurred when, between shows, he was abducted from his motel room and held for ransom.

Several days later, unharmed, his kidnapers released him after his father met their demands and paid a $240,000 ransom. The men were ultimately captured. Their ensuing trial was something of a sensation. Despite defense claims that the kidnaping had been a hoax, and Frank, Jr. an accomplice in what they contended was a publicity stunt, they were all convicted in Los Angeles Superior Court. All this was given considerable and lurid press and television coverage.

The incident, however, was quickly forgotten and young Frank resumed his career. Because of his weekly appearance on a summertime replacement show on television he became a popular attraction in that medium and guest-starred on most of the big-time variety shows.

Before principal photography was completed on *Step Lively*, Frank and a host of stars, including Bob Hope, appeared on a war bond benefit show dedicated to celebrating President Roosevelt's birthday. The following March he began a new radio show while still the sometimes-star of "Your Hit Parade."

He was on his overseas tour when *Step Lively* was released that June. RKO, more than gratified with the box-office returns, signed him to a seven year contract. Then, just before his record-breaking third appearance at the Paramount, he was invited to the White House to meet the man whom he had named his son after: Franklin D. Roosevelt. Two close friends, restauranteur Toots Shor and comedian Rags Ragland, accompanied him.

"He kidded me about the art of how to make girls faint," Frank told the newsmen who, with one exception, were all anxious to give him favorable coverage. "But," Frank added, "he didn't ask me to sing." The only unfavorable report of his visit with President Roosevelt appeared in the column of Washington journalist Westbrook Pegler. Pegler, a long-time critic of the New Deal, added Frank's name to his long list of people he took delight in deflating. And more often than not he merely referred to him as "The Hoboken 4-F."

Frank apparently took great delight in baiting Pegler too. Because, a few weeks later, at a Democratic rally in Madison Square Garden, he was a featured singer and a strong supporter of FDR's decision to campaign for a fourth term. In future presidential campaigns Frank gave untiringly of his time and talent on behalf of two other Democratic candidates, Harry S. Truman and John F. Kennedy. It wasn't until the 1970s that he switched party affiliations and helped re-elect Republican Ronald Reagan as Governor of California. That political turnabout ended

a long, and not always good-natured, feud with one of Westbrook Pegler's pets—John Wayne.

Politics, however, has not been the only cause to which he has devoted much of his time, talent and money. He's always a soft touch and an eager worker on behalf of charitable organizations and, with the possible exception of Bob Hope, he has contributed more than anybody else in show business to worthwhile causes. Unlike many celebrities he always minimizes these efforts with remarkable self-effacement. He's much happier reading about allusions to his underworld associates and his intimate connections with alleged members of the Mafia.

These paradoxical inclinations have continuously made him the center of some controversy. His career follows an inexorable pattern of turning dissenters into defenders; acquaintances into bitter enemies; and his undeniable friends to speculating whether or not they know him as well as they think they do. One close friend observed: "He's a simple guy who likes to appear complex—or maybe it's the other way around!"

Another Sinatra paradox: never learning to read music. This inability did not deter him from conducting the Los Angeles Symphony Orchestra, at the Hollywood Bowl. Critics were derisive but, because of a capacity turnout, the occasion turned into an event thereby enabling the Symphony to end a season profitably—instead of artistically well-realized but financially disappointing. He later conducted an album of Alec Wilder's music which Wilder himself rather liked ("What was so good about it was that it was so musical. Frank felt music and he listened carefully to the soloists and he built up a wonderful rapport with them and the other musicians."). Another of his curious musical contributions was writing lyrics for a very popular ballad, "This Love of Mine."

Axel Stordahl had been Tommy Dorsey's musical arranger but he left to become Frank's arranger. But Petrillo's ban, which lasted until a few days after the 1945 Armistice, prevented Stordahl from working on Frank's early Columbia recordings. During these years of union restrictions *Metronome* magazine announced that Frank had won their best male singer poll for the fourth straight year.

At this point Louis B. Mayer became so interested in Frank that he wasn't content until he managed to buy his RKO contract and add his name to the MGM galaxy. Mayer used him to good advantage as a shy and lovesick sailor in *Anchors Aweigh*. The score included two notable Sinatra songs—"I Fall in Love Too Easily" and "The Charm of You"—both memorably performed. *Anchors Aweigh* had many things going for it—Technicolor, Kathryn Grayson, innovative choreography by Gene Kelly, including a marvelous sequence wherein he dances with animated cartoon characters, and a generally insouciant score and screenplay. Although one of the most

On the set of *Till the Clouds Roll By*.

popular films of 1945, it was almost two years before Frank was on screen again.

This occurred when, along with most of MGM's musical talents, he contributed one song, "Ol' Man River," to part of the finale of *Till the Clouds Roll By*, a tribute to Jerome Kern's career which, as it should be, is loaded with songs and only occasionally burdened with a tediously fictitious script. He fared much better in *It Happened in Brooklyn*, although the Jule Styne-Sammy Cahn score was one of this talented team's less inspired creations.

On radio Frank changed his brand of cigarettes from Lucky Strike to Old Gold and did a season of programs for them. Years later, one of the many guest stars to appear on that show, former "Ooomph Girl" Ann Sheridan, listening to the latest Sinatra recording during rehearsals of her TV series, commented, "That guy still gives me goose pimples—all over! The radio show I did with him was one of the zaniest and happiest times I had in Hollywood."

By the time he switched back to Luckies and resumed as star of "Your Hit Parade," his popularity as the best male singer had dropped to second place. Billy Eckstine was the number one boy. The new edition added Axel Stordahl's arrangements and the singing talents of Doris Day. But it was the same old formula and the same stilted musical policy until all three of them rebelled. The sponsors and program directors finally saw the light and the show underwent a complete musical renovation. The results were gratifying but too late to help Frank immediately regain his *amour-propre* as number one singing star.

While co-starring on "Your Hit Parade," Doris Day gushed: "Frank is so wonderful! He's a wonderful guy to work with. I really owe him so much. He wanted me on the show. I suppose they could have had a lot of gals with bigger names, but he wanted me. Just watching him and working with him is a lot of help to any singer. He's so relaxed; he gave me confidence. He'll do anything for you. He's just the sweetest and greatest person I've ever known in the business."

Seven years later, however, when Miss Day co-starred with him in *Young At Heart*, she had cause to change her tune. Their clashes of personality and temperaments were daily occurrences reported by Louella Parsons and Hedda Hopper with monotonous regularity. None of this is evident on screen. Doris and Frank made an appealing team with exactly the right "chemistry." *Young At Heart* was as popular as *Four Daughters*, an earlier film version in which John Garfield and Priscilla Lane, in the same roles, catapulted to stardom.

When he returned for his encore engagement on "Your Hit Parade," his marriage and his star status were in jeopardy. He made a valiant attempt to solve both dilemmas.

None too happy with the properties Louis B. Mayer was offering as subsequent screen vehicles, he asked to be loaned to his old studio RKO to play a straight dramatic role, as a priest, in *Miracle of the Bells*. Not a few people thought his judgment faulty and tried to dissuade him.

Miracle of the Bells had been a best-selling novel but much of its reader appeal was due to author Russell Janney's introspective narrative. The screen play, devised by Ben Hecht and Quentin Reynolds, never quite overcame that obstacle. Competing for acting honors with Fred MacMurray, Valli, and Lee J. Cobb, Frank gave a plausible and well-thought out performance. He also sang one song—"Ever Homeward." The press and the public became aware of his dramatic potential but, because *Miracle* failed to ring any box-office bells, studio officials were inclined to denigrate this facet of Frank's talents.

And when MGM starred him in *The Kissing Bandit* even his musical comedy abilities appeared dubious. He considers *The Kissing Bandit* the nadir of his screen career and nobody argues that appraisal.

Rumors began circulating as early as 1946 that all was not well between Frank and Nancy. Reports of his late hours of carousing and long absences from home were all well publicized with such emphasis there was little cause to doubt these reports. But a reconciliation with Nancy caused gossips to pause and re-evaluate their domestic situation. Then, on June 20, 1948, their second daughter, Christine, was born.

To her playmates and classmates, however, she was always Tina, the shy Sinatra. But, by the time she was twenty, she too had succumbed to the lure of show business. As a member of a film crew, she spent the summer of 1968 touring Europe and the Far East gathering footage for a unique series of television travelogs and documentaries.

Later Tina said, "We're all little pieces of Daddy and I seem to follow his dramatic inclinations." Since then she acted in various television dramas: in a Western telefilm she gave an exceptional performance in a very difficult role. Nevertheless, Tina is less compulsively ambitious than her brother and sister. She can remember that when she was an impressionable youngster her father's career was not going too well and in her young mind she may well have associated that with the fact her parents had parted and divorced.

For several years prior to his legal separation from Nancy, Frank had been linked romantically with Lana Turner, Marilyn Maxwell, and a host of beautiful starlets and eager sycophants anxious to see their name in print.

Nancy was painfully aware of the opportunities and temptations Frank encounterd every moment he was away from her. Intuition told her that these peccadilloes could be tolerated and that no matter how much she suffered it was best not to dignify them with acknowledgement. She knew his career was floundering and such escapades were necessary to his ego. Instinctively, however, she also came to realize that his infatuation for Ava Gardner could not be ignored.

Ironically, it was St. Valentine's Day of 1950 when she announced: "Unfortunately, my married life with Frank Sinatra has become unhappy. We have therefore separated and I have requested my attorney to work out a property settlement. I do not contemplate a divorce." To keep herself occupied, she enrolled as a special UCLA student and, among other things, she took a course in music appreciation.

The following April she did file for a divorce. The same week, by mutual agreement, MGM released Frank from his contract which still had several years to go.

His campaign for more worthwhile scripts, and Louis B. Mayer's insistence that his personal life had become too public became insuperable. His displeasure had much less basis, in fact, than Mayer's. His last two MGM films were both worthwhile. In *Take Me Out to the Ball Game*, a pleasant period musical, he co-starred with Esther Williams and Gene Kelly; *On The Town*, an uninhibited

After divorcing Nancy, and before marrying Ava Gardner, he occasionally dated Lana Turner.

With Ava Gardner

screen version of the Broadway show, ranks among the best musicals ever produced in Hollywood. But, in each instance Frank was second banana to buoyant, high-spirited Gene Kelly.

Kelly expressed surprise over Frank's decision and thought MGM was foolish to allow him to depart. "He's the hardest worker I've ever known," Kelly said. "I think he's a great singer and has what it takes to make a fine actor. He has a native talent that shows up in his singing and an acting talent that makes you believe what he's doing."

Howard Hughes, impressed with Frank's native *off-screen* talents, hired him, in 1948, to co-star with Jane Russell and Groucho Marx in *It's Only Money*. After viewing the completed film, however, RKO officials decided it would be an act of public charity to shelve it. It was released in 1951 as *Double Dynamite*. Frank's unpopularity is only part of the reason it failed.

His reception at London's Palladium, in July 1950, was enthusiastic but not overwhelming. He then became engrossed with the idea of doing a weekly television series that debuted that December and struggled through two stormy seasons. A few months later he left Columbia

Records. Disenchanted with the financial returns on his recordings, he was also unsusceptible to suggestions that songs and arrangements he was using were musically inferior. His last Columbia recording was a plaintive ballad, "Why Try to Change Me Now."

While still happily married to Nancy, he had moved his family from Toluca Lake to a large estate in the Holmby Hills section of Beverly Hills. One of their neighbors, Barbara Stanwyck, became a close friend of Nancy's. Another neighbor, with whom Frank felt an immediate rapport, and enjoyed a lasting friendship, was Humphrey Bogart.

Bogart, and a close circle of friends, including his wife, Lauren Bacall, were the Hollywood rebels whose code of behavior branded them anti-establishment. Frank became a part of the group which columnists, anxious to preserve the myth that Hollywood was and always would be the entertainment capital of the world, at first disdained and later nicknamed "The Beverly Hills Rat Pack." Their pranks, philosophies and drinking bouts at Romanoff's, and later at Chasen's, captured the admiration and the imagination of the public. But the close knit clan, which denied their existence right up to the time of

14

Bogart's death, rejected all opportunities to increase their ranks as many crestfallen personalities and celebrities were to discover.

Soon after his divorce was final, Frank married Ava Gardner, on November 7, 1951, at the West Germantown, Pennsylvania, home of radio executive Isaac Levy.

At the time of her first encounter with Frank, Ava Gardner was on the threshold of international stardom and rapidly approaching the apogee of her celebrated beauty. She had already been married to bandleader Artie Shaw, as had Lana Turner, and to Mickey Rooney. Soon after meeting Frank, she broke up with Johnny Stompanato, once described by mobster Mickey Cohen as "a gigolo-about-town," who was soon cultivated by a former reject of Frank's, Lana Turner. Ava always maintained, with some justification, that she had nothing whatever to do with his marital rift. Following his separation from Nancy, she was reported with him in New York, Mexico, England, and Spain, where she was filming exteriors on *Pandora and the Flying Dutchman*. His sudden arrival, it has been said, was motivated by gossip that Ava was being romanced by bullfighter Mario Cabre, who had a small role in the film.

During his years as Ava's husband, Frank discovered what it's like to be on the shady side of the limelight. CBS had cancelled his television show. He suffered physical disabilities after a hemorrhage of blood vessels in his vocal apparatus that noticeably affected his voice and the quality of his singing. His divorce and division of community property depleted him financially and he was behind in income tax payments. His only film offer, which he accepted, was the lead in a Universal film, *Meet Danny Wilson*, playing a shady nightclub singer involved with the underworld. The script seemed patterned after a conception of his life most of the public, because of his bad press relations, believed to be an accurate one. Not without cinematic interest, *Meet Danny Wilson* was too modestly produced and indifferently directed to create any kind of Sinatra renaissance.

Although he signed a long term contract with Capitol Records immediately upon leaving Columbia, which included clauses that enabled him to make his own selections, give final approval to musical arrangements and choice of conductor, it was some time before he produced a hit record for them. Prophetically, this was "I'm Walking Behind You" which, at this conjuncture, was exactly what he was doing.

He accompanied Ava to Africa while she made *Mogambo* with Clark Gable and Grace Kelly. It had already been filmed before, as *Red Dust* with Gable and Jean Harlow, and as *Congo Maisie* with Ann Sothern, but John Ford's direction, and authentic locales, made it seem new and exciting on screen.

He spent his days reading, watching his wife work, and exploring the Kenya savannah. At night, drinking and relaxing around a campfire, he regaled John Ford and Gable, who became an immediate friend, with tales of his early experiences in Hoboken. He also mentioned that a book he just finished reading, and which Columbia Studios had purchased for filming, contained a character with whom he felt a close identity. He also thought it was the part he had been born to play. But, he reasoned, his present unpopularity and his past screen work would automatically cancel any opportunity he might have had to test for it. Besides, the president of Columbia Studios Harry Cohn had already announced he wanted Eli Wallach for the role of Angelo Maggio in *From Here to Eternity*.

Gable suggested that if he really wanted the part, and believed himself good enough to play it, he was a fool not to go after it. Gable also told him something he remembered throughout his subsequent career: "Talent is the least important thing a performer needs, but humility is one thing he must have."

Humbled but hopeful, he returned to Hollywood and through his agent he was able to make a screen test for the role. His arrival went almost unnoticed by the press. And there were no swooning bobby-soxers to meet and mob him. Nevertheless, he was determined to prove, especially to himself, that he had not already sung his swan song.

THE SWINGING YEARS

Producer Buddy Adler, and Harry Cohn, began publicizing pre-production plans on *From Here to Eternity* early in 1953. It was announced that Joan Crawford would be the promiscuous army wife, Karen; Eli Wallach would be Angelo; and Gladys George the madame of a North Hotel Street whorehouse in Honolulu. Joan Crawford liked the script but finally declined because she was psychologically unable to bring herself to take second billing to Burt Lancaster, already signed to play Milton Warden. Director Fred Zinnemann was somewhat relieved because he wanted to cast the feminine roles against type. He selected Deborah Kerr as the erring wife and Donna Reed, whose career until then consisted of sweet, girl-next-door roles, as Alma, the prostitute who called herself Lorene. Over mild Adler-Cohn objections, he also cast character actress Barbara Morrison, who fitted author James Jones' conception of the madame to perfection, in the part previously promised to Gladys George.

Zinnemann, Cohn, and Adler, impressed with Frank's screen test, sent a cable to Africa, where he had returned after Ava suffered a miscarriage, to let him know he had the part.

With Ava Gardner shortly after their marriage.

Their decision, and his compelling performance, which won him a "Best Supporting Actor" Academy Award, put him back in show business. His $8000 gamble, the salary he agreed to work for, paid off. Within two years he was again earning a million dollars annually. Shortly afterward, because of shrewd business investments, he more than doubled that.

He was musically back in tune with his Capitol recordings. Nelson Riddle replaced Axel Stordahl as his arranger. His moody and dreamy interpretation of lyrics, backed by strings, was replaced with a new jazz beat that helped him achieve a new tempo. His voice, no longer as personal, had a mature and universal appeal. Every phrase he sang carried the authority of experience and optimism of someone dedicated to proclaiming the eternal verities of the heaven-and-hell emotion called love.

The only sour notes in his life: his mercurial marital status and a lawsuit involving a film role.

In the latter he alleged that he had a verbal agreement with Harry Cohn that he would play the lead in *On The Waterfront*, which, instead, was given to Marlon Brando. The subsequent settlement he received was small compensation for not getting a role he considered worthy of his newly acclaimed acting ability.

He joined Ava in England after completing *From Here to Eternity* but their fights, never too private, were soon common knowledge. After returning to New York, where he fulfilled a sensational nightclub engagement, they drifted apart, reunited, and finally, after two stormy years, went their separate ways. He was seldom without a feminine companion, but Toots Shor, his old friend, confided to a columnist: "I think he's still carrying a torch for Ava."

He's always had an aversion to discussing his private life, which as all columnists and writers know, is absolutely maniacal. On rare occasions he's been known to recall some incident of his childhood or an association with another celebrity but he never discusses his affairs of the heart. That aspect of his life is inviolate. Whenever his romances are discussed it's up to the woman involved to do it.

Almost equally hostile about protecting her privacy, Ava contends that the reason she elected to live in Spain was that it was the only country where her wishes are respected. Once, in a moment of unusual candor, she speculated on one of the causes of their estrangement: "Everything seemed to go wrong after we lost the baby we both wanted so much."

It wasn't until 1957 that she finally got around to getting a divorce, in Mexico. Several years prior to that she filed in Nevada and remained there for the duration of residency requirements necessary to get a decree. But she never picked up the final papers. Once free, she said,

"When he was down he was sweet but when he got back up he was hell." Those close to her report they are now friendly but seldom see each other.

Less curious and more understandable is his amiable relationship with Nancy. "If I hadn't held to friendship with Frank," she said, not too long ago, "and made him welcome in our home, I couldn't have lived with my conscience. Children need two parents. Whenever there's some special problem of discipline, I've been able to call their father and say, 'I think this is something you should handle. I can't be the ogre all the time.' And always, Frank has come over."

The girl whom his friends believed would be the one to make him forget Ava was an American beauty with a British title, Lady Adelle Beatty. They first met in 1958 and until shortly before her marriage to film director Stanley Donen in 1960 the romance was considered the "real thing." For almost those entire two years whenever Lady Beatty announced she was on the way to Nassau she would turn up in Hollywood, Las Vegas, New York, or Miami, where, coincidentally, Frank had a nightclub engagement. She never made it to the Bahamas the entire time and her only excuse for not doing so was a discreet observation that "I just like music."

More a figment of Louella Parsons' fancy than fact, was her *exclusive* report that Frank would marry Humphrey Bogart's widow Lauren Bacall. She rather liked the idea; he did not.

His private life, which has always seemed a full-time occupation, caused one friend to remark, "He does better at making out *accidentally* than Hugh Heffner does on purpose." Whatever his alleged sybaritical indulgences were, however, they did not affect his professional productivity.

On screen he played a cold-blooded political assassin in *Suddenly* (1954) and, after completing *Young At Heart*, he played Nathan Detroit in Samuel Goldwyn's lavish version of Frank Loesser's musical classic, *Guys and Dolls*. He was not impressed with his co-star Marlon Brando who had won an Oscar for his method-acting in *On The Waterfront*. Two years later, much to his continuous satisfaction, he got a role at Columbia that Brando had wanted: the lead in *Pal Joey*.

Between these musicals he made seven other films. *The Tender Trap* was a triumphant return to MGM; a dramatic role in *Not As A Stranger* allowed him time to clown between scenes with co-star Robert Mitchum; *The Man with the Golden Arm* brought him a "Best Actor" Oscar nomination; a vulgar musicalization of *The Philadelphia Story*, called *High Society*, had him work with idol Bing Crosby and good-friend Grace Kelly; *The Pride and the Passion*, filmed mostly in Spain, teamed him with Sophia Loren and Cary Grant in a spectacle about Napo-

With Donna Reed on the set of *From Here to Eternity* (1953).

Oscar winners Sinatra and Donna Reed, with a previous winner, Mercedes McCambridge.

17

leonic warfare; but *The Joker Is Wild*, based on the career of his friend, comedian Joe E. Lewis, gave him one of his all-time best songs, "All the Way," and one of his best roles.

His least successful film of this period is *Johnny Concho*, a somewhat ridiculous western which he financed and produced. He also owned a percentage of *Pal Joey*, a free-wheeling adaptation of John O'Hara's account of a nightclub bum with a knack for bringing out the worst in women that had shocked and captivated audiences when it played Broadway in the last days before the war. Gene Kelly, his eventual co-star, and champion, originated the role.

A quartet of films he either personally produced or wholly financed, *Ocean's Eleven*, *Sergeants Three*, *Robin and the Seven Hoods*, and *Four For Texas*, are nothing more than expensively mounted "home movies" in which he employed, and clowned with, some of the members of The Clan: Sammy Davis, Jr., Joey Bishop, Dean Martin, and Peter Lawford. Nobody, including the critics, took them very seriously. *Ocean's Eleven* made a little money but the other three were tax write-offs.

The Clan became the new nomenclature of Bogart's Beverly Hills Rat Pack after his death and Frank became its Chairman of the Board. Other members now included were Tony Curtis, songwriters Sammy Cahn and Jimmy Van Heusen, agent Irving Lazar, and Harry Kurnitz. Non-member Shirley MacLaine was known as their mascot. Noticeably absent from the new ranks were three original members: Spencer Tracy, Katharine Hepburn, and Lauren Bacall.

One of Shirley MacLaine's earliest admirers and promoters, Frank insisted on her being co-starred in *Some Came Running*. In addition to disagreements with director Vincente Minnelli, the people of Madison, Indiana, where much of it was filmed on location, also took a very stuffy attitude about the off-camera doings of Frank and another co-star, Dean Martin.

But the folks at Miami Beach, and its environs, accustomed to seeing him about town, or headlining a show at one of the posh hotels, were too sophisticated to pay much attention to him or the cast and crew working there on *A Hole in the Head*. Aside from singing "High Hopes," he didn't seem too interested in what he was doing either. Edward G. Robinson and Carolyn Jones had no trouble stealing the show.

Nothing diverted his attention while on locations in Burma, Thailand, and Ceylon while making *Never So Few*, including his co-star, Gina Lollobrigida. Even though the cast also includes Steve McQueen and Peter Lawford, the film is notable because of Frank's excellent performance.

Besides her unbilled "guest" appearance in *Ocean's Eleven*, Shirley MacLaine worked with him in *Can-Can*.

While it was in production at 20th Century-Fox, a studio visitor was Soviet Premier Nikita Khrushchev. Shirley danced for him and Marilyn Monroe gave him her autograph. While all this was happening, Frank was concentrating on another cast member, Juliet Prowse.

A talented dancer with the same kind of beauty and elfin charm that made Leslie Caron so captivating, Miss Prowse was auspiciously showcased in *Can-Can*. And, while their romance blossomed, newsmen thought her television appearances, nightclub appearances, and film appearances, noteworthy.

When the bloom faded, Dorothy Provine, whose forté is acting, replaced her in Frank's fickle affections but their *vis-à-vis* didn't last as long as her *Roaring Twenties* TV series. When last seen, she was doing television commercials.

Around the time when John Wayne was completing *The Alamo*, Frank announced he had purchased William Bradford Huie's controversial book, *The Execution of Private Slovik*, and hired former black-listed writer Albert Maltz to adapt it for the screen. Wayne, politically right-wing, and Russell Birdwell, whom he hired to do a special press campaign on *The Alamo*, both voiced loud objections. They were not alone. The furor in the press, church groups, veteran organizations, and Congress, caused him to change his mind. He paid Maltz off, cancelled their project, and said he would abide by public opinion although he personally felt he was the best writer for the job.

He did, however, produce a film immediately afterward, *X-15*, which United Artists released. It made a little money.

He was also Spencer Tracy's well-paid co-star in *The Devil At Four O'Clock*, partly filmed in Hawaii.

After that he began a vigorous campaign to help elect John F. Kennedy to the presidency. By organizing everybody in show business who claimed loyalty to the Democratic Party he was able to raise a reported two million dollars for them by arranging $100-a-plate dinners and star-studded political rallies. At all such events he was the most popular and electrifying entertainer.

And he was always exciting on stage at the Sands Hotel in Las Vegas where he owns a piece of the action. For a decade or more, his semi-annual appearances there were sellout engagements. Just so the competitor hotels and casinos wouldn't feel too left out of things while he was in town, he lost most of his astronomical salary at one of their gambling tables. When other corporate investors in The Sands heard about this they refused to allow him to gamble on credit in his own hotel.

Most of his Capitol recordings, still exciting to listen to, were all top-selling albums although none of them ever quite sold a million copies which would have earned him a Gold Record Award. The irony of this seems even more blatant when non-singers like Rex Harrison, via the original cast recording of *My Fair Lady*, do achieve that distinction.

He left Capitol in late 1960 and formed his own company, Reprise, which, about three years later, became incorporated with Warner Bros. Records. He's one of their largest stockholders.

His immediate success with his first Reprise albums was echoed by his superb performance in John Frankenheimer's harrowing and macabre film, *The Manchurian Candidate*. Like *Suddenly*, it deals with political assassination. Besides some tense dramatic encounters, Frank, and Janet Leigh, the ex-wife of Clan member Tony Curtis, also engaged in some insinuating dialog sequences reminiscent of the Bogart-Bacall exchanges in *The Big Sleep*.

About a year after *The Manchurian Candidate* was released, President Kennedy was assassinated. Many who saw the film could not help remembering how close it came to anticipating the actual tragedy. The distributor, United Artists, rejected theatre owners' demands for a re-issue and shelved it indefinitely. Years later, when it was re-released, its brutal impact was still overpowering.

In 1965, besides playing a starring role in *Von Ryan's Express*, he produced, co-directed and starred in *None But the Brave*. His then-current son-in-law Tommy Sands had a featured role. Another featured player in the cast, actor-producer and close friend Brad Dexter said of him, "He has an insatiable desire to live every moment to its fullest because, I guess, he feels that right around the corner is extinction."

It was a most apropos observation because he was fifty years old and he was in love with Mia Farrow.

A popular co-star of the long running TV soap opera *Peyton Place*, Mia, the daughter of the late film director John Farrow and Maureen O'Sullivan, and less than half his age. More than a few observers opined that he would have been wiser falling in love with her widowed mother, the still lovely actress who gained screen prominence playing Jane in the Johnny Weissmuller *Tarzan* films made at MGM.

After his experience as "Mr. Ava Gardner," close associates claimed he would never again marry anyone interested in a career. For this reason, friends insisted, he broke up with Juliet Prowse and Dorothy Provine. And until July 17, 1966, the day when she married him in Jack Entratter's Las Vegas home, Mia Farrow told everyone that being his wife was more important to her than a career.

After their marriage, and a trip to England, where he filmed *The Naked Runner*, he discovered she had changed her mind.

He contracted with 20th Century-Fox to make three films and part of this agreement included a role for his

With director George Sidney on the set of *Pal Joey* (1957).

With Spencer Tracy on location for *The Devil at 4 O'Clock* (1961).

19

With Laurence Harvey on location for *The Manchurian Candidate* (1962).

At the film industry's tribute to Jack Warner, the "last of the great moguls." With them is Ted Ashley, who succeeded Warner as head of the Warner Bros. Studios.

With director Mark Robson on location for *Von Ryan's Express* (1965).

On location, in 1965, for *Assault on a Queen.*

With poet Rod McKuen in 1969.

With wife Mia Farrow at a reception for *Tony Rome*.

bride in one of them, *The Detective*, in which he plays a New York policeman. She seemed bored while accompanying him on location to Florida where *Tony Rome*, and later its sequel, *Lady in Cement*, was filmed. In both films he seemed to enjoy his role as a Miami private eye. She, however, did not seem very content to stand idly by so she contracted with Paramount to play the lead in Roman Polanski's *Rosemary's Baby*.

That film remained in production long over the estimated time schedule. Frank, filming *The Detective* on location in New York, suffered a great deal of embarrassment and harassment when it reached near completion and Mia had still not reported for work. Disappointed, and visibly disenchanted, he had her replaced by Jacqueline Bisset. Their ultimate separation, and divorce, was bitter.

His subsequent television specials, mostly one-man shows, had the luster of brilliance only a genius of showmanship can radiate. Repeated viewings of them continually generate pleasure and excitement.

Frank made what was to have been his last professional nightclub appearance during the summer of 1970 at Caesars Palace in Las Vegas. The engagement ended abruptly after an altercation with a casino pit boss who refused him the privilege of gambling on credit. His departure, a two-way

With Rosalind Russell, just before his last public appearance at the 50th Anniversary benefit show of the Motion Picture and Television Relief Fund (1971).

21

Gregory Peck presenting Sinatra the Jean Hersholt Humanitarian Award in 1971.

Kennedy Center honoree Sinatra and Ronald and Nancy Reagan pay tribute to fellow honoree Virgil Thomson as Elia Kazan, Barbara Sinatra (partly hidden), Katherine Dunham and James Stewart join in on the applause at the December 1983 awards ceremony.

loss for Caesars Palace, was another headline maker.

Back in Hollywood, Sinatra was rumored to have been approached to do a movie about a maverick cop named Harry Callahan. The film was to be called *Dirty Harry*. Frank opted for another "dirty" character—a scrungy saddle tramp in the Old West. So he did *Dirty Dingus Magee*. It was admired by only his closest friends. It would also sour him on filmmaking for some time. It's interesting to speculate about Sinatra's career had he become Dirty Harry. And about Clint Eastwood's.

Sinatra's "retirement" came with a *Life* Magazine cover story and a gala farewell appearance at a benefit concert at the Dorothy Chandler Pavilion in Los Angeles in mid-June

1971. Retirement apparently did not suit Francis Albert Sinatra and he was back in action again by 1973 with the widely-heralded album "Ol' Blue Eyes Is Back," followed by his headline-making Main Event tour the next year along with a live album from Madison Square Garden. Actually he had never left the scene, except for cutting back for a while on concert appearances. His charity activities, at his own insistence never given much publicity, took precendence. At the 1971 Oscar ceremony, he had been given the Jean Hersholt Humanitarian Award; in 1972 the State of Israel Medallion of Valor.

He returned to films briefly in 1974 as one of the hosts of the MGM salute to itself and to moviegoers everywhere, *That's Entertainment!* In July 1976, he married again. The new Mrs. S. was (and still is) the former Barbara Blakely, a one-time showgirl who had been wed to Zeppo Marx and who certainly knew and understood Frank's world. The next year, he was devastated by the airplane death of his beloved mother Dolly.

During the 1970s, he not only put himself increasingly into the public arena, but also in politics. Shifting from left to right, primarily because of his snub by the Kennedys in

1962 (he had supported Humphrey and participated in his campaign race against Robert Kennedy), he again became a darling of the White House after enthusiastically embracing Richard Nixon. (In 1981, the Republicans called on Sinatra to stage the Reagan Inauguration ceremonies.) His on-going feud with the press continued apace and he was especially miffed at writers Maxine Cheshire and Kitty Kelley, the latter having done a hatchet job of a book on him.

Filmwise, he made his first television movie, *Contract on Cherry Street*, in 1977, although he had acted on TV on-and-off through the years, beginning with his role as Stage Manager in the demi-musical *Our Town* in the 1950s and continuing with occasional dramatic appearances on the weekly anthology show in 1957-58 which he hosted. (In 1987, he made an acclaimed guest appearance as a tenacious, over-the-hill detective on "Magnum, P.I.")

He made his first theatrical film in a decade, playing a cop in *The First Deadly Sin*, a muddled 1980 movie which gave him personally good notices, and he continued his round of charity concerts including yearly sold-out events at Radio City Music Hall, made several more albums, and began concert appearances in arenas across the country and even internationally. His appearance at the inauguration of the "integrated" Sun City, a Club Med complex in the South African enclave of Bophuthatswana, brought him the emnity of anti-Apartheidists the world over; his one-man "Concert for the Americas" performance opening an outdoor stadium in the Dominican Republic as a goodwill ambassador of sorts was captured on tape for showing on American TV and later on home video. These tours culminated with "The Ultimate Event" concerts coast to coast in 1988 with Sammy Davis, Jr. and Liza Minnelli (replacing Dean Martin). In 1989, the tour took him to Japan, Australia, England, and much of the Continent and became available first as a pay-per-view television event and then for Showtime.

In 1983, Sinatra was one of the honorees at the Kennedy Center Honors for his lifetime achievement in the arts.

During the late 1980s, plans were announced by CBS Television for a six-hour mini-series based on Frank Sinatra's life. Daughter Tina was to produce, with Frank's apparent blessings. Casting rightly became a problem, with three actors to play Sinatra at various phases of his career. And who would do the singing? The project, as the '90s approach, remains unrealized.

It is difficult to think of Francis Albert Sinatra, the Chairman of the Board, as he has come to be called in show business, old blue eyes as fans still call him, the man who was once simply "The Voice," in retirement and senior citizenship. To one and all, he shall always be young at heart.

With Sammy Davis, Jr. and Liza Minnelli on the occasion of "The Ultimate Event" in 1988—the tour, and later the television special.

The guest of honor entertains at the Variety Club's "All-Star Party for Frank Sinatra" in 1983, telecast on the eve of his birthday by CBS.

LAS VEGAS NIGHTS · 1941

With Connie Haines (*left*). In the foreground are Virginia Dale, Phil Regan, Bert Wheeler, Constance Moore, Tommy Dorsey and Lillian Cornell

CAST

A Paramount Picture. Directed by Ralph Murphy. Produced by William LeBaron. Original screenplay by Ernest Pagano and Harry Clork. Additional dialogue by Eddie Welch. Musical director, Victor Young. Musical advisor, Arthur Franklin. Musical numbers staged by LeRoy Prinz. Incidental score by Phil Boutelje and Walter Scharf. Musical arrangements by Axel Stordahl, Victor Young, Charles Bradshaw, Leo Shuken, and Max Terr. Director of photography, William C. Mellor. Film editor, Arthur Schmidt. Art directors, Hans Dreier and Earl Hedrick. Sound by Harold Lewis and Walter Oberst. Assistant director, Edward Selven. Running time, 89 minutes.

Norma Jennings, CONSTANCE MOORE; *Stu Grant,* BERT WHEELER; *Bill Stevens,* PHIL REGAN; *Mildred Jennings,* LILLIAN CORNELL; *Patsy Lynch,* VIRGINIA DALE; *Hank Bevis,* HANK LADD; *Katy,* BETTY BREWER; *William Stevens, Sr.,* HENRY KOLKER; *Gloria Stafford,* FRANCETTA MALLOY; *Maitre D',* EDDIE KANE; *Hat Check Girl,* ELEANOR STEWART; *Cigarette Girl,* WANDA MC KAY; *Croupier,* JACK MULHALL; *Judge Elkins,* RICHARD CARLE; *Mexican Trio:* NICK MORO (guitar & violin), FRANK YACONELLI (concertina), EARLE DOUGLAS (guitar); *Girls with Bill:* CATHERINE CRAIG, MARCELLE CHRISTOPHER, ELLA NEAL, JEAN PHILLIPS; Red Donahue and His Mule "Uno" and Tommy Dorsey and His Orchestra.

Sinatra's song: "I'll Never Smile Again" by Ruth Lowe. (*Sinatra appeared only as the male soloist with Dorsey's orchestra.*)

STORY

Stu Grant, vaudevillian, lands in Las Vegas with three sisters, who are singers; they are broke, but the girls have a claim to an uncle's estate. The girls win some money in a gambling casino, and put their winnings in the custody of Stu, who gambles most of it away, but there is enough left for them to start a night club of their own. The club is wrecked, and a shyster lawyer attempts to cheat the sisters of their inheritance, but they are able to sell it advantageously to a Los Angeles real estate operator, who happens to be the hero's father.

REVIEWS

"On account of Tommy Dorsey and his band being hopefully but vainly involved, there may be some mild jitterbug interest in Paramount's *Las Vegas Nights*, which settled heavily upon the screen of the Paramount Theatre yesterday. But from every other possible source of friendship, its expectation of favor is virtually nil. For there is precious little humor, little life, little anything save an excess of dullness in this labored musical show about a troupe of indigent entertainers adrift in the Nevada gambling town."

Bosley Crowther, *The New York Times*

"*Las Vegas Night*s is weak entertainment. The laughs are few and the dull stretches are many and long. The plot is strictly off the elbow and the narrative and musical items are haphazardly interwoven. . . . It's Tommy Dorsey's first try at a feature picture. His orchestra makes pleasant listening so long as it remains in a familiar groove."

Odec., Variety

SHIP AHOY · 1942

A Metro-Goldwyn-Mayer Picture. Directed by Edward Buzzell. Produced by Jack Cummings. Screenplay by Harry Clork. Additional material by Harry Kurnitz and Irving Brecher. Based on a story by Matt Brooks, Bradford Ropes, and Bert Kalmar. Music supervised and conducted by George Stoll. Musical arrangements by Axel Stordahl, Sy Oliver, Leo Arnaud, George Bassman, and Basil Adlam. Incidental score by George Bassman, George Stoll, and Henry Russell. Directors of photography, Leonard Smith and Robert Planck. Film editor, Blanche Sewell. Art directors, Cedric Gibbons and Harry McAfee. Set decorations by Edwin B. Willis. Recording director, Douglas Shearer. Gowns by Kalloch. Musical presentations by Merrill Pye. Dances directed by Bobby Connolly. Assistant director, Al Shenberg. Running time, 95 minutes.

CAST

Tallulah Winters, ELEANOR POWELL; *Merton K. Kibble*, RED SKELTON; *Skip Owens*, BERT LAHR; *Fran Evans*, VIRGINIA O'BRIEN; *H. U. Bennett*, WILLIAM POST, JR.; *Stump*, JAMES CROSS; *Stumpy*, EDDIE HARTMAN; *Art Higgins*, STUART CRAWFORD; *Dr. Farno*, JOHN EMERY; *Pietro Polesi*, BERNARD NEDELL; *Inspector Davis*, MORONI OLSEN; *Grimes*, RALPH DUNN; *Flammer*, WILLIAM TANNEN; *Nurse*, MARY TREEN; *Captain C. V. O'Brien*, RUSSELL HICKS; *Koro Sumo*, PHILIP AHN; *Felix*, NESTOR PAIVA; *Waldo*, BOBBY LARSON; *Waldo's Mother*, MARISKA ALDRICH; *Dr. Loring*, JOHN DILSON; *Mrs. Loring*, BARBARA BEDFORD; *Kibble's Secretaries:* CAROL HUGHES, GLADYS BLAKE, MARY CURRIER; *Agent in Puerto Rico*, ADDISON RICHARDS; *Lt. Cmdr. Thurston*, GRANDON RHODES; *Waiters:* GRANT WITHERS, OTTO REICHOW; *Girls:* HILLARY BROOKE, NATALIE THOMPSON; and Tommy Dorsey and His Orchestra.

Sinatra's songs: "The Last Call for Love" by Burton Lane, E. Y. Harburg, and Margery Cummings. "Poor You" by Burton Lane and E. Y. Harburg.

STORY

Tallulah Winters, star of a dancing troupe, leaves by ship with her company and Tommy Dorsey's band to put

Virginia O'Brien, Tommy Dorsey, Buddy Rich (drums), The Pied Pipers (behind piano), Connie Haines and Frank Sinatra (leaning on piano)

With pianist Joe Bushkin and The Pied Pipers (Chuck Lowry, Jo Stafford, Clark Yocum, Hal Hopper)

on a show at a floating nightclub in Puerto Rico. She is deceived into carrying along a magnetic mine, believing that she is serving her country by doing so. Her luggage, containing the mine, is misplaced with that of Merton K. Kibble, a hypochondriac daredevil-fiction writer. Eventually realizing that she has been duped by foreign agents, Tallulah dance-taps out a message in Morse code, and the agents are captured.

REVIEWS

"As a further selling point the exhibitor can point out that Tommy Dorsey and his orchestra are in the picture, and not just for one appearance either. They are around quite a deal and that fact should be of interest to Dorsey fans. The music is very good and some of the pieces will be heard on the 'Hit Parade.'"

P.C.M., Jr., *Motion Picture Herald*

"Eleanor Powell has never stepped more delightfully than in her dazzling routine around the ship's swimming pool. . . . The music to which she dances is provided by Tommy Dorsey and his orchestra, and certainly no one needs to be told of the preeminence Dorsey and his band have deservedly won as drawing cards. . . . The drummer and vocalist with Dorsey's orchestra have their moments."

The Hollywood Reporter

"Dorsey's own tromboning, Ziggy Elman's trumpet, Buddy Rich's drum work, and Frank Sinatra's singing, latter doing 90% of the vocalizing in the film and doing it well, stands out."

Scho., *Variety*

REVEILLE WITH BEVERLY · 1943

A Columbia Picture. Directed by Charles Barton. Produced by Sam White. Original screenplay by Howard J. Green, Jack Henley, and Albert Duffy. Musical director, Morris Stoloff. Director of photography, Philip Tannura. Film editor, James Sweeney. Art director, Lionel Banks. Set decorator, Joseph Kish. Sound recorder, Jack Goodrich. Assistant director, Rex Bailey. Running time, 78 minutes.

CAST

Beverly Ross, ANN MILLER; *Barry Lang*, WILLIAM WRIGHT; *Andy Adams*, DICK PURCELL; *Vernon Lewis*, FRANKLIN PANGBORN; *Mr. Kennedy*, TIM RYAN; *Eddie Ross*, LARRY PARKS; *Mrs. Ross*, BARBARA BROWN; *Mr. Ross*, DOUGLAS LEAVITT; *Evelyn Ross*, ADELE MARA; *Canvassback*, WALTER SANDE; *Stomp McCoy*, WALLY VERNON; *Mr. Smith*, ANDREW TOMBES; *Elsie*, IRENE RYAN; *Elmer*, DOODLES WEAVER; *Mrs. Browning*, VIRGINIA SALE; *Laura Jean*, SHIRLEY MILLS; and Bob Crosby and His Orchestra; Freddie Slack and His Orchestra, with Ella Mae Morse; Duke Ellington and His Orchestra; Count Basie and His Orchestra; Frank Sinatra, Mills Brothers, The Radio Rogues.

Sinatra's song: "Night and Day" by Cole Porter.

STORY

Beverly Ross, one-time salesgirl in a record shop, substitutes for a radio announcer on a dawn platter program. She plays popular songs instead of classical recordings, aiming the program at the boys in nearby Army camps. By the end of the first week, her fan mail is jamming the local post office. Eddie Ross, a rich inductee, switches identity with his former chauffeur who is also in the camp, makes a play for Beverly, and eventually wins her.

REVIEWS

"Ann Miller plays Beverly to score on abilities, apart from her dancing. In fact, she taps only in the finale, a breathless routine to the tune of *Thumbs Up for V for Victory*. When she airs the recordings, the disc irises out into the performance of the band, the Frank Sinatra number being especially smoothly staged."

The Hollywood Reporter

"It's all painfully inept in the writing, production, and, with few exceptions, in performance. The single excuse, the hot swing by the various bands and the Sinatra vocal, will be good for box office, but won't satisfy even the jitterbug customers, since every one of the names offers only a single number."

Hobe, *Variety*

"And this Frank Sinatra! Well, I am convinced there has been nothing like him since goldfish-eating. He even out-manias the chain letter rage and the Rudy Vallee crush of 15 years ago. And for the life of me, I can't tell you why. He is a slight young man given to violent sport jackets. He sings, yes—with an almost studied affectation of zombie mannerisms. His voice is pleasant enough—a kind of moaning baritone with a few trick inflections that involve going off-key at turning points in the melody.

"*Reveille with Beverly* is his first movie, so it is reportable news that at each moan and trick-turn of the Sinatra voice, in fact each time he so much as turns his dead-pan head or flickers an eye-lid, the adolescent set goes absolutely nuts! They squeal with delight; they rock and moan and make little animal cries. When he is finished, they are emotionally spent."

John T. McManus, *PM*

With Barbara Hale and Michele Morgan

HIGHER AND HIGHER · 1943

An RKO Radio Picture. Produced and directed by Tim Whelan. Associate producer, George Arthur. Screenplay by Jay Dratler and Ralph Spence. Additional dialogue by William Bowers and Howard Harris. Based on the play by Gladys Hurlbut and Joshua Logan. Musical director, Constantin Bakaleinikoff. Orchestral arrangements by Gene Rose. Musical arrangements for Frank Sinatra by Axel Stordahl. Incidental score by Roy Webb, orchestrated by Maurice de Packh. Vocal arrangements by Ken Darby. Musical numbers staged by Ernst Matray. Director of photography, Robert DeGrasse. Film editor, Gene Milford. Art directors, Albert S. D'Agostino and Jack Okey. Set decorators, Darrell Silvera and Claude Carpenter. Gowns by Edward Stevenson. Sound recorders, Jean L. Speak and James G. Stewart. Assistant director, Clem Beauchamp. Running time, 90 minutes.

Millie, MICHELE MORGAN; *Mike*, JACK HALEY; *Frank*, FRANK SINATRA; *Drake*, LEON ERROL; *Mickey*, MARCY MC GUIRE; *Fitzroy Wilson*, VICTOR BORGE; *Sandy*, MARY WICKES; *Mrs. Keating*, ELISABETH RISDON; *Catherine Keating*, BARBARA HALE; *Marty*, MEL TORME; *Byngham*, PAUL HARTMAN; *Hilda*, GRACE HARTMAN; *Oscar*, DOOLEY WILSON; *Miss Whiffin*, IVY SCOTT; *Mr. Green*, REX EVANS; *Hotel Manager*, STANLEY LOGAN; *Sarah, Maid*, OLA LORRAINE; *Mr. Duval*, KING KENNEDY; *Announcer*, ROBERT ANDERSEN; *Bridesmaids:* ELAINE RILEY, SHIRLEY O'HARA, DOROTHY MALONE, DAUN KENNEDY.

Sinatra's songs (by Jimmy McHugh and Harold Adamson): "You Belong in a Love Song," "I Couldn't Sleep a Wink Last Night," "A Lovely Way to Spend an Evening," "The Music Stopped," and "I Saw You First."

With Dooley Wilson and Michele Morgan

STORY

A houseful of servants face the loss of their long over-due wages when their employer, Drake, admits bankruptcy. Led by the valet, Mike, the servants scheme to pass off Millie, the scullery maid, as Drake's debutante daughter, hoping she will snare a wealthy husband and solve their financial problems. Frank, a well-to-do young fellow who lives next door, is considered a likely prospect as a suitor for the pseudo-heiress. Another target is "nobleman" Fitzroy Wilson, but he proves to be as phony as the "debutante." The servants connive to present Mille at the Debutantes' Ball, but their plans are haunted by Mrs. Keating, a society matron who has plans for her own debutante daughter Catherine. Millie's deception misfires when Mike, with whom she has long been in love, discovers the emotion is mutual. Catherine wins Frank. Finally, with the discovery of a secret storeroom filled with enough old liquor to restore the family fortune, Drake and his retinue decide to open a tavern.

REVIEWS

"The crooner certainly doesn't fulfill the cinema's traditional idea of a romantic figure which may be a break for him eventually. He plays himself in *Higher and Higher*, appears more at ease than we expected and should find his place as a film personality with careful choice of subjects. Crosby did it, didn't he?"

John L. Scott, *Los Angeles Times*

"The camera captures an innate shyness in the singer who has uniquely become an idol of the airlanes and the bobby-sock trade. Under the direction and production presentation by Tim Whelan, he impresses an audience as a regular guy who has retained his modest bewilderment concerning the fame that has just happened to happen to him. Perhaps Whelan couldn't have changed Sinatra's naturally retiring personality, but wisely he doesn't attempt to parade him as a fictional character. People who have never understood his appeal to swooning fans, have even resented him, will have no trouble in buying the guy they meet on the screen here."

The Hollywood Reporter

"It is through no fault of Jack Haley's or Michele Morgan's or Leon Errol's or even Frank Sinatra's that *Higher and Higher*, a loose adaptation of the Broadway musical, is not a particularly engaging film. The main trouble lies in the book, which is just another unlikely and inconsistent movie-musical affair. Mr. Sinatra comes out fine. He has some acting to do, and he does it."

David Lardner in *The New Yorker*

With Marcy McGuire in the "I Saw You First" number

With Mary Wickes, Jack Haley, Michele Morgan and Marcy McGuire

With Mary Wickes, Michele Morgan and Jack Haley

With Michele Morgan

With Jack Haley and Barbara Hale

With Gloria De Haven

STEP LIVELY · 1944

An RKO Picture. Directed by Tim Whelan. Produced by Robert Fellows. Screenplay by Warren Duff and Peter Milne. Based on the play Room Service *by John Murray and Allen Boretz. Musical director, Constantin Bakaleinikoff. Orchestral arrangements by Gene Rose. Musical arrangements for Frank Sinatra by Axel Stordahl. Vocal arrangements by Ken Darby. Musical numbers created and staged by Ernst Matray. Director of photography, Robert DeGrasse. Film editor, Gene Milford. Art directors, Albert S. D'Agostino and Carroll Clark. Set decorators, Darrell Silvera and Claude Carpenter. Gowns by Edward Stevenson. Sound recorders, Jean L. Speak and James G. Stewart. Assistant director, Clem Beauchamp. Running time, 88 minutes.*

CAST

Glen, FRANK SINATRA; *Miller,* GEORGE MURPHY; *Wagner,* ADOLPHE MENJOU; *Christine,* GLORIA DE HAVEN; *Gribble,* WALTER SLEZAK; *Jenkins,* EUGENE PALLETTE; *Binion,* WALLY BROWN; *Harry,* ALAN CARNEY; *Dr. Glass,* GRANT MITCHELL; *Miss Abbott,* ANNE JEFFREYS; *Mother,* FRANCES KING; *Father,* HARRY NOBLE; *Country Yokel,* GEORGE CHANDLER; *Louella,* ROSEMARY LA PLANCHE; *Louise,* SHIRLEY O'HARA; *Lois,* ELAINE RILEY; *Telephone Operator,* DOROTHY MALONE; *Doorman,* FRANK MAYO.

Sinatra's songs (by Jule Styne and Sammy Cahn):

"Come Out, Come Out, Wherever You Are," "Where Does Love Begin?," "As Long as There's Music," and "Some Other Time."

STORY

Glen, a young country bumpkin from Oswego who dreams of becoming a playwright, has sent his play, along with $1500 toward its production, to a slick Broadway producer named Miller. Arriving in New York to learn how his play is progressing, Glen finds Miller interned in a Manhattan hotel because of a large, unpaid bill, rehearsing another script with twenty-two hungry actors. A man named Jenkins, representing a mysterious backer, appears with a check for $50,000 and a protégé, Miss Abbott, who falls for Glen. The check, however, is rubber, and Miller and his aides, Binion and Harry, become intent on getting their new musical on the boards within five days in order to beat the check when it bounces back from a San Francisco bank. At the same time, Miller attempts to dodge Gribble, the hotel's harassed, slow-witted manager, and Wagner, the irascible hotel chain supervisor and efficiency expert. Miller also tries to evade the persistent playwright, but then discovers the young man has a voice that makes women swoon, and prevails upon Glen to take over the leading role in his musical. The playwright-turned-crooner is an overnight success, saves the show, and wins Christine, the girl he loves.

With Anne Jeffreys

With Walter Slezak and George Murphy

REVIEWS

"*Step Lively* is not a very good dish for Sinatra, although it demonstrates that he has far more performing range and assurance than many might have suspected. As a film, it is strictly a cream puff, nicely flavored and well baked."

Howard Barnes, *New York Herald Tribune*

"The old George Abbott play, *Room Service*, has been resurrected for an RKO remake, with song trimming palpably designed to fit Frank Sinatra. As a tailormade vehicle it's somewhat loosely fitted but in the main it will please. It's good summer film fare, and riding the Sinatra crest right now it's sure to do well. . . . Sinatra, an important property now to RKO and Metro (where he is on loan), handles himself with ease but still needs some camera assists."

Abel, *Variety*

"With the Sinatra Swoon & Squeal Society in force at the Palace Theatre, where *Step Lively* is displaying their idol under favorable screen conditions, it is not always possible to pay attention to the picture. Whenever Mr. Sinatra does anything the slightest bit endearing, his followers let forth such an ear-piercing shriek that further

With Walter Slezak, Alan Carney, Wally Brown, George Murphy, Adolphe Menjou and Gloria De Haven

calm judgment is out of the question. This is usually followed by loud and oppositious noises from sailors and others pretending to excess masculinity, and the result is a portion of bedlam. Fortunately, *Step Lively*, the movie version of the hectic Broadway hit, *Room Service*, is itself no shrinking violet that rough usage withers. Much of the footage is slap-happy farce that could be appreciated in a boiler factory. ... Sinatra himself, cast in the modest role of the young playwright whose money and play have been taken without compensation, is better than in his previous movie efforts. He looks better, acts better, and sings in the manner that has made him famous. If it were not for the rampant demonstrations of his fanatics, there would be little to hold against him. ... Apparently the Voice is here to stay, and if the progress continues, the experience will not be as trying as anticipated, providing the incidental squeals can be tuned out."

Archer Winsten, *New York Post*

"As shuddering exhibitors remember from his first picture, Sinatra's name on the marquee is sufficient to guarantee lipsticky posters on the outside, moaning galleryites within."

Time

With Eugene Pallette, George Murphy, Anne Jeffreys, Wally Brown, Alan Carney and Gloria De Haven

Singing "What Makes the Sunset?"

ANCHORS AWEIGH · 1945

With Kathryn Grayson, Gene Kelly and Dean Stockwell

A Metro-Goldwyn-Mayer Picture. Technicolor. Directed by George Sidney. Produced by Joe Pasternak. Screenplay by Isobel Lennart. Based on a story by Natalie Marcin. Music supervised and conducted by George Stoll. Frank Sinatra's vocal arrangements by Axel Stordahl. Kathryn Grayson's vocal arrangements by Earl Brent. Incidental score by George Stoll and Calvin Jackson. Orchestrations by Ted Duncan, Joseph Nussbaum, Robert Franklyn, and Wally Heglin. Dance sequences created by Gene Kelly. Directors of photography, Robert Planck and Charles Boyle. Film editor, Adrienne Fazan. Art directors, Cedric Gibbons and Randall Duell. Set decorators, Edwin B. Willis and Richard Pefferle. Sound recorder, James Z. Flaster. Costumes by Irene and Kay Dean. Makeup by Jack Dawn. Assistant director, George Rheim. Color consultant, Henri Jaffa. "Tom & Jerry" cartoon directed by Fred Quimby. Running time, 143 minutes.

CAST

Clarence Doolittle, FRANK SINATRA; Susan Abbott, KATHRYN GRAYSON; Joseph Brady, GENE KELLY; Himself, JOSE ITURBI; Donald Martin, DEAN STOCKWELL; Girl from Brooklyn, PAMELA BRITTON; Police Sergeant, RAGS RAGLAND; Cafe Manager, BILLY GILBERT; Admiral Hammond, HENRY O'NEILL; Carlos, CARLOS RAMIREZ; Police Captain, EDGAR KENNEDY; Bertram Kraler, GRADY SUTTON; Admiral's Aide, LEON AMES; Little Girl Beggar, SHARON MC MANUS; Radio Cop, JAMES FLAVIN; Studio Cop, JAMES BURKE; Hamburger Man, HENRY ARMETTA; Iturbi's Assistant, CHESTER CLUTE; Movie Director, WILLIAM FORREST; Assistant Director, RAY TEAL; Bartender, MILTON KIBBEE; Studio Waitress, RENIE RIANO; Butler, CHARLES COLEMAN; Soldiers: GARRY OWEN, STEVE BRODIE.

Sinatra's songs: "We Hate to Leave," "What Makes the Sunset?," "The Charm of You," "I Begged Her," and "I Fall in Love Too Easily" by Jule Styne and Sammy Cahn; "Lullaby" ("Wiegenlied") by Johannes Brahms.

With Kathryn Grayson

With Gene Kelly and Dean Stockwell

43

With Gene Kelly

With Pamela Britton

STORY

Clarence and Joseph, two sailors on shore leave, spend their holiday in Hollywood. They meet a pretty movie player, Susan Abbott, who lives with her little nephew. Joseph has always had a way with the ladies, and he tries to get his shy shipmate Clarence to fall in love with Susan, and she with him. But his scheming boomerangs when he himself falls for Susan, and she confesses he's the one she really prefers. Clarence, meanwhile, has forgotten to be shy, and has lost his heart to a girl from Brooklyn. When the sailors go back to their ship, they've both got new romances on shore.

REVIEWS

"Surprise revelation of the picture is the team of Frank Sinatra and Gene Kelly, who go through a remarkable variety of paces. This consists of songs, humor, and even dancing. For both of them, too. Sinatra does a good job in a duo with Kelly."

Edwin Schallert, *Los Angeles Times*

"The superb dances which Gene Kelly creates and executes are perhaps the most memorable moments of a memorable evening. All the world knows Frank Sinatra can sing; now it turns out that he can act, too. His characterization of Kelly's shipmate is delightful."

Thalia Bell, *Motion Picture Herald*

"It has sock artists, sock tunes and sock dances, all given by three stars who are tops in their individual lines: Frank Sinatra, Kathryn Grayson, and Gene Kelly are just what the doctor ordered to help you spend a pleasant afternoon or evening."

Louella O. Parsons, *Los Angeles Examiner*

With Gene Kelly, Dean Stockwell and Rags Ragland

With Gene Kelly and Kathryn Grayson

With Kathryn Grayson, Gene Kelly and Pamela Britton

THE HOUSE I LIVE IN · 1945

An RKO Radio Picture. Directed by Mervyn LeRoy. Produced by Frank Ross. Original screenplay by Albert Maltz. Musical director, Axel Stordahl. Incidental score by Roy Webb. Film editor, Philip Martin, Jr. Running time, 10 minutes.

Sinatra's songs: "If You Are But a Dream" by Nathan J. Bonx, Jack Fulton, and Moe Jaffe (adapted from Anton Rubinstein's "Romance"); "The House I Live In" by Earl Robinson and Lewis Allan.

STORY

In a radio rehearsal studio, Sinatra sings "If You Are But a Dream." The song completed, the band leader calls for a few minutes rest and Sinatra steps out into an adjoining alley for a breath of air. He comes upon a group of boys chasing and beating another boy—"because we don't like his religion."

Sinatra talks to them, straightens them out a bit, and turns back to the studio doorway. "Hey, what do *you* do for a living?" yells one boy, and Sinatra replies, "I sing." Another says, "Aw, you're kidding," and Sinatra answers, "No, I'll show you," and sings "The House I Live In."

REVIEWS

"... a film that packs more power, punch and solid substance than most of the featres ground each year out of Hollywood. The picture's message is Tolerance. Its medium is song. And its protagonist is Frank Sinatra—the bow-tied, fan-eared, scrawny-necked idol of the bobbie soxers, who has, amazingly, grown within a few short years from a lovelorn microphone-hugging crooner to become one of filmdom's leading and most vocal battlers for a democratic way of life.

Mr. Sinatra takes his popularity seriously. More, he attempts to do something constructive with it. Millions, young and old, who will not or cannot read between the lines of their daily newspapers and are blind to the weed-like growth of bigotry and intolerance planted by hate-ridden fanatics, will listen carefully to what Mr. Sinatra has to say in this short film."

Cue

"*The House I Live In* is a worthy, heartfelt short on religious and racial tolerance. The main trouble is that those who need it—the race-rioting bigots and barfly commandos—will doubtless think it is meant for someone else.

This well-meaning project ... part of a larger Sinatra crusade ... was staged with free help from topflight Hollywood talent. They got the idea for the picture when they learned that Sinatra had been making spontaneous visits to high schools where he preached little sermons on tolerance. The short's message should be clear enough to anyone."

Time

NOTE: *The House I Live In* received a Special Award from the Academy of Motion Picture Arts and Sciences.

TILL THE CLOUDS ROLL BY · 1946

A Metro-Goldwyn-Mayer Picture. Technicolor. Directed by Richard Whorf. Produced by Arthur Freed. Screenplay by Myles Connolly and Jean Holloway. Adapted by George Wells from an original story by Guy Bolton. Based on the life and music of Jerome Kern. Music supervised and conducted by Lennie Hayton. Orchestrations by Conrad Salinger. Incidental score by Conrad Salinger, Lennie Hayton, and Roger Edens. Additional orchestrations by Robert Franklyn, Wally Heglin, Leo Shuken, Sidney Cutner, and Ted Duncan. Vocal arrangements by Kay Thompson. Musical numbers staged and directed by Robert Alton. Judy Garland's numbers directed by Vincente Minnelli. Directors of photography, Harry Stradling and George Folsey. Film editor, Albert Akst. Art directors, Cedric Gibbons and Daniel B. Cathcart. Set decorators, Edwin B. Willis and Richard Pefferle. Recording supervisor, Douglas Shearer. Costume supervisor, Irene; women's costumes by Helen Rose; men's costumes by Valles. Makeup by Jack Dawn. Special effects by Warren Newcombe. Montages by Peter Ballbusch. Hair styles by Sydney Guilaroff. Assistant director, Wally Worsley. Color consultant, Henri Jaffa. Running time, 137 minutes.

CAST

Guest Star, JUNE ALLYSON; *Sally*, LUCILLE BREMER; *Marilyn Miller*, JUDY GARLAND; *Magnolia**, KATHRYN GRAYSON; *James I. Hessler*, VAN HEFLIN; *Julie**, LENA HORNE; *Band Leader*, VAN JOHNSON; *Guest Star*, ANGELA LANSBURY; *Gaylord Ravenal**, TONY MARTIN; *Ellie**, VIRGINIA O'BRIEN; *Julie Sanderson*, DINAH SHORE; *Guest Star*, FRANK SINATRA; *Jerome Kern*, ROBERT WALKER; *Mrs. Jerome Kern*, DOROTHY PATRICK; *Dance Specialty*, GOWER CHAMPION; *Dance Specialty*, CYD CHARISSE; *Charles Frohman*, HARRY HAYDEN; *Oscar Hammerstein*, PAUL LANGTON; *Victor Herbert*, PAUL MAXEY; *Dance Specialty*, RAY MC DONALD; *Mrs. Muller*, MARY NASH; *Joe**, CALEB PETERSON; *Hennessey*, WILLIAM "BILL" PHILLIPS; *Sally as a girl*, JOAN WELLS; *Specialty*, THE WILDE TWINS; *Cecil Keller*, REX EVANS; *Dance Specialty*, MAURICE KELLY; *Orchestra Conductor*, RAY TEAL; *Frohman's Secretary*, BYRON FOULGER; *Captain Andy**, WILLIAM HALLIGAN; *Steve**, BRUCE COWLING.

Sinatra's song: "Ol' Man River" by Jerome Kern and Oscar Hammerstein II.

* in *Show Boat* number.

STORY

After the successful opening night of *Show Boat* on Broadway, Jerome Kern attends a party in his honor and then asks his chauffeur to drive to an old New York brownstone house, the scene, as he remembers, of his beginning his career as an aspiring song writer. Generously interspersed with Kern numbers, the story goes on to tell how Kern attained success in the theatre, married happily, and eventually came to Hollywood and MGM Studios, where *Show Boat* was being filmed.

REVIEW

"Of course *Ol' Man River* gets a big play, being put on early by Caleb Peterson and chorus and late in the show by Frank Sinatra. Both versions are creditably done and are calculated to meet any divergence of audience preference in the singing of *Ol' Man River*."

Variety

"The story itself, not unlike most film biographies, is a success story—told simply and unaffectedly, and not in the embarrassingly fawning fashion characteristic of certain other recent endeavors along these lines. . . . It's a glorious, lively and grand entertainment, not to be missed."

Cue

"As for drama—whatever drama the story lacks may be found in the Music Hall's audience. Since Van Johnson, Van Heflin, Robert Walker, Lena Horne, Dinah Shore, June Allyson, Judy Garland—and Frank Sinatra—are billed, and since each of these has his own coterie, and since their size is not constant, there is no way of knowing in advance which of these artists will arouse the most shrieks. The suspense, therefore, is terrific. Being a Sinatra fan myself, I am proud to report that at the performance I participated in, my man won by thousands of decibels."

Cecelia Ager, *PM*

"Frank Sinatra wanted to sing 'Ol' Man River,' and Kern said he thought that would be a good idea. Oscar Hammerstein, who collaborated with Kern on lots of musicals, including *Show Boat*, thought so too.

" 'My idea with that song,' said Kern, 'was to have a rabbity little fellow do it—somebody who made you believe he was tired of livin' and scared of dyin'. That's how you do it, Frankie.' "

Amy Porter, *Collier's*

T HAPPENED IN BROOKLYN · 1947

With Jimmy Durante

With Gloria Grahame

With Kathryn Grayson

A Metro-Goldwyn-Mayer Picture. Directed by Richard Whorf. Produced by Jack Cummings. Screenplay by Isobel Lennart. Based on an original story by John McGowan. Musical supervision, direction, and incidental score by Johnny Green. Orchestrations by Ted Duncan. Frank Sinatra's vocal orchestrations by Axel Stordahl. Musical numbers staged and directed by Jack Donohue. Piano solos arranged and played by Andre Previn. Director of photography, Robert Planck. Film editor, Blanche Sewell. Art directors, Cedric Gibbons and Leonard Vasian. Set decorators, Edwin B. Willis and Alfred E. Spencer. Makeup by Jack Dawn. Recording supervisor, Douglas Shearer. Assistant director, Earl McEvoy. Running time, 104 minutes.

CAST

Danny Webson Miller, FRANK SINATRA; *Anne Fielding,* KATHRYN GRAYSON; *Jamie Shellgrove,* PETER LAWFORD; *Nick Lombardi,* JIMMY DURANTE;

Nurse, GLORIA GRAHAME; *Rae Jakobi,* MARCY MC GUIRE; *Digby John,* AUBREY MATHER; *Mrs. Kardos,* TAMARA SHAYNE; *Leo Kardos,* BILLY ROY; *Johnny O'Brien,* BOBBY LONG; *Police Sergeant,* WILLIAM HAADE; *Canon Green,* LUMSDEN HARE; *Fodderwing,* WILSON WOOD; *Mr. Dobson,* RAYMOND LARGAY; *Captain,* WILLIAM TANNEN; *Driver,* AL HILL; *Cop,* DICK WESSEL; *Corporal,* LENNIE BREMEN; *Soldier,* BRUCE COWLING; *Printer,* MITCHELL LEWIS.

Sinatra's songs: "Brooklyn Bridge," "I Believe," "Time After Time," "The Song's Gotta Come from the Heart," and "It's the Same Old Dream" by Jule Styne and Sammy Cahn; "La Ci Darem la Mano" by Mozart; "Black Eyes" (in Russian).

STORY

Danny Miller, a returned G.I., has no family, and it seems the only thing he is in love with is the Brooklyn Bridge. He bunks in with an old pal, Nick Lombardi, jan-

With Kathryn Grayson and Peter Lawford

With Peter Lawford

itor at New Utrecht High School, where Anne Fielding is a teacher. Both Danny and Anne are disillusioned but aspiring singers. Jamie Shellgrove, scion of a titled English family, arrives in New York with a song he has written, and it is finally performed successfully in a school-children's recital. Jamie and Anne fall in love, and Danny suddenly remembers happily a certain nurse he once knew who hails from Brooklyn. So everybody is in love, and happy.

REVIEW

"*It Happened in Brooklyn* couldn't happen any place except Hollywood. . . . Sinatra becomes a smoother performer every time out."

Newsweek

"This lively, pleasant and altogether unselfconscious cinematic romp, set in the booby-hatch of Brooklyn, may not win a Pulitzer Prize as highbrow literary entertain-ment; but for simple, straightforward, unadulterated movie fun, its uncomplicated plot and slaphappy comedy-line formula are sheer magic."

Cue

"I suppose the big revelation of *It Happened in Brooklyn,* aside from little Miss Grayson being the niftiest Lakme in the business if not the most bell-like, is the way Frank Sinatra seems to have loosened up and got into the swing of things as a film player and even as a comedian. Things look promising for Frankie-boy in films even if his wooing notes should one day peter out."

John McManus, *PM*

"Frank, of course, thrills the customers with his vocal-izing, but it's his naturalness and easy-going charm that begets applause. It just seems like all of a sudden it's spring and Frankie is an actor. His comical duet with Durante provoked great whoops of approval from the boys and girls out front."

Sara Hamilton, *Los Angeles Examiner*

THE MIRACLE OF THE BELLS · 1948

An RKO Radio Picture. Directed by Irving Pichel. Produced by Jesse L. Lasky and Walter MacEwen. Screenplay by Ben Hecht and Quentin Reynolds. Additional material for Frank Sinatra's sequences by DeWitt Bodeen. Based on the novel by Russell Janney. Music by Leigh Harline. Director of photography, Robert de Grasse. Film editor, Elmo Williams. Art director, Ralph Berger. Costumes by Renie. Makeup by Karl H. Herlinger, Jr. Hair stylist, Annabelle Levy. Musical director, C. Bakaleinikoff. Dance director, Charles O'Curran. Sound recorder, Philip N. Mitchell. Assistant director, Harry D'Arcy. Production manager, Fred Fleck. Running time, 120 minutes.

CAST

Bill Dunnigan, FRED MacMURRAY; *Olga Treskovna*, ALIDA VALLI; *Father Paul*, FRANK SINATRA; *Marcus Harris*, LEE J. C COBB; *Orloff*, HAROLD VERMILYE; *Father Spinsky*, CHARLES MEREDITH; *Tod Jones*, JIM NOLAN; *Anna Klovna*, VERONIKA PATAKY; *Ming Gow*, PHILIP AHN; *Dolan*, FRANK FERGUSON; *Dr. Jennings*, FRANK WILCOX; *Koslick*, RAY TEAL; *Katie*, DOROTHY SEBASTIAN; *Tom Elmore*, BILLY WAYNE; *Freddy Evans*, SYD SAYLOR; *Milton Wild*, TOM STEVENSON; *Grave Digger*, IAN WOLFE; *Slenzka*, OLIVER BLAKE; *Max*, GEORGE CHANDLER; *Martha*, REGINA WALLACE; *Worshippers:* FRANKLYN FARNUM, SNUB POLLARD, BETH TAYLOR; Narrated by QUENTIN REYNOLDS.

Sinatra's song: "Ever Homeward" by Kasimierz Lubomirski, Jule Styne, and Sammy Cahn.

With Fred MacMurray and Alida Valli

STORY

Bill Dunnigan, a theatrical press agent, comes to Coaltown, Pennsylvania, to bury Olga Treskovna beside her coal-miner father, a death-bed promise he had made her, the one girl he has loved. Bill had first met Olga when she was in burlesque, and she had confessed at once her burning desire to be a great dramatic actress. But, as Bill tells Father Paul of the little struggling St. Michael's Church, a terminal disease burned feverishly within Olga, too, and although Bill had got her a big role in a Hollywood super feature, she only barely finished the part before she died of tuberculosis. Marcus Harris, the producer, has determined to shelve the film on the theory that the public will never accept a picture with a star who has died. Bill tries to gain publicity by having the bells of Coaltown ring for four days, but Harris remains firm in his decision not to release the film. Then worshippers at morning Mass at St. Michael's note how the statues of St. Michael and the Virgin have turned on their bases to face

With Fred MacMurray

With Fred MacMurray

With Fred MacMurray and Alida Valli

Olga's coffin. Although Father Paul has a realistic explanation for the "miracle," he does not spoil public emotion, and when commentators like Quentin Reynolds tell the world of the good that has come to Coaltown, Marcus Harris changes his mind and decides to release Olga's picture.

REVIEWS

"Sinatra wisely doesn't attempt to "act" at all. His portrayal has the virtue of simplicity. His one song, *Ever Homeward*, is unaccompanied."

Philip K. Scheuer, *Los Angeles Times*

"Beyond these two principals, some words must also be set down for Frank Sinatra as Father Paul, the priest of the little mining town church. I cannot, however, think of the precise words at this minute. Since Crosby also played a cleric in a couple of pictures, I suppose Sinatra is entitled to have his fling, too. At least one of them by this time should be a monsignor."

Leo Mishkin, *New York Morning Telegraph*

"From the Russell Janney best-seller, Ben Hecht and Quentin Reynolds have fashioned a sentimental story with an inspirational message. Its chief asset is the cast, comprising Fred MacMurray as a press agent, Valli as a flickering star on the Hollywood horizon, Frank Sinatra as a soft-spoken priest, and Lee J. Cobb as a picture producer. . . . As for Frankie turning his collar around to play the part of Father Paul, in some quarters he may be accused of copying Crosby in *Going My Way*."

Photoplay

56

THE KISSING BANDIT: 1948

A Metro-Goldwyn-Mayer Picture. Technicolor. Directed by Laslo Benedek. Produced by Joe Pasternak. Original screenplay by Isobel Lennart and John Briard Harding. Music supervised and conducted by George Stoll. Musical arrangements by Leo Arnaud. Incidental score by George Stoll, Albert Sendrey, Scott Bradley, and Andre Previn. Additional orchestrations by Albert Sendrey, Calvin Jackson, Conrad Salinger, Robert Van Eps, Paul Marquardt, and Earl Brent. Dance director, Stanley Donen. Director of photography, Robert Surtees. Film editor, Adrienne Fazan. Art directors, Cedric Gibbons and Randall Duell. Set decorators, Edwin B. Willis and Jack D. Moore. Costumes by Walter Plunkett. Makeup by Jack Dawn. Hair stylist, Sydney Guilaroff. Special effects by A. Arnold Gillespie. Sound recorder, Wilhelm W. Brockway. Assistant director, Marvin Stuart. Production manager, Sergei Petschnikoff. Color consultant, Henri Jaffa. Running time, 102 minutes.

CAST

Ricardo, FRANK SINATRA; *Teresa,* KATHRYN GRAYSON; *Chico,* J. CARROL NAISH; *Isabella,* MILDRED NATWICK; *Don José,* MIKHAIL RASUMNY; *General Torro,* BILLY GILBERT; *Bianca,* SONO OSATO; *Colonel Gomez,* CLINTON SUNDBERG; *Count Belmonte,* CARLETON YOUNG; *Juanita,* EDNA SKINNER; *Guitarist,* VICENTE GOMEZ; *Pepito* HENRY MIRELEZ; *Pablo,* NICK THOMPSON; *Francisco,* JOSE DOMINGUEZ; *Lotso,* ALBERT MORIN; *Esteban,* PEDRO REGAS; *Postman,* JULIAN RIVERO; *Fernando,* MITCHELL LEWIS; *Grandee,* BYRON FOULGER; and RICARDO MONTALBAN, ANN MILLER, CYD CHARISSE in "Dance of Fury" by Nacio Herb Brown.

Sinatra's songs: "What's Wrong with Me?", "If I Steal a Kiss," and "Senorita" by Nacio Herb Brown and Edward Heyman; "Siesta" by Nacio Herb Brown and Earl Brent.

STORY

Ricardo, a young Boston business school graduate, comes to old California in the days of the grandees to take over his late father's innkeeping business. His departed father, he quickly learns, was really a bandit, and the men of the old gang are waiting for Ricardo to get back into a flourishing business. Also, Ricardo's father left all the ladies of the ranchos he robbed with a kiss they could never forget. Ricardo is hard put to it in order to keep up his father's reputation until he meets Teresa, daughter of the don who rules the territory. Ricardo and his head man Chico impersonate tax collectors expected from Spain, and are caught and disclosed as phonies. But love conquers all, and at the final fade-out Ricardo is free, forgiven, and has won the beautiful Teresa.

REVIEWS

"The Kissing Bandit is a sock musical show in which those intrinsic ingredients—story, comedy, music, romance, and action—are blended to a rare degree of perfection. They are put together in a pattern more closely approximating operetta than the usual film musical pattern. . . . Frank Sinatra, playing the undernourished bandit, is just wonderful. He handles the comedy falls and romantic scenes with equal ease, and of course his warbling is just what the fans expect."

The Hollywood Reporter

"The frenzied members of Frankie's Fan Clubs are not going to be very happy about their Mr. Sinatra's latest picture. In this lavish but limping Technicolored musical of Spanish California in the 1830s, Frankie plays a mousey little man who masquerades as a notorious and quite romantic bandit. Never any great shakes as a comic, Mr. Sinatra is further handicapped by a weak script, silly dialogue and uncertain direction."

Cue

With Kathryn Grayson

With Sono Osato and J. Carrol Naish

"Lavish, laugh-laden and lithesome is this filmusical which in story, mountings and music leans toward the operetta technique. The plot was cleverly contrived to fit the acting and singing talents of Frank Sinatra so that his appearance in the title role is sufficiently tongue-in-cheek to make it acceptable—even ingratiating."

Box Office

**TAKE ME OUT
TO THE BALL GAME · 1949**

A Metro-Goldwyn-Mayer Picture. Technicolor. Directed by Busby Berkeley. Produced by Arthur Freed. Screenplay by Harry Tugend and George Wells. Based on a story by Gene Kelly and Stanley Donen. Music supervised and conducted by Adolph Deutsch. Incidental score by Roger Edens. Orchestral arrangements by Adolph Deutsch, Conrad Salinger, Robert Franklyn, Paul Marquardt, Alexander Courage, Axel Stordahl, and Leo Arnaud. Vocal arrangements by Robert Tucker. Dance directors, Gene Kelly and Stanley Donen. Director of photography, George Folsey. Film editor, Blanche Sewell. Art directors, Cedric Gibbons and Daniel B. Cathcart. Set decorators, Edwin B. Willis and Henry W. Grace. Costumes by Helen Rose and Valles. Makeup by Jack Dawn. Hair stylist, Sydney Guilaroff. Special effects by Warren Newcombe. Montages by Peter Ballbusch. Sound recorder, James K. Brock. Assistant director, Dolf Zimmer. Production manager, Sergei Petschnikoff. Color consultant, James Gooch. Running time, 93 minutes.

CAST

Dennis Ryan, FRANK SINATRA; K. C. Higgins, ESTHER WILLIAMS; Eddie O'Brien, GENE KELLY; Shirley Delwyn, BETTY GARRETT; Joe Lorgan, EDWARD ARNOLD; Nat Goldberg, JULES MUNSHIN; Michael Gilhuly, RICHARD LANE; Slappy Burke, TOM DUGAN; Zalinka, MURRAY ALPER; Nick Donford, WILTON GRAFF; Henchman, MACK GRAY; Henchman, CHARLES REGAN; Steve, SAUL GORSS; Karl, DOUGLAS FOWLEY; Dr. Winston, EDDIE PARKES; Cop in Park, JAMES BURKE; Specialty, THE BLACKBURN TWINS; Senator Catcher, GORDON JONES; Acrobat, HENRY KULKY; Photographer, WILLIAM TANNEN; Teddy Roosevelt, ED CASSIDY; Umpire, DICK WESSEL; Umpire, PAT FLAHERTY; Girls on Train: VIRGINIA BATES, JOI LANSING.

Sinatra's songs: "Take Me Out to the Ball Game" by Albert von Tilzer and Jack Norworth; "Yes, Indeedy," "O'Brien to Ryan to Goldberg," "The Right Girl for Me," and "It's Fate, Baby, It's Fate" by Roger Edens, Betty Comden, and Adolph Green; "Strictly U.S.A." by Roger Edens.

STORY

Vaudeville's most popular song-and-dance team, Dennis Ryan and Eddie O'Brien, spend every summer as star members of the Wolves baseball team. A pretty new manager, K. C. Higgins, comes on the scene, and both Eddie and Dennis are much smitten by her charms. Eddie, however, not only gets involved with a two-timing gambling king, Joe Lorgan, who is out to wreck the Wolves, but he takes on a job at night directing a night club chorus. Miss Higgins benches Eddie for breaking training. On the day of the big game, Lorgan tries to keep a repentant Eddie from getting into the play, but fails. Eddie helps the Wolves win the pennant. He also wins Miss Higgins, while Dennis realizes that Shirley, who has been aggressively pursuing him, is worthy of succumbing to. He has thought her fast, but now realizes she's the gal for him.

With Gene Kelly, Esther Williams, Jules Munshin and Betty Garrett

With Gene Kelly

With Betty Garrett and Esther Williams

REVIEWS

"For all its high spots, the show lacks consistent style and pace, and the stars are forced to clown and grimace much more than becomes their speed. Actually, the plotted humor is conspicuously bush-league stuff. Don't be surprised if you see people getting up for a seventh-inning stretch."

Bosley Crowther, *The New York Times*

"*Take Me Out to the Ball Game* is a lazy Technicolored cine-musical aimed squarely and accurately at the summer box office. Set in the nostalgic days of the modified bustle, its story is wonderfully easy to follow; it involves Frank Sinatra and Gene Kelly in a whirl of songs and dances that are easy to forget."

Time

"Frank Sinatra and Gene Kelly are no strangers to the jobs of sharing stellar honors, and the addition of Esther Williams makes their engaging talents seem that much brighter. Sinatra sings and gags his way through a most pleasant role, and Kelly steps out to knock the folks dead with his terrific dancing. The boys are given an elegant set of songs by Betty Comden, Adolph Green, and Roger Edens, to say nothing of the title tune by Albert von Tilzer and Jack Norworth."

The Hollywood Reporter

With Gene Kelly

ON THE TOWN · 1949

With Gene Kelly

With Betty Garrett, Ann Miller, Jules Munshin, Vera-Ellen and Gene Kelly

CAST

A Metro-Goldwyn-Mayer Picture. Technicolor. Directed by Gene Kelly and Stanley Donen. Produced by Arthur Freed. Screenplay by Adolph Green and Betty Comden, from their musical play based on an idea by Jerome Robbins. Music supervised and conducted by Lennie Hayton. Orchestral arrangements by Conrad Salinger, Robert Franklyn, and Wally Heglin. Vocal arrangements by Saul Chaplin. Incidental score by Roger Edens, Saul Chaplin and Conrad Salinger. Music for "Miss Turnstiles" Dance and "A Day in New York" Ballet by Leonard Bernstein. Director of photography, Harold Rosson. Film editor, Ralph E. Winters. Art directors, Cedric Gibbons and Jack Martin Smith. Set decorators, Edwin B. Willis and Jack D. Moore. Costumes by Helen Rose. Makeup by Jack Dawn. Hair stylist, Sydney Guilaroff. Special effects by Warren Newcombe. Sound recorder, John A. Williams. Assistant director, Jack Gertsman. Production manager, Hugh Boswell. Color consultants, Henri Jaffa and James Gooch. Running time, 98 minutes.

Gabey, GENE KELLY; *Chip*, FRANK SINATRA; *Brunhilde Esterhazy*, BETTY GARRETT; *Claire Huddesen*, ANN MILLER; *Ozzie*, JULES MUNSHIN; *Ivy Smith*, VERA-ELLEN; *Madame Dilyovska*, FLORENCE BATES; *Lucy Shmeeler*, ALICE PEARCE; *Professor*, GEORGE MEADER.

Sinatra's songs: "New York, New York" and "Come Up to My Place" by Leonard Bernstein, Adolph Green, and Betty Comden; "You're Awful," "On the Town," and "Count on Me" by Roger Edens, Adolph Green, and Betty Comden.

STORY

Three sailors, Gabey, Chip, and Ozzie, set out to do New York in 24 hours of shore leave. All want to find the right girl, and the hunt is on right away in Gabey's behalf for the girl who is "Miss Turnstiles," the representative working girl. Gabey finds her; Chip finds that a

With Betty Garrett, Ann Miller, Jules Munshin, Vera-Ellen and Gene Kelly

With Gene Kelly, Betty Garrett, Florence Bates, Jules Munshin and Ann Miller

With Jules Munshin, Ann Miller, Betty Garrett and Gene Kelly

In the "Count on Me" number, with Betty Garrett, Ann Miller, Gene Kelly, Jules Munshin and Alice Pearce

Going primitive with Jules Munshin as Ann Miller sings "Prehistoric Man"

With Jules Munshin and Gene Kelly

female taxi driver named Brunhilde Esterhazy goes for him in a big way; and Ozzie links up with an anthropological student, Claire Huddesen. The six go on the town, and during their 24 hours miss nothing—the Empire State Building, Statue of Liberty, Grant's Tomb, Radio City, Fifth Avenue, Coney Island—every place that's a landmark. After 24 hours, they return to their ship, all agree that New York, New York is one helluva town.

REVIEWS

"*On the Town* brings airy imagination and solid showmanship to the kind of movie that needs it most: the musical. The film avoids such standard cine-musical trappings as hothouse splendor, the lumbering backstage story and the curious notion that the script ought to give performers a pseudo-logical excuse to burst into song & dance. Instead, by combining a fluid cinematic approach and slick Broadway professionalism, Co-Directors Gene Kelly and Stanley Donen have turned out a film so exuberant that it threatens at moments to bounce right off the screen."

Time

"New Yorkers away from the home base will probably put *On the Town* at the head of the list as a 1949 musical film. About gobs and gals, this MGM production applies the old chase formula to a tour of the big city. It is bright, spectacular, action-filled, and bursting at times with humor."

Edwin Schallert, *Los Angeles Times*

"*On the Town* has one ingredient no musical should be without, and that is pace. It has it in unbelievable quantity. The story of three sailors on a 24-hour leave in New York City, it packs the high spots of those 24 hours into an hour and a half of film that leaves you spinning and breathless."

Ann Helming, *Hollywood Citizen-News*

"The pep, enthusiasm and apparent fun the makers of *On the Town* had in putting it together comes through to the audience and gives the picture its best asset. B.o. outlook is good as entertainment values are sturdy for a tune-film entry. Picture is crammed with songs and dance numbers, the book is sufficient to carry it along, the Technicolor hues are topflight, and the cast hard-working."

Brog, *Variety*

With Jane Russell

DOUBLE DYNAMITE · 1951

With Nestor Paiva and Joe Devlin

With Groucho Marx

With Groucho Marx and Jane Russell

An RKO Radio Picture. Directed by Irving Cummings. Produced by Irving Cummings, Jr. Screenplay by Melville Shavelson. Additional dialogue by Harry Crane. From an original story by Leo Rosten, based on a character created by Mannie Manheim. Music by Leigh Harline. Director of photography, Robert de Grasse. Film editor, Harry Marker. Art directors, Albert S. D'Agostino and Feild M. Gray. Set decorators, Darrell Silvera and Harley Miller. Makeup supervisor, Gordon Bau. Sound recorders, Phil Brigandi and Clem Portman. Assistant director, James Lane. Music conducted by C. Bakaleinikoff. Running time, 80 minutes.

CAST

Mildred (Mibs) Goodhug, JANE RUSSELL; *Emile J. Keck*, GROUCHO MARX; *Johnny Dalton*, FRANK SINATRA; *Bob Pulsifer, Jr.*, DON MC GUIRE; *R. B. Pulsifer, Sr.*, HOWARD FREEMAN; *Bookie*, NESTOR PAIVA; *Mr. Kofer*, FRANK ORTH; *J. L. McKissack*, HARRY HAYDEN; *Baganucci*, WILLIAM EDMUNDS; *Tailman*, RUSSELL THORSON; *Frankie Boy*, JOE DEVLIN; *Max*, LOU NOVA; *Santa Claus*, CHARLES COLEMAN; *Little Old Lady*, IDA MOORE; *Mr. Hartman*, HAL K. DAWSON; *Messenger*, GEORGE CHANDLER; *Maitre D'*, JEAN DE BRIAC.

Sinatra's songs: "Kisses and Tears" and "It's Only Money" by Jule Styne and Sammy Cahn.

With Jane Russell and Groucho Marx

With Groucho Marx

STORY

Johnny Dalton and Mildred, the girl he loves, are tellers in a bank, but even their combined salaries don't provide enough for them to marry and live comfortably. Their friend Emile, a hash slinger, half in jest, urges Johnny to rob a bank in order to gain happiness, but Johnny, shocked, won't listen to him. Johnny does come to the rescue of a bookie, who out of gratitude makes a bet in Johnny's name on a horse, and parlays the winning for Johnny to $60,000. Happily, Johnny buys a new car and a mink coat for Mildred, only to find that the bank officials where he works have uncovered a shortage of $75,000. Johnny is thus afraid to make known his good luck. Mildred is accused of embezzlement, because of the shortage which showed up on her machine; but charges are dropped when it is discovered that Mildred's adding machine has gone wild and is making nothing but addition errors. Johnny tells everybody of his luck, and Mildred and he marry.

REVIEWS

"Of the three stars—Groucho gets the best opportunity to shine. The magnificent Marx would be a comedy delight just running through the alphabet. Jane Russell turns on the beauty and Sinatra the charm—as expected."

Dorothy Manners, *Los Angeles Examiner*

"*Double Dynamite*, originally called *It's Only Money*, got its new title as a leering tribute to the extraordinary

69

physical endowments of actress Jane Russell. The movie, however, cheats on RKO's full-bosomed advertising. Actress Russell is cast as a demure bank clerk named Mibs Goodhug, who aspires to nothing more glamorous than marriage with Frank Sinatra, the bank teller in the next cage."

Time

"Sinatra and Marx do yeoman comedy labors, and Miss Russell seems nicely type-cast."

Jesse Zunser, *Cue*

"*Double Dynamite* ... is prevented from slipping into the category of ordinary film comedy by the sly buffoonery of capable Groucho Marx. His inimitable manner of tossing a line or word into an otherwise dull tableau accounts for a great deal of the picture's yak value. And li'l ol' Frankie Sinatra, who is held down to two songs, displays quite a knack himself in getting rid of some funny tag lines."

Howard McClay, *Los Angeles Daily News*

"Miss Russell, per usual, looks okay and part is no strain on her acting ability. Sinatra, too, isn't called upon for any more than a haphazard performance, but he handles himself well enough. Marx is the picture's standout, dishing out his familiar line of patter for number of laughs."

Variety

MEET DANNY WILSON · 1951

A Universal-International Picture. Directed by Joseph Pevney. Produced by Leonard Goldstein. Associate producer and original screenplay by Don McGuire. Musical director, Joseph Gershenson. Musical numbers staged by Hal Belfer. Director of photography, Maury Gertsman. Film editor, Virgil Vogel. Art directors, Bernard Herzbrun and Nathan Juran. Set decorators, Russell A. Gausman and Julia Heron. Gowns by Bill Thomas. Makeup by Bud Westmore. Hair stylist, Joan St. Oegger. Sound recorders, Leslie I. Carey and Richard De Weese. Special photography by David S. Horsley. Assistant directors, Frank Shaw and Les Warner. Dialogue director, Les Urbach. Unit production manager, Edward Dodds. Running time, 88 minutes.

With Alex Nicol and Shelley Winters

CAST

Danny Wilson, FRANK SINATRA; *Joy Carroll*, SHELLEY WINTERS; *Mike Ryan*, ALEX NICOL; *Nick Driscoll*, RAYMOND BURR; *Tommy Wells*, TOMMY FARRELL; *T. W. Hatcher*, VAUGHN TAYLOR; *Sergeant*, DONALD MAC BRIDE; *Marie*, BARBARA KNUDSON; *Cab Driver*, CARL SKLOVER; *Gus*, JOHN DAY; *Heckler*, JACK KRUSCHEN; *Turnkey*, TOM DUGAN; *Joey Thompson*, DANNY WELTON; *Mother Murphy*, PAT FLAHERTY; *Bandleader*, CARLOS MOLINA; *Lieutenant Kelly*, GEORGE ELDRIDGE; *Emerson*, BOB DONNELLY; *Truck Driver*, JOHN INDRISANO; *Nightclub Patron*, TONY CURTIS.

Sinatra's songs: "You're a Sweetheart" by Jimmy McHugh and Harold Adamson; "Lonesome Man Blues" by Sy Oliver; "She's Funny That Way" by Richard Whiting and Neil Moret; "A Good Man Is Hard to Find" by Eddie Green; "That Old Black Magic" by Harold Arlen and Johnny Mercer; "When You're Smiling" by Mark Fisher, Joe Goodwin, and Larry Shay; "All of Me" by Seymour Simons and Gerald Marks; "I've Got a Crush on You" by George and Ira Gershwin; "How Deep Is the Ocean?" by Irving Berlin.

With Raymond Burr, Shelley Winters and Alex Nicol

With Alex Nicol

STORY

Danny Wilson and Mike Ryan are barely making it as singer and pianist at some cheap beer joints, when they meet songstress Joy Carroll. She introduces them to Nick Driscoll, a racketeer night club owner, who thinks Danny's voice so promising that he sets up a verbal contract calling for 50 per cent of all Danny's future earnings. Danny becomes a big success, and both Mike and he vie for Joy Carroll's favor; she, however, loves only Mike. Nick has to go into hiding from the law, but he continues to hound Danny for his promised percentage,

With Shelley Winters

which now amounts to big money. Nick threatens to harm Danny, but Mike interferes, taking the bullet intended for Danny. In revenge, Danny hunts Nick down, meeting him at night in deserted Wrigley Field, where they shoot it out, and Danny kills Nick.

REVIEWS

"Title role is tailor-made for Sinatra and he plays it to the hilt with an off-hand charm that displays the various facets of his personality. . . . Nine tunes are in the score for Sinatra to work over and several draw reprises. Songs are all standards that Sinatra has sold effectively in the past and they listen well."

Brog, *Variety*

"Frank Sinatra is obviously unfair to himself in *Meet Danny Wilson*. For Danny's rise to fame and fortune as crooner and bobby-sox idol is so much like Frankie's that the parallel is inescapable."

Philip K. Scheuer, *Los Angeles Times*

"*Meet Danny Wilson* pictures the rise of a brash but likable young crooner to the special fame that only bobby-soxers can bestow. Apart from romantic and melodramatic trimmings that it borrows elsewhere, the story cribs so freely from the career and personality of Frank Sinatra that fans may expect Ava Gardner to pop up in the last reel. What sharpens the illusion is the playing of Crooner Danny Wilson by Crooner Sinatra himself."

Time

With Shelley Winters

With Alex Nicol and Shelley Winters

"He (Sinatra) is responsible for most of the picture's interest, a convincing portrayer of a nasty little success boy and, as usual, a finely relaxed singer of some excellent popular songs."

Newsweek

"Probably nobody is more surprised in *Meet Danny Wilson* to learn that Frank Sinatra can act than its pugnacious, obstreperous hero, Frank Sinatra, himself. In a complete reversal of his usual roles—but in what may be a perfect example of type-casting—Frank plays a nasty-tempered crooner who can't get started in his crooning profession until he sells a chunk of himself to a night-club gangster; and then proceeds to jam up his own life and the lives of friends who try to lend him a hand."

Cue

"As for Sinatra, the actor, for the first time on the screen he seems completely at ease, and sure of himself and what he is doing.

"There may be other reasons for this, but chiefly, I suspect, it is because the role of Danny Wilson quite openly parallels Sinatra's own career in many instances, and in a sense, therefore, he is just being himself."

Kay Proctor, *Los Angeles Examiner*

Singing "A Good Man Is Hard to Find" with Shelley Winters

FROM HERE TO ETERNITY · 1953

With Don Dubbins and Montgomery Clift

With Montgomery Clift

A Columbia Picture. Directed by Fred Zinnemann. Produced by Buddy Adler. Screenplay by Daniel Taradash. Based on the novel by James Jones. Music supervised and conducted by Morris Stoloff. Background music by George Duning. Orchestrations by Arthur Morton. Song "Re-enlistment Blues" by James Jones, Fred Karger, and Robert Wells. Director of photography, Burnett Guffey. Film editor, William Lyon. Art director, Cary Odell. Set decorator, Frank Tuttle. Gowns by Jean Louis. Makeup by Clay Campbell. Hair stylist, Helen Hunt. Sound recorder, Lodge Cunningham. Assistant director, Earl Bellamy. Technical adviser, Brig. Gen. Kendall J. Fielder, U.S. Army, Ret. Running time, 118 minutes.

CAST

Sgt. Milton Warden, BURT LANCASTER; *Robert E. Lee Prewitt*, MONTGOMERY CLIFT; *Karen Holmes*, DEBORAH KERR; *Lorene*, DONNA REED; *Angelo Maggio*, FRANK SINATRA; *Capt. Dana Holmes*, PHILIP OBER; *Sgt. Leva*, MICKEY SHAUGHNESSY; *Mazzioli*, HARRY BELLAVER; *Sgt. "Fatso" Judson*, ERNEST BORGNINE; *Cpl. Buckley*, JACK WARDEN; *Sgt. Ike Galovitch*, JOHN DENNIS; *Sal Anderson*, MERLE TRAVIS; *Sgt. Pete Karelsen*, TIM RYAN; *Treadwell*, ARTHUR KEEGAN; *Mrs. Kipfer*, BARBARA MORRISON; *Annette*, JEAN WILLES; *Sgt. Baldy Dhom*, CLAUDE AKINS; *Sgt. Turp Thornhill*, ROBERT KARNES; *Sgt. Henderson*, ROBERT WILKE; *Cpl. Champ Wilson*, DOUGLAS HENDERSON; *Sgt. Maylon Stark*, GEORGE REEVES; *Friday Clark*, DON DUBBINS; *Cpl. Paluso*, JOHN CASON; *Georgette*, KRISTINE MILLER; *Capt. Ross*, JOHN BRYANT; *Sandra*, JOAN SHAWLEE; *Jean*, ANGELA STEVENS; *Lieut. Colonel*, WILLIS BOUCHEY; *Major Stern*, TYLER MC VEY.

76

From Here to Eternity won eight Oscars in the 1953 Academy Awards: Best picture, direction, screenplay, photography, film editing, sound, supporting actress (Donna Reed), and supporting actor (Frank Sinatra).

STORY

In the summer of 1941, Robert E. Lee Prewitt is transferred to Schofield Barracks, Honolulu. He is an ace bugler, but has been broken in his old outfit from corporal to buck private because another soldier has been ranked above him as head bugler. Right away, Prewitt runs into new trouble in Honolulu. The commanding officer Captain Dana Holmes knows that Prewitt was a top middleweight boxer in his former outfit, and expects him to fight for his company. Prewitt refuses, because he had once blinded a sparring partner and has vowed never again to fight. For this Prewitt is accorded the "treatment" by the members of his company; the only man who befriends him is a tough little private, Angelo Maggio. First Sergeant Milton Warden, contemptuous of Captain Holmes, makes a play for Holmes' beautiful wife Karen, and the two fall quickly in love. Prewitt falls in love with Lorene, a pretty prostitute who is interested only in making enough money to return to the States and marry a rich, respectable husband. Maggio gets into trouble and is thrown into the stockade, where he is brutally treated and then mortally injured by Sgt. "Fatso" Judson. Maggio manages to escape, and dies in the arms of his friend Prewitt, who vows vengeance and kills "Fatso" in a knife duel. But Prewitt is wounded badly and hides out AWOL in Lorene's apartment. On the morning of December 7, 1941, the Japanese pull their

With Montgomery Clift, Burt Lancaster and
Mickey Shaughnessy

With Joan Shawlee and Montgomery Clift

sneak attack on Pearl Harbor. Prewitt is killed accidentally, trying to get back to camp; Warden forgets love
and romance for professional soldiering. Karen and
Lorene ironically return to the States on the same ship,
and Lorene introduces herself as the grieving fiancee of
Prewitt, "fighter-pilot killed during the attack on Pearl
Harbor."

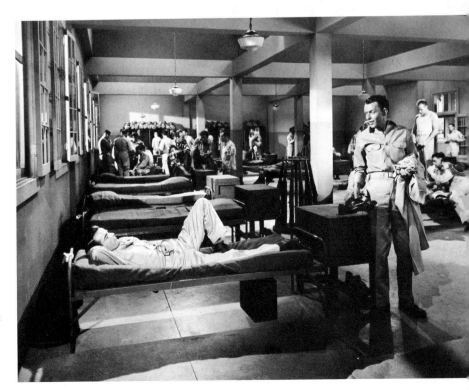

With Montgomery Clift

REVIEWS

"Frank Sinatra, a crooner long since turned actor, knew what he was doing when he plugged for the role of Angelo Maggio in the screen version of James Jones's best seller *From Here to Eternity*. It shouldn't come as a surprise that Sinatra—who flew from Africa and his wife, Ava Gardner, to make a Hollywood screen test—distinguishes himself in the part of a tough little Italian-American in the U.S. Army. Sinatra can act when the mood is on him, and when the writing is good."

Newsweek

"As you can see, *From Here to Eternity* has a fairly yeasty content, and in the way of other gratifications it reveals that Frank Sinatra, in the part of Mr. Clift's friend who winds up in the stockade, is a first-rate actor. Directed by Fred Zinnemann, the work often has the same effectively spare quality that made Mr. Zinnmann's *High Noon* an impressive business, and the general atmosphere of Honolulu on the soldiers' nights out is quite convincing. Some of the episodes are perhaps excessively brutal, but Mr. Zinnemann is not, after all, trying to portray the activities of a Beaver Patrol. What he has done is give us a glimpse of the military that is very rare."

The New Yorker

"And now for Frank Sinatra as Maggio. I have deliberately left him till last, since it is visible even from here that he will be among the first next Academy time. He is simply superb, comical, pitiful, childishly brave, pathetically defiant. Prew (Clift) is able to absorb 'the treatment' the Army dishes out to him for his rebelliousness. Poor little Maggio succumbs to it, and Sinatra makes his death scene one of the best ever photographed."

Ruth Waterbury, *Los Angeles Examiner*

"Frank Sinatra does Private Maggio like nothing he has ever done before. His face wears the calm of a man who is completely sure of what he is doing as he plays it straight from Little Italy. . . . The performers have that curious and captivating air which Director Zinnemann calls 'behaving, rather than acting,' an artless-seeming form of art that he followed in such notable films as *The Search, The Men, The Member of the Wedding*."

Time

With Montgomery Clift

With Paul Frees

SUDDENLY · 1954

With Nancy Gates and James Gleason

A Libra Production. Released by United Artists. Directed by Lewis Allen. Produced by Robert Bassler. Original screenplay by Richard Sale. Music by David Raksin. Director of photography, Charles G. Clarke. Film editor, John F. Schreyer. Art director, Frank Sylos. Set decorator, Howard Bristol. Wardrobe by Jack Masters. Makeup by Bill Buell. Sound recorder, Joe Edmonson. Assistant director, Hal Klein. Second assistant director, Erich Von Stroheim, Jr. Production manager, Charles Hall. Running time, 77 minutes.

CAST

John Baron, FRANK SINATRA; *Tod Shaw*, STERLING HAYDEN; *Pop Benson*, JAMES GLEASON; *Ellen Benson*, NANCY GATES; *Dan Carney*, WILLIS BOUCHEY; *Pidge Benson*, KIM CHARNEY; *Jud Hobson*, JAMES LILBURN; *Benny Conklin*, PAUL FREES; *Bart Wheeler*, CHRISTOPHER DARK; *Slim Adams*, PAUL WEXLER; *Wilson*, KEN DIBBS; *Haggerty*, CLARK HOWATT; *Bebob*, CHARLES SMITH; *Burge*, DAN WHITE; *Hawkins*, RICHARD COLLIER; *First Driver*, ROY ENGEL; *Second Driver*, TED STANHOPE; *Kaplan*, CHARLES WAGGENHEIM; *Trooper*, JOHN BERARDINO.

STORY

On a quiet Saturday afternoon, three men arrive in the small town of Suddenly, California. They are John Baron, Bart Wheeler, and Benny Conklin, and they have come to kill the president of the United States as he leaves his special train for a fishing trip. They take over a house with a sniper's view of the railroad station and make prisoners of the occupants: Pop Benson, a retired secret service man, his daughter-in-law Ellen, and Ellen's young son Pidge.

When secret service chief Dan Carney and Sheriff Tod Shaw go to the house on a security check, Carney is killed and Shaw wounded and made prisoner. Jud Hobson, a TV repairman, comes in response to an earlier call, and he too is held captive. Hearing Baron's plan, Ellen is horrified; widowed by the Korean War, she is

With Kim Charney, Nancy Gates and Sterling Hayden

With Nancy Gates

81

opposed to violence of any kind. Shaw and Pop try to reason with Baron, but he is not a man of reason; he is determined to be "a somebody." He was, in his words, "a nobody" until World War II, when a gun was put in his hands. He won the Silver Star for wiping out a force of Germans, and when he came out of the Army he aimed to continue being "somebody." Now he is being paid $500,000 to kill the president.

Benny, sent to the station to check the train's schedule, shoots a suspicious deputy and is killed by police. Hobson has furtively connected the TV set with the table holding the assassin's rifle, and when Wheeler tests the sight he is electrocuted. Enraged, Baron kills Hobson and turns on the others. Threatened with the death of all those she holds dear, Ellen herself seizes a fallen gun and shoots Baron. The president's train, signaled by officers, passes through its scheduled stop without pausing.

REVIEWS

"As the assassin in the piece, Sinatra superbly refutes the idea that the straight-role potentialities which earned an Academy Award for him in *From Here to Eternity* were one-shot stuff. In *Suddenly*, the happy-go-lucky soldier of *Eternity* becomes one of the most repellent killers in American screen history. Sneeringly arrogant in the beginning, brokenly whimpering at the finish, Sinatra will astonish viewers who flatly resent bobby-soxers' idols."

Newsweek

With Nancy Gates, Kim Charney and Sterling Hayden

With Sterling Hayden

With Nancy Gates

"Unpredictable Frank Sinatra, in still another quick change, makes his bow as, of all things, a Mickey Spillane-type killer in *Suddenly*. . . . The one-time crooner who went on to win Academy honors as an actor brings spine-chilling reality to the role of the crack-brained hired gunman who heads a gang out to assassinate the president of the United States."

Wylie Williams, Hollywood *Citizen-News*

"Frank Sinatra's name will be a valuable asset in boosting the b.o. chances of the slick exploitation feature, which twirls about a fantastic plot to assassinate the president of the U.S. . . . Sinatra plays his role flamboyantly, while Hayden enacts his with repression as he seeks the weak link in the other's seeming strength. Both score heavily, and they get top support from a competent cast."

Whit, *Variety*

"*Suddenly* provides an excellent and welcome opportunity for song-and-dance man Frank Sinatra to prove again that the dramatic talent he suggested in *Meet Danny Wilson*, and which came to richer fruition in *From Here to Eternity* is a solid and potentially richer talent than many suspected. In *Suddenly* Sinatra bears a full load as its star and dominating character. He holds the screen and commands it with ease, authority, and skill that is, obviously, the result of care, study, work, and an intelligent mind."

Cue

YOUNG AT HEART · 1955

An Arwin Production. Released by Warner Bros. WarnerColor; print by Technicolor. Directed by Gordon Douglas. Produced by Henry Blanke. Adaptation by Liam O'Brien from the screenplay Four Daughters *by Julius J. Epstein and Lenore Coffee. Based on the* Cosmopolitan *magazine story "Sister Act" by Fannie Hurst. Music supervised, arranged and conducted by Ray Heindorf. Piano solos played by Andre Previn. Director of photography, Ted McCord. Film editor, William Ziegler. Art director, John Beckman. Set decorator, William Wallace. Wardrobe by Howard Shoup. Makeup by Gordon Bau. Special effects by H. F. Koenekamp. Sound recorders, Leslie G. Hewitt and Charles David Forrest. Assistant director, Al Alleborn. Color consultant, Philip Jefferies. Running time, 117 minutes.*

With Gig Young

CAST

Laurie Tuttle, DORIS DAY; *Barney Sloan,* FRANK SINATRA; *Alex Burke,* GIG YOUNG; *Aunt Jessie,* ETHEL BARRYMORE; *Fran Tuttle,* DOROTHY MALONE; *Gregory Tuttle,* ROBERT KEITH; *Amy Tuttle,* ELISABETH FRASER; *Robert Neary,* ALAN HALE, JR.; *Ernest Nichols,* LONNY CHAPMAN; *Bartell,* FRANK FERGUSON; *Mrs. Ridgefield,* MARJORIE BENNETT; *Doctor,* JOHN MAXWELL; *Husband,* WILLIAM MC LEAN; *Wife,* BARBARA PEPPER; *Girl,* ROBIN RAYMOND; *Fat Man,* TITO VUOLO; *Fat Man's Wife,* GRAZIA NARCISO; *Porter,* IVAN BROWNING; *Minister,* JOE FORTE; *Bartender,* CLIFF FERRE; *Conductor,* HARTE WAYNE.

Sinatra's songs: "Young at Heart" by Johnny Richards and Carolyn Leigh; "Someone to Watch Over Me" by George and Ira Gershwin; "Just One of Those Things" by Cole Porter; "One for My Baby" by Harold Arlen and Johnny Mercer; "You, My Love" by Mack Gordon and James Van Heusen.

With Doris Day

STORY

In a small Connecticut town, the three Tuttle sisters live a quiet, homey life with their father and aunt. Along comes Alex Burke, a handsome young composer who sets everybody aflutter, especially Laurie. Then Barney Sloan shows up, called in by Alex to arrange a musical comedy Alex is writing. A saloon pianist and music arranger, Barney is a moody and frustrated genius from the gutter. Cynical about life and bitter about his bad luck, he is convinced the fates have conspired against him: He responds to Laurie's carefree cheerfulness and falls in love with her, although Laurie and Alex plan to marry.

85

On her wedding day, Laurie learns that her sister Fran loves Alex, and she runs away with Barney to the city, where they are married. Fate is not kind to either of them in the big city, but despite much heartache Laurie comes to love Barney. Yet with no faith in himself, Barney can't believe that Laurie really loves him, and he decides to step out of her life. He attempts suicide in a deliberate car accident, and it is only after surviving the near-fatal crash that he comes to recognize the truth. Barney's bad breaks come to an end as he and Laurie start life anew.

REVIEWS

"The story is a very free adaptation of the one that was filmed before the war as *Four Daughters*, in which the late John Garfield made his first [*sic*] screen appearance. That was the part that woke up that film, and the equivalent one, played by Frank Sinatra, does the same

With Doris Day

for this. There is no need any longer to insist on the acting ability of Mr. Sinatra; he has a limited range, but within that range he is very good indeed. The fact that he sings too—and in that particular way—is irrelevant."

Punch (London)

"The sentiments of this wide-eyed romance have become a bit tarnished with age, and the present performance of it is not as crisp as the first one was. But some brightness and charm still linger in this *Little Women* tale brought up to date, and Miss Day and Mr. Sinatra deliver some added musical sentiments appropriately."

Bosley Crowther, *The New York Times*

"*Young at Heart* proves that Hollywood has not lost its knack for making indifferent new pictures out of good old pictures. This is a remake of *Four Daughters* with one daughter missing, Frank Sinatra in the old John Gar-

field cynic-at-the-piano part, and Doris Day playing whichever one of the Lane Sisters broke her heart over him. Miss Day delivers a fresh-faced and warmhearted performance. Sinatra, although he smokes enough cigarettes for six cynics, doesn't burst from the screen with the old Garfield excitement, but he obliges with *Just One of Those Things* and *Someone to Watch Over Me* to carry us along the way."

Lee Rogow, *The Saturday Review*

"Romance in drama and song is effectively sold by Doris Day and Frank Sinatra in this slickly framed Warner Bros. offering. . . . For both Miss Day and Sinatra, *Young at Heart* is a topflight credit. They give the songs the vocal touch that makes them solid listening, and score just as strongly on the dramatics, seemingly complementing each other in their scenes together to make the dramatic heart tugs all the more effective."

Brog, *Variety*

With Gig Young, Doris Day, Frank Ferguson and Elisabeth Fraser

With Charles Bickford

NOT AS A STRANGER · 1955

A Stanley Kramer Production. Released by United Artists. Produced and directed by Stanley Kramer. Screenplay by Edna and Edward Anhalt. Based on the novel by Morton Thompson. Music composed and conducted by George Antheil. Orchestrations by Ernest Gold. Director of photography, Franz Planer. Film editor, Fred Knudtson. Production design by Rudolph Sternad. Art director, Howard Richmond. Set decorator, Victor Gangelin. Costume supervisor, Joe King. Gowns by Don Loper. Makeup by Bill Wood. Hair stylist, Esperanza Corona. Sound recorder, Earl Snyder. Production assistant, Sally Hamilton. Assistant director, Carter DeHaven, Jr. Production manager, John E. Burch. Dialogue director, Anne Kramer. Technical advisers, Morton Maxwell, M.D., Josh Fields, M.D., and Marjorie Lefevre, R.N. Running time, 135 minutes.

CAST

Kristina Hedvigson, OLIVIA DE HAVILLAND; Lucas Marsh, ROBERT MITCHUM; Alfred Boone, FRANK SINATRA; Harriet Lang, GLORIA GRAHAME; Dr. Aarons, BRODERICK CRAWFORD; Dr. Runkleman, CHARLES BICKFORD; Dr. Snider, MYRON MC CORMICK; Job Marsh, LON CHANEY; Ben Cosgrove, JESSE WHITE; Oley, HARRY MORGAN; Brundage, LEE MARVIN; Bruni, VIRGINIA CHRISTINE; Dr. Dietrich, WHIT BISSELL; Dr. Lettering, JACK RAINE; Miss O'Dell, MAE CLARKE.

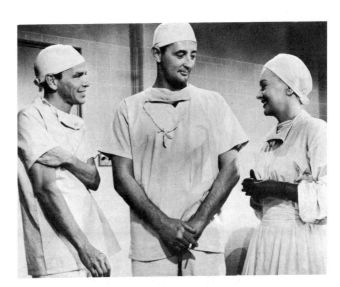

With Robert Mitchum and Olivia de Havilland

With Lee Marvin and Jerry Paris (left), and Robert Mitchum (right)

With Robert Mitchum

89

STORY

Lucas Marsh is a dedicated student of medicine, and rather than be discharged from medical school because he cannot pay his tuition, he married a mature nurse, Kristina Hedvigson, when he learns she has a great deal of money. When Lucas graduates, he goes with his wife to a small town, where he becomes assistant to Dr. Runkleman. A wealthy woman is attracted to Lucas, but drops him when she realizes he has guilt feelings about her. Lucas, in his total dedication, makes many errors—and Kristina and he quarrel, and she asks him to leave her. Lucas does not know his wife is three months pregnant, and his best friend, Dr. Boone, tells him the truth. Dr. Runkleman has a serious heart attack, and Marsh makes a miscalculation on the operating table, and Runkleman dies. Lucas returns humbly to Kristina, knowing he is neither infallible nor perfect, and, above all, needs her love.

REVIEWS

"This is an interesting but not a very pleasant story. Though he plays the role written for him with a remote intensity that comes close to perfection, there was always the danger that Mitchum would seem as cold to the audience as he does to the other characters, particularly since Miss de Havilland is so appealing and womanly. Producer-director Stanley Kramer has avoided this by seeing to it that the spectators are thoroughly entertained during the first half of the film by Frank Sinatra in the role of a lovable young cynic to whom the study of medicine is more or less a lark. Sinatra, who seems to become a better actor with each successive part, is simply terrific."
Jack Moffitt, *The Hollywood Reporter*

"Producer Stanley Kramer, a man with a penchant for offbeat choices, took Morton Thompson's best-selling novel of a young doctor as the occasion of his own directional debut. . . . Sinatra is another of the players who comes close to doing a little picture stealing."
Land, *Variety*

"But Kramer has directed all of this with a documentarian's objectivity and with sensitivity. The result, enhanced by an all-star cast that includes Olivia de Havilland, Robert Mitchum, Frank Sinatra, Gloria Grahame, and Charles Bickford, is a kind of super-suds—the very finest consistency, but still soap."
Arthur Knight, *The Saturday Review*

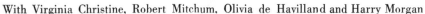

With Virginia Christine, Robert Mitchum, Olivia de Havilland and Harry Morgan

With Debbie Reynolds

THE TENDER TRAP · 1955

With David Wayne

With Debbie Reynolds

A Metro-Goldwyn-Mayer Picture. Eastman Color; CinemaScope. Directed by Charles Walters. Produced by Lawrence Weingarten. Screenplay by Julius J. Epstein. Based on the play by Max Shulman and Robert Paul Smith. Music composed and conducted by Jeff Alexander. Orchestrations by Will Beittel. Director of photography, Paul C. Vogel. Film editor, John Dunning. Art directors, Cedric Gibbons and Arthur Lonergan. Set decorators, Edwin B. Willis and Jack D. Moore. Costumes by Helen Rose. Makeup by William Tuttle. Hair stylist, Sidney Guilaroff. Recording supervisor, Dr. Wesley C. Miller. Assistant director, Joel Freeman. Color consultant, Charles K. Hagedon. Running time, 111 minutes.

CAST

Charlie Y. Reader, FRANK SINATRA; *Julie Gillis*, DEBBIE REYNOLDS; *Joe McCall*, DAVID WAYNE; *Sylvia Crewes*, CELESTE HOLM; *Jessica Collins*, JARMA LEWIS; *Poppy Matson*, LOLA ALBRIGHT; *Helen*, CAROLYN JONES; *Sam Sayers*, HOWARD ST. JOHN; *Sol Z. Steiner*, JOEY FAYE; *Mr. Loughran*, TOM HELMORE; *Director*, WILLARD SAGE; *Ballet Actor*, MARC WILDER; *Audition Dancer*, JACK BOYLE; *Eddie*, JAMES DRURY; *Mr. Wilson*, BENNY RUBIN; *Stage Manager*, REGINALD SIMPSON; *TV Announcer*, GIL HARMAN; *Society Reporter*, MADGE BLAKE; *Elevator Boy*, WILSON WOOD; *Doormen:* FRANK SULLY, GORDON RICHARDS; *Cab Drivers:* LENNIE BREMEN, DAVE WHITE.

Sinatra's song: "(Love Is) The Tender Trap" by James Van Heusen and Sammy Cahn.

STORY

Joe McCall, on vacation from marriage, arrives in New York to visit his old friend, theatrical agent Charlie Reader. Amazed at the procession of girls—Poppy, Jessica, Helen, Sylvia—at Charlie's beck and call, Joe believes he has found Utopia, but Charlie professes equal envy of Joe's married life. At a dance audition, Charlie meets Julie Gillis, a young girl with definite ideas about marriage and even a timetable worked out for catching a husband. Charlie begins dating her, despite Joe's warnings that she is a marriage trap. Climaxing what she believes to be a successful campaign, Julie informs Charlie that he must give up his other girls so she can marry him. Shocked, Charlie exclaims, "Who *asked* you?"

Then suddenly one day Charlie finds that the girls he took for granted are unavailable. In a panic for companionship, he proposes to both Sylvia *and* Julie on the same night. Learning of Charlie's dual engagement, Julie storms out of his apartment, and Charlie apologizes to Sylvia, admitting that he really loves only Julie. Joe, long smitten by Sylvia, then proposes to her, but she gently tells him she doesn't love him, and he prepares to return to his wife. In the elevator, Sylvia meets a Mr. Loughran, who asks her to dinner and eventually to the altar. At the wedding, Sylvia throws her bouquet to Charlie, who takes it to Julie's, tosses it to her. He has, finally, been tenderly trapped.

REVIEWS

"Screen comedy is often old-time slap-stick or the equivalent of the blue comedian in the music hall (suitably

With Debbie Reynolds and Benny Rubin

With Celeste Holm and David Wayne

With Debbie Reynolds, Celeste Holm and David Wayne

adapted for the majority of world censors). It is refreshing to find a film like *The Tender Trap*—even if it does owe its origin to the stage. This may not be good cinema; but it is good entertainment for those who relish the Thurber style of humour .... Frank Sinatra sings only one song and it is a pleasant surprise to find him such an accomplished comedian."

Peter G. Baker, *Films and Filming*

"MGM's screen version of *The Tender Trap* allows another matinee idol, Frank Sinatra, to show again that in addition to possessing whatever it is that it takes he also has acting ability."

Kenneth Coyte, *The Saturday Review*

"As a matter of fact, his performance is well-nigh a perfect demonstration of the sort of flippant, frantic thing he can do best. It catches the nervous, restless Frankie at the top of his comedy form. Indeed, it is probably in his timing that his excellence with the quip is achieved, and this leads one to wonder how much his training as a singer contributed to what he is."

Bosley Crowther, *The New York Times*

With David Wayne

With Marlon Brando

GUYS AND DOLLS · 1955

With Johnny Silver and Stubby Kaye

Sky Masterson (Marlon Brando) offers to bet Nathan Detroit (Frank Sinatra) that he can't remember the color of his bow tie. Unable to steal a peek. Nathan declines the wager.

Singing "Sue Me" with Vivian Blaine

With Sheldon Leonard, B. S. Pully and George E. Stone

A Samuel Goldwyn Production. Released by Metro-Goldwyn-Mayer. Eastman Color; CinemaScope. Directed by Joseph L. Mankiewicz. Produced by Samuel Goldwyn. Screenplay by Joseph L. Mankiewicz. From the musical play, book by Jo Swerling and Abe Burrows, music and lyrics by Frank Loesser. Based on the story "The Idyll of Miss Sarah Brown" by Damon Runyon. Music supervised and conducted by Jay Blackton. Orchestral arrangements by Skip Martin, Nelson Riddle (for Sinatra), Alexander Courage, and Albert Sendrey. Background music adapted by Cyril J. Mockridge, assisted by Herbert Spencer. Director of photography, Harry Stradling. Film editor, Daniel Mandell. Production design by Oliver Smith. Art director, Joseph Wright. Set decorator, Howard Bristol. Choreography by Michael Kidd. Costumes by Irene Sharaff. Makeup by Ben Lane. Hair stylist, Annabell. Special photographic effects by Warren Newcombe, Mark H. Davis, and Irving G. Ries. Sound recorders, Fred Lau, Roger Heman, and Vinton Vernon. Assistant director, Arthur S. Black, Jr. Color consultant, Alvord L. Eiseman. Running time, 150 minutes.

With Vivian Blaine

97

CAST

Sky Masterson, MARLON BRANDO; *Sarah Brown*, JEAN SIMMONS; *Nathan Detroit*, FRANK SINATRA; *Miss Adelaide*, VIVIAN BLAINE; *Lt. Brannigan*, ROBERT KEITH; *Nicely-Nicely Johnson*, STUBBY KAYE; *Big Jule*, B. S. PULLY; *Benny Southstreet*, JOHNNY SILVER; *Harry the Horse*, SHELDON LEONARD; *Rusty Charlie*, DAN DAYTON; *Society Max*, GEORGE E. STONE; *Arvid Abernathy*, REGIS TOOMEY; *General Cartwright*, KATHRYN GIVNEY; *Laverne*, VEDA ANN BORG; *Sister Agatha*, MARY ALAN HOKANSON; *Angie the Ox*, JOE MC TURK; *Brother Calvin*, KAY KUTER; *Mission Member*, STAPLETON KENT; *Cuban Singer*, RENEE RENOR; *Louie*, JOHN INDRISANO; *Pitch Man*, EARLE HODGINS; *Waiter*, HARRY TYLER; and THE GOLDWYN GIRLS.

Sinatra's songs: "The Oldest Established (Permanent Floating Crap Game in New York)," "Guys and Dolls," "Adelaide," and "Sue Me" by Frank Loesser.

STORY

Nathan Detroit, proprietor of "the oldest established permanent floating crap game in New York," needs a grand in order to pay for a place that will be safe from the cops. He bets long-shot gambler Sky Masterson that he can't take Sergeant Sarah Brown, of the Save-a-Soul Mission, to Havana. Sky knows that Sister Sarah's mission is a flop, and he promises her that her next prayer meeting will be filled with "genuine sinners" if she'll fly to Havana and have dinner with him there. Sister Sarah is game, but once in Havana, she falls for booze, the moonlight—and Sky. He, moved by her attractive innocence, brings her back to New York without seducing her.

Sky then risks his bankroll against every gambler's pledge to attend the prayer meeting—and wins. The mission is filled with dutiful sinners. Even Nathan Detroit is converted and marries Miss Adelaide, to whom he's been engaged for fourteen years, and Sky and Sarah also wed.

REVIEWS

"The Detroit role is a breeze for Frank Sinatra, and he plays it as casually as if he were eating a banana split, stopping only long enough to put an extra throb into his voice for the one new tune added to the original Frank Loesser score, *Adelaide*."

Louella O. Parsons, *Los Angeles Examiner*

"I am not quite sure whether it is the Goldwyn touch or the Mankiewicz stamp that has been put upon *Guys and Dolls*, but of one thing I'm certain: the two should collaborate more often. . . . Sinatra is Sinatra and in this is perfect. A couple of songs are left out, but no real harm done."

Hollis Alpert, *The Saturday Review*

"In a recent picture, Frank Sinatra advises another character on how to put over a song. 'Exterior schmaltz

is no good,' he says, 'real schmaltz has to come from the heart.' He uses the same philosophy to put over the humor of Nathan Detroit. Never knocking himself out for a laugh, he plays the gambler as an earnest, worried man, with a peculiar idiom that comes naturally to him. He takes great pride in trivialities and his mind is forever seeking angles. He is always a man and never a buffoon. And, of course, the way he can tailor a Frank Loesser song is nobody's business but his own."

Jack Moffitt, *The Hollywood Reporter*

With Johnny Silver

With Johnny Silver and Stubby Kaye

With Vivian Blaine

With Kim Novak

THE MAN WITH
THE GOLDEN ARM · 1955

A Carlyle Production. Released by United Artists. Produced and directed by Otto Preminger. Screenplay by Walter Newman and Lewis Meltzer. Based on the novel by Nelson Algren. Music composed and conducted by Elmer Bernstein. Orchestrations by Frederick Steiner. Director of photography, Sam Leavitt. Film editor, Louis R. Loeffler. Art director, Joseph Wright. Set decorator, Darrell Silvera. Costume supervisor, Mary Ann Nyberg. Men's wardrobe, Joe King. Women's wardrobe, Adele Parmenter. Makeup by Jack Stone, Bernard Ponedel, and Ben Lane. Hair stylists, Helene Parrish and Hazel Keats. Sound recorder, Jack Solomon. Music editor, Leon Birnbaum. Assistant directors, Horace Hough and James Engle. Production manager, Jack McEdward. Producer's assistant, Maximilian Slater. Running time, 119 minutes.

With Kim Novak

CAST

Frankie Machine, FRANK SINATRA; *Zosh,* ELEANOR PARKER; *Molly,* KIM NOVAK; *Sparrow,* ARNOLD STANG; *Louie,* DARREN MC GAVIN; *Schwiefka,* ROBERT STRAUSS; *Drunky,* JOHN CONTE; *Vi,* DORO MERANDE; *Markette,* GEORGE E. STONE; *Williams,* GEORGE MATHEWS; *Dominowski,* LEONID KINSKEY; *Bednar,* EMILE MEYER; *Himself,* SHORTY ROGERS; *Himself,* SHELLY MANNE; *Piggy,* FRANK RICHARDS; *Lane,* WILL WRIGHT; *Kvorka,* TOMMY HART; *Antek,* FRANK MARLOWE; *Meter Reader,* JOE MC TURK; *Chester,* RALPH NEFF; *Bird Dog,* ERNEST RABOFF; *Vangie,* MARTHA WENTWORTH; *Junkie,* JERRY BARCLAY; *Taxi Driver,* LENNIE BREMEN; *Suspenders,* PAUL E. BURNS; *Landlord,* CHARLES SEEL.

Sinatra received an Academy nomination; the Award went to Ernest Borgnine for *Marty.*

With Leonid Kinskey and Eleanor Parker

STORY

After six months in Lexington, where he was "cured" of drug addiction, Frankie Machine returns to his old haunts in Chicago. He is greeted by a friend, Sparrow, and by Louie, a pusher, who offers a free "fix" that Frankie declines. He goes home to his wife Zosh, a petulant girl in a wheelchair, and tells her that he's going to be a drummer, but Zosh wants things to be as they were before Frankie went away—when he dealt poker at Schwiefka's so deftly he was known as "the man with the golden arm." So Frankie, reminded that he "crippled" Zosh in a drunk-driving accident, goes back to the dealer's slot. At the Club Safari he meets and falls for a B-girl, Molly, but tells her he cannot leave Zosh so long as she is "helpless." He tries to practice drumming at home, but Zosh nags him so about the noise that he

With Kim Novak and John Conte

102

With Darren McGavin
and Robert Strauss

With Eleanor Parker

With John Conte and Kim Novak

With Kim Novak

accepts Molly's invitation to practice at her place. He even gets an audition date and quits Schwiefka, but is conned into "one more game," dealing against a pair of well-heeled gamblers, and succumbs to Louie's offer of a fix. Caught cheating, he is beaten up, and at the audition he needs a fix so badly that his hands shake and he fails miserably.

Louie goes to Frankie's rooms and finds Zosh on her feet. When he threatens to reveal that Zosh can walk, she pushes him down a stairwell to his death. Seeking relief from his increasing pain, Frankie goes to Molly, who tells him he is suspected of killing Louie. Not daring to face the police as he is, Frankie agrees to the "cold turkey" cure—there days of anguished withdrawal. He suffers,

crawls, weeps and prowls in Molly's locked room, threatening to kill her, begging her to kill him, finally falling unconscious. At the end of the third day he awakens haggard and weak, but triumphant. He goes to tell Zosh that he must go away to save himself, but will send money for her care. Zosh jumps up to follow him, sees police in the hallway, and in panic throws herself to the alley below. Zosh dies with Frankie at her side, and he walks slowly away, followed by Molly.

REVIEWS

"There's one dramatic justification: Sinatra gives a near-great performance. He is the only one, in a company that includes as many wrong as right castings, who does."

Philip K. Scheuer, *Los Angeles Times*

"Frank Sinatra, who has continually amazed me with his acting ability, continues to amaze me in *The Man with the Golden Arm.* This is a rather glum chronicle of the life of a hophead in Chicago. Like one of the waits between trains there, it goes on practically forever, but Mr. Sinatra does very well as the fellow with the payoff mitt."

John McCarten, *The New Yorker*

"As Frankie, the card dealer so good they called him 'the man with golden arm,' Frank Sinatra is terrifying in the vividness of his portrayal of a junkie trying to get that monkey off his back. He runs the shaky gamut from quiet confidence, uncertainty, bravado, fright, apprehension, and terror, through the range of the junkie's need, desire, satisfaction and ecstasy—and then into the private hell reserved for all such. It's quite a performance Frankie gives—and something of a revelation too."

Cue

"No small part of the complex emotional coloration that we feel toward Frankie Machine comes from a truly virtuoso performance by Frank Sinatra. The thin, unhandsome one-time crooner has an incredible instinct for the look, the gesture, the shading of the voice that suggest tenderness, uncertainty, weakness, fatigue, despair. Indeed he brings to the character much that has not been written into the script, a shade of sweetness, a sense of edgy indestructibility that actually creates the appeal and intrinsic interest of the role. But he is also an actor of rare ability. His scene in the jail with a junkie screaming for a fix in the same cell, the scene of his own first fix in Louie's room—both played in huge, searching close-ups—and the terrible writhing agony of the 'cold turkey' treatment are conveyed with clinical realism."

Arthur Knight, *The Saturday Review*

With Robert Strauss (*left*)
and Arnold Stang (*with glasses*)

With Kim Novak

MEET ME IN LAS VEGAS · 1956

A Metro-Goldwyn-Mayer Picture. Eastman Color; CinemaScope. Directed by Roy Rowland. Produced by Joe Pasternak. Original screenplay by Isobel Lennart. Music supervised and conducted by George Stoll. Music for "Frankie and Johnny" ballet adapted by Johnny Green. Lena Horne's number arranged and conducted by Lennie Hayton. Orchestrations by Albert Sendrey and Skip Martin. Songs by Nicholas Brodszky and Sammy Cahn. Dances and musical numbers created and staged by Hermes Pan. "Rehearsal Ballet" and "Sleeping Beauty Ballet" created and staged by Eugene Loring. Vocal supervision by Robert Tucker. Music coordinator, Irving Aaronson. Director of photgraphy, Robert Bronner. Film editor, Albert Akst. Art dirctors, Cedric Gibbons and Urie McCleary. Set decorators, Edwin B. Willis and Richard Pefferle. Costumes by Helen Rose. Makeup by William Tuttle. Hair stylist, Sydney Guilaroff. Special effects by Warren Newcombe. Recording supervisor, Dr. Wesley C. Miller. Assistant director, George Rhein. Color consultant, Charles K. Hagedon. Running time, 112 minutes.

CAST

Chuck Rodwell, DAN DAILEY; Maria Corvier, CYD CHARISSE; MC at Silver Slipper, JERRY COLONNA; Maria's Manager, PAUL HENREID; Guest Star at Sands, LENA HORNE; Guest Star at Sands, FRANKIE LAINE; Japanese Girl, MITSUKO SAWAMURA; Miss Hattie, AGNES MOORHEAD; Sari Hatvany, LILI DARVAS; Tom Culdane, JIM BACKUS; Lotsi, OSCAR KARLWEIS; Lilli, LILIANE MONTEVECCHI; Kelly Donavan, CARA WILLIAMS; Young Groom, GEORGE CHAKIRIS; Young Bride, BETTY LYNN; Themselves, THE SLATE BROTHERS; Conductor, PETE RUGOLO; Specialty Dancer, JOHN BRASCIA; Worried Boss, JOHN HARDING; Croupier, BENNY RUBIN; Meek Husband, JACK DALY; Bossy Wife, HENNY BACKUS; Prince Charming, MARC WILDER.

Unbilled guest appearances

FRANK SINATRA, DEBBIE REYNOLDS, TONY MARTIN, PETER LORRE, VIC DAMONE, ELAINE STEWART.

With Cyd Charisse and Dan Dailey

Main and end title songs sung (off-screen) by the Four Aces. New lyrics by Sammy Cahn for "Frankie and Johnny" sung (off-screen) by Sammy Davis, Jr.

STORY

Rancher Chuck Rodwell, losing at roulette, grabs the hand of ballerina Maria Corvier "for luck" as she passes the table. He wins. Thereafter he is loath to let go of either the hand or the girl.

As Chuck and Maria walk through the Sands Hotel, we get a back view of a man about to play a slot machine. Chuck takes out a coin and puts it in the machine, holding Maria's hand for luck. The machine hits the jackpot. As money cascades onto the floor, the astonished player turns around. It's Sinatra.

REVIEWS

"This film, one of the most entertaining movie packages of the year, is set in that wondrous Never-Never Land of the west, the gambling paradise of the nation. The story's nonsense, but it's pleasant nonsense—and so glossed over with Technicolored glitter and glamor, with dazzling sights and sounds, gags and girls, color and excitement and fun and frolic, as to be well-nigh irresistible."

Cue

"*Meet Me in Las Vegas* is the sprightliest musical to come along in years . . . It is overloaded with talent—most of all in beauty, dancing ability, sex appeal, and a hitherto undiscovered flair for comedy—the talent of Cyd Charisse . . . Guest stars pop in and out with specialties of their own . . . Not rating program mention at all, but spotted around the plush Sands Hotel, are Frank Sinatra, Debbie Reynolds, Vic Damone, Peter Lorre, and Tony Martin."

Philip K. Scheuer, *Los Angeles Times*

JOHNNY CONCHO · 1956

With Phyllis Kirk

With Howard Petrie

With Keenan Wynn

With William Conrad, Willis
Bouchey and Christopher Dark

110

A Kent Production. Released by United Artists. Directed by Don McGuire. Produced by Frank Sinatra. Associate producer, Henry Sanicola. Screenplay by David P. Harmon and Don McGuire. Based on the story "The Man Who Owned the Town" by David P. Harmon. Music composed and conducted by Nelson Riddle. Orchestrations by Arthur Morton. Director of photography, William Mellor. Film editor, Eda Warren. Art director, Nicolai Remisoff. Set decorator, Gustav Bernsten. Costumes by Gwen Wakeling. Makeup by Bernard Ponedel and Ernest J. Park. Hair Stylist, Patricia Westmore. Sound recorders, Dean Thomas and Robert Roderick. Music editor, Leon Birnbaum. Production supervisor, James Vaughn. Assistant director, Emmett Emerson. Running time, 84 minutes.

CAST

Johnny Concho, FRANK SINATRA; *Barney Clark,* KEENAN WYNN; *Tallman,* WILLIAM CONRAD; *Mary Dark,* PHYLLIS KIRK; *Albert Dark,* WALLACE FORD; *Walker,* CHRISTOPHER DARK; *Helgeson,* HOWARD PETRIE; *Sam Green,* HARRY BARTELL; *Judge Tyler,* DAN RUSS; *Sheriff Henderson,* WILLIS BOUCHEY; *Duke Lang,* ROBERT OSTERLOH; *Mason,* LEO GORDON; *Sarah Dark,* DOROTHY ADAMS; *Pearl Lang,* JEAN BYRON; *Lem,* CLAUDE AKINS; *Jake,* JOHN QUALEN; *Pearson,* WILFRED KNAPP; *Benson,* BEN WRIGHT; *Bartender,* JOE BASSETT.

STORY

Johnny Concho is the young, aggressive brother of the top gunman of Cripple Creek, Arizona, in 1875. The gunman is killed in a duel, and the town turns to Johnny, because Cripple Creek has been taken over by the gunman's killers, Tallman and Walker. The town wants Johnny to avenge his brother's death. Johnny, afraid, runs away, but can find peace and understanding nowhere. A girl, Mary Dark, and a gun-toting preacher, Barney Clark, persuade Johnny that what he is really running away from is his own manhood. And so Johnny returns to Cripple Creek, tells the citizens that they should get rid of fear and oppression. In a showdown battle with the gunmen Johnny is wounded, but the aroused citizenry take care of the villains—and Johnny finds himself accepted as a person in his own right, a man who does not live in the shadow of his brother.

REVIEWS

"The picture, oddly enough, plays and feels more like an off-Broadway, one-set staged show than a movie Western. The slim cast stands and moves about in dim lighting and stagey sets. Frank Sinatra as both star and producer does pretty well by himself. As actor, he delivers himself excellently in the earlier scenes as the ratty little bully, card cheat, and coward, but weakens a bit when the acting demands get tough as he moves toward reformation."

Cue

"The film apparently represents two wish fulfillments of every Hollywood star—to boss his own company and to play a cowboy. Sinatra has, on the whole, done better with the second wish than the first: Performing competently if never brilliantly, he at least causes one to dislike him at the start and pull for him at the finish, which is what one is supposed to do. And his modesty has charm."

Philip K. Scheuer, *Los Angeles Times*

"The chief fault in the production is that Sinatra is made to appear for roughly the first third of the picture in a highly unfavorable light. Nothing he can do in the remainder of the film can overcome that initial impression that Johnny Concho is nothing but a nasty little bully and even the knowledge of what makes him act that way does not make him much more sympathetic."

The Hollywood Reporter

With Phyllis Kirk

With William Conrad and Willis Bouchey

With Grace Kelly

HIGH SOCIETY · 1956

A Metro-Goldwyn-Mayer Picture. Technicolor; Vista-Vision. Directed by Charles Walters. Produced by Sol C. Siegel. Screenplay by John Patrick. Based on the play, The Philadelphia Story by Philip Barry. Music supervised and adapted by Johnny Green and Saul Chaplin. Orchestra conducted by Johnny Green. Orchestral arrangements by Conrad Salinger and Nelson Riddle. Additional orchestrations by Robert Franklyn and Albert Sendrey. Musical numbers staged by Charles Walters. Director of photography, Paul C. Vogel. Film editor, Ralph E. Winters. Art directors, Cedric Gibbons and Hans Peters. Set decorators, Edwin B. Willis and Richard Pefferle. Costumes by Helen Rose. Makeup by William Tuttle. Recording supervisor, Dr. Wesley C. Miller. Special effects by A. Arnold Gillespie. Hair stylist, Sydney Guilaroff. Assistant director, Arvid Griffen. Color consultant, Charles K. Hagedon. Running time, 107 minutes.

CAST

C. K. Dexter-Haven, BING CROSBY; *Tracy Lord*, GRACE KELLY; *Mike Connor*, FRANK SINATRA; *Liz Imbrie*, CELESTE HOLM; *George Kittredge*, JOHN LUND; *Uncle Willie*, LOUIS CALHERN; *Seth Lord*, SIDNEY BLACKMER; *Himself*, LOUIS ARMSTRONG; *Mrs. Seth Lord*, MARGALO GILLMORE; *Caroline Lord*, LYDIA REED; *Dexter-Haven's Butler*, GORDON RICHARDS; *The Lords' Butler*, RICHARD GARRICK; *Uncle Willie's Butler*, REGINALD SIMPSON; *Mac*, RICHARD KEENE; *Editor*, PAUL KEAST; *Parson*, HUGH BOSWELL; *Matrons:* RUTH LEE, HELEN SPRING.

Sinatra's songs, by Cole Porter: "Who Wants to Be a Millionaire?" "You're Sensational," "Well, Did You Evah?" and "Mind If I Make Love to You?"

STORY

Terribly rich and terribly Newport rich Tracy Lord has three men in her life: her ex-husband, C. K. Dexter-Haven, who still calls her Sam; her husband-to-be, George Kittredge; and a charming but brash reporter, Mike Connor, who is on hand to cover her forthcoming wedding for a pictorial magazine. Tracy gets tight with Connor, and dives into a swimming pool, from which she is rescued by him. She tries to go through with her marriage to stuffy George Kittredge, but her eyes have been opened—and she realizes she's no icy virgin on a pedestal, but a real woman still in love with her ex-husband. Dexter-Haven and she re-marry.

With Margalo Gillmore
Sidney Blackmer, Celeste Holm,
Grace Kelly and John Lund

With Bing Crosby

With Grace Kelly

116

With Celeste Holm, Grace Kelly and Margalo Gillmore

With Celeste Holm

REVIEWS

"Fortified with a strong Cole Porter score, film is a pleasant romp for cast toppers Bing Crosby, Grace Kelly, and Frank Sinatra who, tactfully, get alphabetical top billing. Their impact is almost equally consistent. Although Sinatra has the top pop tune opportunities, the Groaner makes his specialties stand up and out on showmanship and delivery, and Miss Kelly impresses as a femme lead with pleasantly comedienne overtones. This is perhaps her most relaxed performance."

Abel, *Variety*

"A covey of ingratiating characters may be flushed in *High Society*, a new-day and mellifluously musical version of *The Philadelphia Story* which Philip Barry wrote back in 1939. The author of this one is John Patrick, and among those present are Frank Sinatra, Bing Crosby, Grace Kelly, Celeste Holm, and Louis Armstrong. If their efforts are perhaps not quite as rewarding as those of the performers in the original movie (as you may remember, Cary Grant and Katharine Hepburn had the leads in that), they are, as I've said, an attractive lot .... The settings, which have been transferred from Philadelphia to New England for the purpose of introducing the Newport Jazz Festival into the act, are gorgeous, and although much is made, in the true Barry pattern, of the troubles of the rich (income taxes and all that), the movie leaves no doubt that money is a nice thing to have around."

The New Yorker

117

With Grace Kelly

With Bing Crosby,
John Lund and Grace Kelly

"Crosby works (although it never looks like it) and the result, especially in a very witty duet, *Well, Did You Evah?* with Sinatra, is wonderful. This is slick, sure directing and great response from two unique stars. Miss Kelly is very good, and she plays with Crosby and Sinatra in a relaxed and delightful way."

The Hollywood Reporter

"There is one delightful duet, however, when Sinatra and Crosby get together for five minutes or so and show solid professionalism in their handling of *What a Swell Party This Is.* If the rest of the movie were up to that level—But it isn't."

Hollis Alpert, *The Saturday Review*

With John Lund and Bing Crosby

With David Niven and Marlene Dietrich

AROUND THE WORLD
IN 80 DAYS · 1956

A Michael Todd Production. Released by United Artists. Eastman Color; Print by Technicolor; Todd-AO. Directed by Michael Anderson. Produced by Michael Todd. Screenplay by James Poe, John Farrow, and S. J. Perelman. Based on the novel by Jules Verne. Music by Victor Young. Associate producer, William Cameron Menzies. Second unit director, Kevin O'Donovan McClory. Director of photography, Lionel Lindon. Film editors, Paul Weatherwax and Gene Ruggiero. Art director, James Sullivan. Set decorator, Ross Dowd. Costume designer, Miles White. Choreographer, Paul Godkin. Sound recorder, Joseph Kane. Special effects, Lee Zavitz. Makeup supervisor, Gustaf Norin. Hair stylist, Edith Keon. Assistant directors, Ivan Volkman, Lew Borzage, Dennis Bertera, and Farley James. Unit manager, Frank Fox. Sound effects editor, Ted Bellinger. Running time, 178 minutes.

CAST

Phileas Fogg, DAVID NIVEN; *Passepartout*, CANTINFLAS; *Princess Aouda*, SHIRLEY MacLAINE; *Inspector Fix*, ROBERT NEWTON.

Cameos

M. Gasse, clerk, Thomas Cook, Paris, CHARLES BOYER; *Station master, Fort Kearney*, JOE E. BROWN; *Girl in railroad station, Paris*, MARTINE CAROL; *Colonel Proctor*, JOHN CARRADINE; *Clerk, Hong Kong steamship office*, CHARLES COBURN; *Official, Great Indian Railway*, RONALD COLMAN; *Steward, "R.M.S. Mongolia"*, MELVILLE COOPER; *Roland Hesketh-Baggott*, NOEL COWARD; *Member of Reform Club*, FINLAY CURRIE; *Inspector, Bombay Police*, REGINALD DENNY; *First Mate, "S.S. Henrietta"*, ANDY DEVINE; *Owner, Barbary Coast saloon*, MARLENE DIETRICH; *Bullfighter, Spain*, LUIS MIGUEL DOMINGUIN; *Coachman, Paris*, FERNANDEL; *Foster, Fogg's ex-valet*, SIR JOHN GIELGUD; *Tart, London*, HERMIONE GINGOLD; *Dancer, Cave of the Seven Winds*, JOSE GRECO; *Sir Francis Cromarty*, SIR CEDRIC HARDWICKE; *Fallentin, member of Reform Club*, TREVOR HOWARD; *Tart, London*, GLYNIS JOHNS; *Train conductor*, BUSTER KEATON; *Tart, Paris*, EVELYN KEYES; *Revivalist group leader, London*, BEATRICE LILLIE; *Japanese steward, "S.S. Carnatic"*, PETER LORRE; *Chief Engineer, "S.S. Henrietta"*, EDMUND LOWE; *Billiard player, Reform Club*, A. E. MATTHEWS; *Drunk, Hong Kong dive*, MIKE MAZURKI; *Colonel, U.S. Cavalry*, TIM McCOY; *Helmsman, "S.S. Henrietta"*, VICTOR McLAGLEN; *Hansom cab driver, London*, JOHN MILLS; *Ralph, a Governor, Bank of England*, ROBERT MORLEY; *British Consul, Suez*, ALAN MOWBRAY; *Captain, "S.S.*

Henrietta", JACK OAKIE; *Bouncer, Barbary Coast saloon*, GEORGE RAFT; *Achmed Abdullah*, GILBERT ROLAND; *Achmed Abdullah's henchman*, CESAR ROMERO; *Piano player, Barbary Coast saloon*, FRANK SINATRA; *Drunk, Barbary Coast saloon*, RED SKELTON; *Member of Reform Club*, RONALD SQUIRE; *Member of Reform Club*, BASIL SYDNEY; *Aged steward, Reform Club*, HARCOURT WILLIAMS; *Prologue Commentator*, EDWARD R. MURROW.

STORY

At the Reform Club in Victorian London, Phileas Fogg boasts over a game of whist that he can circle the globe in a mere eighty days. The other club members challenge his claim and wager £20,000 that he is wrong. Accepting the bet, Fogg leaves with his servant, Passepartout. The two men travel by every known means of locomotion, and meet with a series of incredible adventures in every land they pass through. An Inspector Fix, convinced that Fogg is wanted for robbing the Bank of England, pursues them.

In India, Fogg rescues a young princess, Aouda, from being burned alive in a suttee ceremony, and she joins the travelers in their daring journey. In San Francisco they encounter a Barbary Coast saloon-keeper (Marlene Dietrich) and her honky-tonk pianist (Frank Sinatra). As Fogg exultantly returns to England, he suddenly is clapped into jail by Fix, who has a warrant for his arrest. By the time Fix discovers his error, Fogg's deadline is up. Consoling himself by arranging for his wedding to the lovely Aouda, Fogg discovers that it is a day earlier than he believed. By traveling eastward he crossed the International Dateline, and he now has ten minutes to spare. Rushing to the Club, he arrives on the dot and wins the £20,000.

REVIEWS

"... it presents a plot that does not falter for an instant, a series of actors and actresses (including Marlene Dietrich, Ronald Colman, Victor McLaglen, Frank Sinatra, Noel Coward, Charles Boyer, Beatrice Lillie, George Raft, John Gielgud—40 of them) who give minute but exquisite characterizations, and includes a travelogue the like of which has never been seen on the screen before."

Good Housekeeping

"Todd himself has done something which has looked to be coming ever since the proscenium-type screen was introduced. He has brought into being a theatrical kind of film entertainment, a kind of show-business bonanza that is going to cause some heavy thinking and reevaluations in movie business circles."

Hollis Alpert, *The Saturday Review*

"Perhaps the simplest explanation is that Mr. Todd didn't think in terms of conventional motion-picture entertainment. He wasn't making a film that had a form. He was using the screen as a canvas on which to mount a giant variety show. . . . What does this prove? Very simply, there are all sorts of ways of doing a show, and Mr. Todd has discovered a good one that is apt for the new giant screen. He has used wit and imagination. Hollywood veterans, please note."

Bosley Crowther, *The New York Times*

With Sophia Loren

THE PRIDE
AND THE PASSION · 1957

With Cary Grant,
the Spanish People,
and The Gun

124

A Stanley Kramer Production. Released by United Artists. Technicolor; VistaVision. Produced and directed by Stanley Kramer. Screenplay by Edna and Edward Anhalt. Based on the novel The Gun by C. S. Forester. Music by George Antheil; orchestrated and conducted by Ernest Gold. Director of photography, Franz Planer. Film editors, Frederic Knudtson and Ellsworth Hoagland. Production design by Rudolph Sternad. Art directors, Fernando Carrere and Gil Parrondo. Costumes by Joe King. Makeup by Bernard Ponedel, John O'Gorman, and Jose Ma Sanchez. Choreographer, Paco Reyes. Special effects by Willis Cook and Maurice Ayers. Sound recorder, Joseph de Bretagne. Assistant director, Carter DeHaven, Jr. Dialogue supervisor, Anne Kramer. Production supervisor, Ivan Volkman. Production manager, Stanley Goldsmith. Military adviser, Lt. Col. Luis Cano. Running time, 132 minutes.

CAST

Captain Anthony Trumbull, CARY GRANT; *Miguel*, FRANK SINATRA; *Juana*, SOPHIA LOREN; *General Jouvet*, THEODORE BIKEL; *Sermaine*, JOHN WENGRAF; *Ballinger*, JAY NOVELLO; *Carlos*, JOSE NIETO; *Jose*, CARLOS LARRANAGA; *Vidal*, PHILIP VAN ZANDT; *Manolo*, PACO EL LABERINTO; *Enrique*, JULIAN UGARTE; *Bishop*, FELIX DE POMES; *Leonardo*, CARLOS CASARAVILLA; *Ramon*, JUAN OLAGUIVEL; *Maria*, NANA DE HERRERA; *Francisco*, CARLOS DE MENDOZA; *French Soldier*, LUIS GUEDES.

STORY

During the Peninsular Wars, climaxing with the Napoleonic campaign in Spain, a tremendous cannon, the ultimate in Spanish ironmongery, has been abandoned by Spanish troops forced to take to their heels upon being defeated by the French legions. Miguel, a Spanish peasant with a real flair for leadership, determines that the cannon must be used to destroy a French-occupied fort. He enlists the aid of the Spanish people in getting the heavy gun to a point outside the fort's walls. Aiding him is Captain Anthony Trumbull, of the English Royal Navy, equally anxious to get the cannon for British use. Miguel is forced to throw in his lot with Trumbull, who is the only man around who knows how to fire the cannon. Juana, a beautiful peasant girl, goes along on the expedition because she is Miguel's woman. Almost at once she is attracted to Trumbull, and he to her. With the aid of hordes of Spanish people, the cannon is transported to outside the walls of Avila, and the bloody siege is fought. Both Miguel and Juana give their lives in the fight, and

With Cary Grant

the victory goes to the Spanish people. Trumbull carries the body of Miguel triumphantly within the walls, and he lays the body of Juana in peace before the statue of Teresa, patron saint of Avila.

REVIEWS

"Plainly, there are more logistics than logic in this film. Without passion and without logic, it merely rambles in the realm of massive display. This is what often happens when producers try to be Cecil B. DeMille."

Bosley Crowther, *The New York Times*

"There is more romance than history in the end-product, and it is an adventure spectacle with an added ingredient—the theme of people rising up from defeat to repel the conqueror. For the latter the big gun serves as an eloquent if rather obvious symbol. As the virtual star the cannon does nobly—if it doesn't exactly out-act Sinatra, Grant, and Miss Loren, it is usually there, like Everest. While the gun deserves a special Academy Award, Mr. Sinatra must be commended for his restrained and appealing *guerillero* leader, Mr. Grant for his stalwart, understated British captain, and Miss Loren for her good looks."

Hollis Alpert, *The Saturday Review*

"Sinatra—despite spit-curl bangs and a put-on accent—expectably works hardest, acts best. Captain Grant suavely keeps trying not to remind himself of Horatio Hornblower. So they finally get the gun to the long shadow of Avila's wall, blast their opening at 1,600 yards, and sliding in on their own blood, overwhelm the hated occupiers. Thus Producer Kramer conquers Napoleon's forces. But somehow the whir of the cameras often seems as loud as the thunderous cannonades. It evidently takes more than dedication, co-operative multitudes and $4,000,000 to shoot history in the face."

Time

With Sophia Loren

"Sinatra is the 'Passion' vis-à-vis Grant's 'Pride.' One is the emotional, zealous, inarticulate Spaniard, driven by blind passion to destruction of the French bastion at Avila. The other is stiff, organized, disciplined—all Government Issue, British style . . . . Sinatra is more colorful, as per script. He looks and behaves like a Spanish rebel leader, earthy and cruel and skilled in handling his men in the primitive warfare. His is a splendid performance."

Gene, *Variety*

THE JOKER IS WILD · 1957

An A. M. B. L. Production. A Paramount release. Vista-Vision. Directed by Charles Vidor. Produced by Samuel J. Briskin. Screenplay by Oscar Saul. Based on the book by Art Cohn. Music composed and conducted by Walter Scharf. Orchestrations by Leo Shuken and Jack Hayes. Orchestral arrangements of songs by Nelson Riddle. Specialty songs and parodies by Harry Harris. Dances staged by Josephine Earl. Director of photography, Daniel L. Fapp. Film editor, Everett Douglas. Art directors, Hal Pereira and Roland Anderson. Set decorators, Sam Comer and Grace Gregory. Costumes by Edith Head. Makeup supervisor, Wally Westmore. Hair stylist, Nellie Manley. Special photographic effects by John P. Fulton. Sound recorders, Harold Lewis and Charles Grenzbach. Assistant director, C. C. Coleman, Jr. Running time, 126 minutes.

CAST

Joe E. Lewis, FRANK SINATRA; *Martha Stewart,* MITZI GAYNOR; *Letty Page,* JEANNE CRAIN; *Austin Mack,* EDDIE ALBERT; *Cassie Mack,* BEVERLY GARLAND; *Swifty Morgan,* JACKIE COOGAN; *Captain Hugh McCarthy,* BARRY KELLEY; *Georgie Parker,* TED DE CORSIA; *Tim Coogan,* LEONARD GRAVES; *Flora,* VALERIE ALLEN; *Burlesque Comedian,* HANK HENRY; *Harry Bliss,* HAROLD HUBER; *Johnson,* NED GLASS; *Dr. Pierson,* NED WEVER; *Mr. Page,* WALTER WOOLF KING; *Allen,* JOHN HARDING; *Runner,* SID MELTON; *Hecklers:* WALLY BROWN, DON BEDDOE, MARY TREEN; *Herself,* SOPHIE TUCKER.

Sinatra's songs: "I Cried for You" by Arthur Freed, Gus Arnheim and Abe Lyman; "If I Could Be with You" by Jimmy Johnson and Henry Creamer; "Chicago" by Fred Fisher; "All the Way" by James Van Heusen and Sammy Cahn (Academy Award for Best Song of 1957).

STORY

Joe E. Lewis is a full-fledged, promising young singer, when he becomes a pawn in a battle between racketeer cafe owners. When he leaves one employer to go to another, he is brutally attacked by mobsters, who slash his throat, cutting his vocal cords. Sophie Tucker helps him back via the burlesque route, and he gains a top place in show business as a solo-humorist. Letty Page, a wealthy society girl, meanwhile has fallen in love with him, and he with her, but she gives up on him when he never gets around to asking her to marry him. A chorus dancer named Martha Stewart marries him, and soon finds that her greatest rival is not another women but booze. She has to walk out on him too, as does his long-suffering best

friend and accompanist, Austin Mack. Alone, Lewis faces himself, and starts on the comeback trail.

REVIEWS

"Frank Sinatra was first to carry the ball with this one, having bought Art Cohn's story of Joe E. Lewis in galley proof form and thereafter taking a key part in the packaging. The objective was a true representation of pixie Lewis, bon vivant and nitery buffoon and acknowledged by many in the trade as doyen of the saloon comedians. It doesn't matter much about this objective, for the fact is that the finished product is a pretty good picture. . . . Sinatra obviously couldn't be made to look like Lewis; any thought of a reasonable facsimile, appearance-wise, is out of the question. And Lewis' style of delivery is unique and defies accurate copying (although some of his on-stage mannerisms are aped by the film's star quite well). But these are minor reservations in light of the major job Sinatra does at being an actor. He's believable and forceful—alternately sympathetic and pathetic, funny and sad."

Gene, *Variety*

With Eddie Albert and Leonard Graves

With Jackie Coogan
and Mitzi Gaynor

With Jeanne Crain

With Jackie Coogan

"As a matter of fact, Sinatra gives a very good performance of Sinatra playing Joe E. Lewis. He has the outer mannerisms down pat and catches the bitter inner restlessness almost too well. This is most evident, significantly, when Frank is being Joe E. at his funniest—in the drunk monologues. When Lewis, highball in hand, is reciting them his natural clown's grin takes the curse off their cynicism; from Sinatra the gags come out bitter and barbed."

Philip K. Scheuer, *the Los Angeles Times*

"Frank Sinatra, whose name popped up among the Top Ten leaders in Quigley Publications' Money-Making Stars poll of exhibitors for the first time last year, plays Joe E. Lewis in the picture, and the performance he gives as the singer-turned-comic is a better piece of acting than he's delivered in the several sympathetically designed characterizations he's been assigned heretofore.

"This time, after the first few sequences, there is mighty little sympathy going for him, and there's none at all when the climactic sequence is run out. But some time between the start of the picture, when he's all-Sinatra, and the end, when he's become all-Lewis, he gets a firm hand on the character he's re-creating and, at the same

With Eddie Albert

With Mitzi Gaynor

With Jeanne Crain

time, the audience he's creating it for. This is the essence of show-business."

William R. Weaver, *Motion Picture Herald*

"One consolation in the glossy gloom of this downbeat drama is that Frank Sinatra has sufficient talent and taste to break through the wall of embarrassment that is bound to arise between an audience and the film case-history of an unanonymous alcoholic. It is also pleasant to note that the horrific bit comes early, is handled with remarkable decorum, and has nothing to do with dipsomania."

Gordon Gow, *Films and Filming*

With Eddie Albert and Beverly Garland

With Sid Melton and Jeanne Crain

With Mitzi Gaynor

With Kim Novak

PAL JOEY · 1957

An Essex-George Sidney Production. A Columbia Release. Technicolor. Directed by George Sidney. Produced by Fred Kohlmar. Screenplay by Dorothy Kingsley. Based on the musical play by John O'Hara (book), Richard Rodgers (music), and Lorenz Hart (lyrics). Music supervised and conducted by Morris Stoloff. Musical arrangements by Nelson Riddle. Music adaptation by George Duning and Nelson Riddle. Orchestrations by Arthur Morton. Director of photography, Harold Lipstein. Film editors, Viola Lawrence and Jerome Thoms. Choreography by Hermes Pan. Art director, Walter Holscher. Set decorators, William Kiernan and Louis Diage. Gowns by Jean Louis. Makeup by Ben Lane. Hair stylist, Helen Hunt. Recording supervisor, John Livadary. Sound by Franklin Hansen. Assistant director, Art Black. Music adviser, Fred Karger. Color consultant, Henri Jaffa. Running time, 111 minutes.

CAST

Vera Simpson, RITA HAYWORTH; *Joey Evans*, FRANK SINATRA; *Linda English*, KIM NOVAK; *Gladys*, BARBARA NICHOLS; *Ned Galvin*, BOBBY SHERWOOD; *Mike Miggins*, HANK HENRY; *Mrs. Casey*, ELIZABETH PATTERSON; *Bartender*, ROBIN MORSE; *Col. Langley*, FRANK WILCOX; *Mr. Forsythe*, PIERRE WATKIN; *Anderson*, BARRY BERNARD; *Carol*, ELLIE KENT; *Sabrina*, MARA MC AFEE; *Patsy*, BETTY UTEY; *Lola*, BEK NELSON; *Barker*, FRANK SULLY; *Shorty*, HENRY MC CANN; *Stanley*, JOHN HUBBARD; *Livingstone*, JAMES SEAY; *Choreographer*, HERMES PAN; *Chef Tony*, ERNESTO MOLINARI.

Sinatra's songs (by Richard Rodgers and Lorenz Hart): "I Didn't Know What Time It Was," "There's a Small Hotel," "I Could Write a Book," "The Lady Is a Tramp," "Bewitched, Bothered and Bewildered," and "What Do I Care for a Dame?"

STORY

Joey Evans, a gilt-edged heel, arrives in San Francisco wearing a tuxedo—but broke. He gets a break at the 626 Club, and almost at once makes the scene with most of the girls in the chorus line. The hold-out is Linda English, a newcomer to night clubs. Joey goes with the band and the girls to perform at a charity given at the Nob Hill mansion of Vera Simpson. Joey recognizes the widowed hostess as the one-time queen stripper Vera Vanessa. Joey and Linda fall in love, but Mrs. Simpson is also very attracted to Joey and finally agrees to set him up in a night club of his own, the Chez Joey. Linda is to have a featured spot in Joey's new floor show, but Vera

Simpson, sensing the bond between the girl and Joey, tells him that Linda must go, or else. Joey calls her bluff, and the Chez Joey does not open. Linda pleads with Vera to give Joey his chance, and Vera promises to do so if Linda will get out of Joey's life. Vera asks Joey to stay, and even promises to make him her husband—but Joey turns her down. He's learned his lesson, and knows Linda is the girl for him.

REVIEWS

"Frankie is perfectly type-cast as Joey, carrying on, in a sense, from his Joey (sic!) Lewis of *The Joker Is Wild*. However, his new Joey is less bitter, at least by comparison. In the beginning, indeed, he seems almost too cocky,

With Barbara Nichols

137

too hep, as if hardly able to keep from breaking himself up at his own audacity.

"This is being Joey even beyond the call of duty; but Frankie is too smart, if not too dedicated, a performer not to knuckle down and come through with the kind of trouping that counts. His Joey is a rat, all right, among mice, but his environment has a lot to do with making him one and you can't quite submerge a sneaking sympathy for the Frankie part of him."

Philip K. Scheuer, *Los Angeles Times*

"First produced on Broadway in 1940, *Pal Joey* is one of the few musical comedies on record with a little heel as a hero. The screen interpretation of the Rodgers and Hart success is a watered-down version of the hard-boiled original about sexy goings-on in dark night clubs. A few of its ribald songs are missing, the lyrics of the other songs have been cleansed, and the story has a 'happy ending.' But its bite remains. Heading up an impressive cast, Frank Sinatra plays Joey with all the brass the role demands. He has a gleam in his eye and a chip on his shoulder, as he portrays this unsavory character who could be so charming—against everybody's better judgment. He tosses off both dames and songs with equal artistry, and almost single-handedly makes *Pal Joey* a wonderfully entertaining movie."

Look

"Sinatra is potent. He's almost ideal as the irreverent, free-wheeling, glib Joey, delivering the rapid-fire cracks in a fashion that wrings out the full deeper-than-pale-blue comedy potentials. Point might be made, though, that it's hard to figure why all the mice fall for this rat. . . . Standout of the score is *Lady Is a Tramp*. It's a wham arrangement and Sinatra gives it power-house delivery. His *Write a Book* is another of the big plusses."

Gene, *Variety*

With Kim Novak

With Rita Hayworth

KINGS GO FORTH · 1958

With Tony Curtis

With Tony Curtis

With Carl Swenson

A Frank Ross-Eton Production. Released by United Artists. Directed by Delmer Daves. Produced by Frank Ross. Screenplay by Merle Miller. Based on the novel by Joe David Brown. Music composed and conducted by Elmer Bernstein. Orchestrations by Leo Shuken and Jack Hayes. Director of photography, Daniel L. Fapp. Associate producer, Richard Ross. Editorial supervisor, William B. Murphy. Art director, Fernando Carrere. Set decorator, Darrell Silvera. Gowns by Leah Rhodes. Makeup by Bernard Ponedel. Assistant director, Edward Denault. Production manager, Richard McWhorter. Running time, 109 minutes.

CAST

Lt. Sam Loggins, FRANK SINATRA; *Sgt. Britt Harris*, TONY CURTIS; *Monique Blair*, NATALIE WOOD; *Mrs. Blair*, LEORA DANA; *Colonel*, KARL SWENSON; *Madame Brieux*, ANNE CODEE; *Corporal Lindsay*, EDWARD RYDER; *Jean Francois*, JACKIE BERTHE; *Old Frenchwoman*, MARIE ISNARD; *Jazz Musicians*: RED NORVO, PETE CANDOLI, MEL LEWIS, RICHIE KAMUCA, RED WOOTEN, JIMMY WEIBLE.

STORY

Lieutenant Sam Loggins and his radio operator Britt Harris are with the American Seventh Army fighting the Germans in southern France. On leave, Sam falls in love with Monique Blair, a beautiful American girl living in Nice with her widowed mother. He asks Monique to marry him, but she refuses, confessing that she is the child of a mixed marriage; her father, whom she dearly loved, was a Negro. Sam is stunned, and then resigned to losing Monique when he sees that she is in love with Britt. Sam tells Britt about Monique's father, but Britt seems to be indifferent.

Then, only a few hours before Sam and Britt are to go on a dangerous mission, Britt admits that he never had any intention of marrying Monique. Sam forces Britt to tell Monique the truth, and she becomes hysterical. Sam vows to kill Britt, but during their mission the Germans do the job for him, and Sam himself loses an arm. After the Armistice, Sam returns to Nice to learn that Monique's mother is dead, and that the girl he silently loves has turned their villa into a school for war orphans.

REVIEWS

"The Thin Singer has never had a more difficult role and he has never more completely mastered a characterization. Might as well admit it, he's a great actor. He makes you love and understand the Yankee lieutenant, a cynical man hardly able to believe himself that he has fallen tenderly in love with the young half-Negress, puzzled by the friendship he feels for the GI 'pal' he intuitively recognizes as a heel."

Dorothy Manners, *Los Angeles Examiner*

"*Kings Go Forth*, glib, happy ending and all, really is the limit. It is time someone debunked this kind of specious, hysterical liberalism. It went out years ago—or should have done. The trouble is that as long as there are directors as technically proficient as Delmer Daves, and actors as hypnotically persuasive as Frank Sinatra—who has every quality but depth and intelligence—audiences will go on accepting this masochistic nonsense."

Peter John Dyer, *Films and Filming*

"The movie *Kings Go Forth* doesn't come close to having the guts of the book by Joe David Brown and the result is a film which is all surface and little depth. . . . It's a strange kind of war the GIs fight in what Author Brown described as 'the champagne war' in Southern France in 1944. During the week, Frank Sinatra's platoon is fighting the Nazis in the mountains. On week ends, Sinatra and buddy Tony Curtis are down on the Riviera on two-day passes, ogling the girls, sipping aperitifs and basking in the sun. . . . The cast's reactions often don't ring true. One doesn't even believe that Sinatra is really stunned, for instance, when he learns that the girl is half Negro. Still, Sinatra is the best of the three."

The Los Angeles *Mirror-News*

"Sinatra, the rough-tough soldier, in action for six months and frustrated in his love for Miss Wood, turns in a capable performance. He's likable, and understandable, and creates sympathy by underplaying the role."

Hift, *Variety*

With Tony Curtis

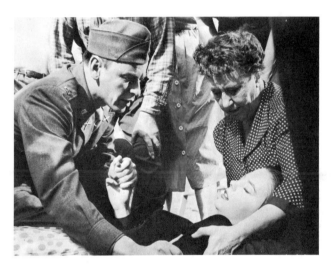

With Anne Codee and Natalie Wood

With Tony Curtis

143

With Dean Martin

SOME CAME RUNNING · 1958

A Metro-Goldwyn-Mayer Picture. MetroColor; Cinema-Scope. Directed by Vincente Minnelli. Produced by Sol C. Siegel. Screenplay by John Patrick and Arthur Sheekman. Based on the novel by James Jones. Music composed and conducted by Elmer Bernstein. Orchestrations by Leo Shuken and Jack Hayes. Director of photography, William H. Daniels. Film editor, Adrienne Fazan. Art directors, William A. Horning and Urie McCleary. Set decorators, Henry Grace and Robert Priestley. Costumes by Walter Plunkett. Makeup by William Tuttle. Recording supervisor, Franklin Milton. Assistant director, William McGarry. Color consultant, Charles K. Hagedon. Song "To Love and Be Loved" by James Van Heusen and Sammy Cahn. Running time, 127 minutes.

With Betty Lou Keim and John Brennan

With William Lockridge and Shirley MacLaine

With Shirley MacLaine

With Shirley MacLaine

With Shirley MacLaine

CAST

Dave Hirsh, FRANK SINATRA; *Bama Dillert,* DEAN MARTIN; *Ginny Moorehead,* SHIRLEY MacLAINE; *Gwen French,* MARTHA HYER; *Frank Hirsh,* ARTHUR KENNEDY; *Edith Barclay,* NANCY GATES; *Agnes Hirsh,* LEORA DANA; *Dawn Hirsh,* BETTY LOU KEIM; *Rosalie,* CARMEN PHILLIPS; *Raymond Lanchak,* STEVEN PECK; *Jane Barclay,* CONNIE GILCHRIST; *Wally Dennis,* JOHN BRENNAN; *Prof. Robert Haven French,* LARRY GATES; *Smitty,* NED WEVER; *Dewey Cole,* DENNY MILLER; *Ted Harperspoon,* DON HAGGERTY; *Al,* WILLIAM SCHALLERT; *Mrs. Stevens,* GERALDINE WALL; *Virginia Stevens,* JANELLE RICHARDS; *Slim,* GEORGE E. STONE; *Judge Baskin,* ANTHONY JOCHIM; *Sister Mary Joseph,* MARION ROSS; *Joe,* RIC ROMAN; *Sheriff,* ROY ENGEL; *Radio Announcer,* ELMER PETERSEN.

STORY

After a long absence, Dave Hirsh returns to his home town in Indiana with an army discharge, an unpublished manuscript, and a good-natured doxy named Ginny who adores him. His older brother Frank is resentful, and Dave in turn hates Frank for consigning him to an orphanage as a child. Gwen French, a college instructor, is intrigued and wants to help Dave with his writing. Bama Dillert, a professional gambler, is delighted, and takes Dave on as a poker-playing, whiskey-drinking partner. Although dying of diabetes, Bama never takes off his hat because he thinks it's bad luck. Dave falls in love with Gwen who encourages his writing and gets his manuscript published, but he cannot melt her sexual coldness, and she refuses to marry him.

Disillusioned, Dave goes on a spree with Ginny and Bama. In Terra Haute, they find Frank's teenage daughter Dawn, who has learned of her father's affair with his secretary and run away from home with her boyfriend Wally. Dave brings the girl home, tells off her parents, and then, over Bama's objections, asks Ginny to marry him. She jumps at the chance, but their marriage is short-lived. Raymond Lanchak, a jealous former boyfriend of Ginny's, arrives in town and attempts to kill Dave at a local carnival. Ginny dies shielding Dave from her ex-lover's gunfire. At Ginny's funeral, Bama pays her a final tribute—he removes his hat.

REVIEWS

"Sinatra moves with impressive speed and precision in every situation, with occasional flashes of humor. It's his picture, but he has distinguished support. Miss MacLaine portrays a young woman out on her own in the world,

With Shirley MacLaine and Betty Lou Keim

who admits she doesn't understand many things, but knows, nevertheless, that she is in love with Sinatra. Her elfin quality shines through the veneer and makes her characterization sympathetic."

James M. Jerauld, *Motion Picture Herald*

"Frank Sinatra and Dean Martin punch over two of their best performances. But the surprise hit is Shirley MacLaine's touching, unforgettable portrait of the crude, pathetic little floozy who falls in love with Frank."

Dick Williams, Los Angeles *Mirror-News*

"Yet as bromide follows bromide, the spectator slowly comes to a drugged realization that the script is not making fun of anybody's beliefs, but simply stating its own. After that, there is nothing to hang around for except occasional flickers of brilliant overacting by Shir-

ley MacLaine, the chance to watch Frank Sinatra play Frank Sinatra, and the spectacle of Director Vincente Minnelli's talents dissolving in the general mess of the story, like sunlight in a slag heap."

Time

"Sinatra plays his role vividly enough, but his is strictly a storybook, or comic book, conception of a dashing, daredevil writer who mixes smoothly with high and low, with gamblers, thugs, bankers, boozers, prostitutes, and social *elegantes*. Everywhere he moves phoney romance and wild melodrama dog his footsteps. By the film's end, *weltschmerzlich*, he picks himself up and wanders on again—surely to literary fame, fortune, and immortality, just like Jack London and Thomas Wolfe, at the very least."

Cue

147

"Sinatra doesn't really ring true in the part of a frustrated author, no matter how many copies of Faulkner and Fitzgerald he is seen taking out of his duffle bag. But the literary business is played down here, and compensation for the film's inadequacies is to be found in Shirley MacLaine's portrait of an over-ripe piece of goods who blows into town from Chicago. She is the brightest feature in a movie which, despite its lack of thematic purpose (or possibly because of it) shows flashes of brilliance."
Newsweek

"Two charter members of Frank Sinatra's Hollywood clan, Shirley MacLaine and Dean Martin, run away with the picture . . . Sinatra, as usual, gives a polished performance; but it is Shirley MacLaine, with a moving portrayal of the giddy and warm-hearted tart that might well win an Academy Award next year, and Dean Martin, with an easy-going portrayal of a superstitious gambler who always keeps his hat on, even in bed, who walk off with the acting honors."
Cosmopolitan

With Carmen Phillips, Steven Peck, Shirley MacLaine and Dean Martin

With Carolyn Jones

A HOLE IN THE HEAD · 1959

A Sincap Production. Released by United Artists. Color by DeLuxe; CinemaScope. Produced and directed by Frank Capra. Screenplay by Arnold Schulman, based on his play. Music by Nelson Riddle. Director of photography, William H. Daniels. Film editor, William Hornbeck. Art director, Eddie Imazu. Set decorator, Fred MacLean. Costumes by Edith Head. Hair stylist, Helene Parrish. Makeup by Bernard Ponedel. Sound by Fred Lau. Assistant directors, Arthur S. Black, Jr., and Jack R. Berne. Production manager, Joe Cook. Running time, 120 minutes.

CAST

Tony Manetta, FRANK SINATRA; *Mario Manetta*, EDWARD G. ROBINSON; *Mrs. Rogers*, ELEANOR PARKER; *Shirl*, CAROLYN JONES; *Sophie Manetta*, THELMA RITTER; *Jerry Marks*, KEENAN WYNN; *Ally Manetta*, EDDIE HODGES; *Dorine*, JOI LANSING; *Mendy*, GEORGE DE WITT; *Julius Manetta*, JIMMY KOMACK; *Fred*, DUB TAYLOR; *Miss Wexler*, CONNIE SAWYER; *Mr. Diamond*, BENNY RUBIN; *Sally*, RUBY DANDRIDGE; *Hood*, B. S. PULLY; *Alice*, JOYCE NIZZARI; *Master of Ceremonies*, PUPI CAMPO.

Sinatra's songs (by James Van Heusen and Sammy Cahn): "All My Tomorrows"; "High Hopes" (Academy Award for Best Song of 1959).

STORY

Tony Manetta is a widower and an impractical daydreamer. He operates a fleabag hotel in Miami Beach, and treats his eleven-year-old son Ally as if he were an adult. Realizing he may lose his hotel, he appeals to Mario, his rich older brother in New York. Mario consents to give him financial assistance, but only in exchange for turning over the son to Mario and his wife in New York, and Tony can't give up his boy. He turns to a rich widow, Mrs. Rogers, but he falls in love with her and can't marry her for money. Tony thinks he's found an angel in an old buddy, Jerry Marks, but only finds himself in more hot water than ever. Desperate, he tries to make his son hate him and *want* to go to New York. But Mario relents, and decides to reform from hard work and become a bum, too. Tony gets the money he needs, and the whole family goes to the beach.

REVIEWS

"But now Mr. Capra is back with us—and not only back, but also in such form as to make one toy vaguely

With Eddie Hodges

With Benny Rubin

151

With Dub Taylor and Eleanor Parker

With Edward G. Robinson

With Keenan Wynn and Joi Lansing

with the notion that maybe it is good for a director to rest a bit once in awhile. For *A Hole in the Head*, which is based on Arnold Schulman's Broadway play and has the carbolic Sinatra playing the character whose head is so endowed, is a thoroughly fresh, aggressive and sardonic comedy of the sort that sets one to thinking about the comedies of the good old days."

Bosley Crowther, *The New York Times*

"A soap-opera plot, if there ever was one. But, having been directed by the 'human-comedy' veteran Frank Capra and acted by those powerful performing personalities Frank Sinatra and Edward G. Robinson, the film turns out to be genuinely entertaining. Sinatra, as the poor man's Hilton, manages to arouse sympathy without employing sentimentality; Robinson, who plays his rich, frugal, sour, advice-giving merchant-brother from New York, displays such finesse as a broad-comedy foil (a new sort of business for the movies' Little Caesar) that he almost steals the show from Sinatra. Not quite, of course. No one these days ever completely steals the show from Sinatra."

Newsweek

"For eight years Hollywood has been unaccountably and, I am sure, needlessly deprived of the know-how of this director, who has left his seriocomic touch on hits from *It Happened One Night* to *Arsenic and Old Lace*. (His last was Crosby's *Here Comes the Groom.*) While he has not performed any major miracle with *A Hole in the Head*, he has at least dressed up a so-so stage comedy with laughs, human interest, a shot of sex, and even a suspicion of a tear toward the close.

"The locale is Miami Beach (in CinemaScope and DeLuxe Color) and the principals are of Italian extraction—a change from the Jewish letter and spirit of the play that, even allowing for the presence of Sinatra, seems to me more of a loss than a gain. As it is, Robinson, called Mario Manetta and playing Frankie's brother, makes little effort to disguise the ethnically Jewish humor of the character originally known as Max. Oh, well, let's say they're typically New Yorkese."

Philip K. Scheuer, *Los Angeles Times*

With Thelma Ritter

153

NEVER SO FEW · 1959

A Canterbury Production. Released by Metro-Goldwyn-Mayer. Metrocolor; CinemaScope. Directed by John Sturges. Produced by Edmund Grainger. Screenplay by Millard Kaufman. Based on the novel by Tom T. Chamales. Music by Hugo Friedhofer; orchestrated by Robert Franklyn; conducted by Charles Wolcott. Director of photography, William H. Daniels. Film editor, Ferris Webster. Art directors, Hans Peters and Addison Hehr. Set decorators, Henry Grace and Richard Pefferle. Gowns for Gina Lollobrigida by Helen Rose. Makeup by William Tuttle. Hair stylist, Sydney Guilaroff. Special effects by Robert R. Hoag and Lee LeBlanc. Recording supervisor, Franklin Milton. Assistant director, Robert E. Relyea. Color consultant, Charles K. Hagedon. Running time, 124 minutes.

With Gina Lollobrigida

CAST

Capt. Tom C. Reynolds, FRANK SINATRA; Carla Vesari, GINA LOLLOBRIGIDA; Capt. Grey Travis, PETER LAWFORD; Bill Ringa, STEVE McQUEEN; Capt. Danny De Mortimer, RICHARD JOHNSON; Nikko Regas, PAUL HENREID; General Sloan, BRIAN DONLEVY; Sgt. Jim Norby, DEAN JONES; Sgt. John Danforth, CHARLES BRONSON; Nautaung, PHILIP AHN; Colonel Fred Parkson, ROBERT BRAY; Margaret Fitch, KIPP HAMILTON; Colonel Reed, JOHN HOYT; Captain Alofson, WHIT BISSELL; Mike Island, RICHARD LUPINO; Billingsly, AKI ALEONG; Dr. Barry, ROSS ELLIOTT; Laurel, LEON LONTOC.

STORY

While fighting the Japs in Burma during World War II with a band of G.I.s and guerrillas, Captains Tom Reynolds and Danny De Mortimer are ordered to take a two-week "holiday" in Calcutta to obtain a doctor and medical supplies for their men. Reynolds acquires a jeep driver named Bill Ringa and a doctor, Captain Grey Travis, who is treating De Mortimer for malaria. At the home of a war profiteer, Nikko Regas, Reynolds meets Regas' mistress Carla Vesari, and when Regas goes to China on business, Reynolds courts Carla, receiving little encouragement. Their leave over, Reynolds and De Mortimer return to the hills, accompanied by Travis and Ringa. As they celebrate Christmas in their camp, they are attacked by the Japanese and Reynolds is wounded. Visited in the hospital by Carla, Reynolds resumes his courtship and Carla is warmer than before.

Recovered, Reynolds joins his men in an attack on a Jap airfield, though without the support promised by Colonel Parkson. After destroying the airstrip, they come upon the convoy that failed to support them—ambushed and massacred by Chinese operating under a warlord.

With Gina Lollobrigida

Reynolds leads his men against the Chinese although it means crossing the Chinese frontier. In a captured Chinese village Reynolds finds American supplies, and licenses issued to warlords by Chungking to raid Allied troops and sell the booty to the Japanese, splitting the take with Chungking! As Reynolds is receiving belated word from Parkson *not* to attack the village, a wounded Chinese kills De Mortimer, and the enraged Reynolds orders all prisoners shot, wiring Chungking and Parkson to "go to hell." Flying back to face a court-martial, Reynolds again meets Carla, rejecting her suggestion to plead "battle fatigue" and her offer to have Regas intercede for him because of his connections' with U.S. brass. After a touchy interview, General Sloan finally backs up Reynolds and puts off the Chungking representative. Carla and Reynolds are briefly reunited before he returns to his men in the hills.

With Gina Lollobrigida and Peter Lawford

With Peter Lawford, Richard Johnson and Steve McQueen

With Gina Lollobrigida

REVIEWS

"Sinatra is in his element, swinging with the plot from tough soldier to teasing lover, and tossing off the smart dialogue in that casual, underplayed way of his."

Kay Proctor, Los Angeles *Examiner*

"War is a messy business, as Frank Sinatra, playing Army Capt. Tom C. Reynolds, and his companions in *Never So Few* graphically re-illustrate, but there's always Gina Lollobrigida to come to, or get together with, or otherwise end a sentence with a proposition. Today this seems like an old-fashioned movie about an old-fashioned war, the kind that Edmund Grainger, its producer, has been turning out intermittently for years (*Flying Tigers, Flying Leathernecks, Sands of Iwo Jima*, etc.). But it is almost sure to be popular."

Philip K. Scheuer, *Los Angeles Times*

"The two co-stars play surprisingly well with each other, with Miss Lollobrigida appearing to greater advantage than she has in some time in an American film. Sinatra gives an earnest and direct performance . . . "

Richard Gertner, *Motion Picture Herald*

"For the first time within recall, an American motion picture has been written and constructed around the rumors (accepted as fact by thousands of G.I.s, and nowadays conveniently forgotten in the interest of 'international amity') that the wartime Nationalist government of Chiang Kai-shek was involved in the sale-for-profit of U.S.-donated arms and materiel to Japanese invaders and Chinese "warlords" (a latter-day euphemism for common bandits). And that far too frequently for comfort, American guns were turned against our own troops in the China-Burma-India jungle area—with Chinese soldiers and/or bandits raiding across the lines, burning, robbing, betraying and murdering our G.I.s."

Cue

"The film provides a catapult to stardom for Steve McQueen, hitherto known principally as a television actor. He has a good part, and he delivers with impressive style."

Powe, *Variety*

With Shirley MacLaine and Louis Jourdan

CAN-CAN · 1960

A Suffolk-Cummings Production. *Released by 20th Century-Fox. Technicolor; Todd-AO. Directed by Walter Lang. Produced by Jack Cummings. Screenplay by Dorothy Kingsley and Charles Lederer. Based on the musical play by Abe Burrows. Songs by Cole Porter. Music arranged and conducted by Nelson Riddle. Vocal supervision by Bobby Tucker. Associate producer, Saul Chaplin. Director of photography, William H. Daniels. Film editor, Robert Simpson. Art directors, Lyle Wheeler and Jack Martin Smith. Set decorators, Walter M. Scott and Paul S. Fox. Dances staged by Hermes Pan. Costumes by Irene Sharaff. Makeup by Ben Nye. Hair stylist, Myrl Stoltz; styling consultant, Tony Duquette. Sound recorders, W. D. Flick and Fred Hynes. Assistant director, Joseph E. Rickards. Color consultant, Leonard Doss. Running time, 130 minutes.*

With Shirley MacLaine and Louis Jourdan

CAST

François Durnais, FRANK SINATRA; *Simone Pistache,* SHIRLEY MacLAINE; *Paul Barriere,* MAURICE CHEVALIER; *Philippe Forrestier,* LOUIS JOURDAN; *Claudine,* JULIET PROWSE; *André, Headwaiter,* MARCEL DALIO; *Orchestra Leader,* LEON BELASCO; *Bailiff,* NESTOR PAIVA; *Jacques, Photographer,* JOHN A. NERIS; *Judge Merceaux,* JEAN DEL VAL; *League President,* ANN CODEE; *Chevrolet,* EUGENE BORDEN; *Recorder,* JONATHAN KIDD; *Adam,* MARC WILDER; *Apache Dancer,* AMBROGIO MALERBA; *Gigi,* CAROLE BRYAN; *Camille,* BARBARA CARTER; *Renée,* JANE EARL; *Julie,* RUTH EARL; *Germaine,* LAURA FRASER; *Gabrielle,* VERA LEE; *Fifi,* LISA MITCHELL; *Maxine,* WANDA SHANNON; *Gisele,* DARLENE TITTLE; *Lili,* WILDA TAYLOR; *Gendarme Dupont,* PETER COE.

Sinatra's songs (by Cole Porter): "I Love Paris," "C'est Magnifique," "Let's Do It," and "It's All Right with Me."

With Maurice Chevalier

STORY

Dancing the can-can has been forbidden by an ancient French law, but lawyer François Durnais takes care of possible police interference with the help of his good friend on the bench, Paul Barriere. Philippe Forrestier joins the court, and tries to get Simone Pistache's café raided and the dancers arrested, but in planning the raid Philippe falls under Simone's spell. François uses this infatuation to help free Simone when the raid does come off, but Philippe, undaunted, proposes marriage. Simone, who really loves François, tries to persuade him to do likewise, but François does not believe that love and marriage can be mixed. François and Barriere cook up a scheme whereby Simone makes a spectacle of herself at a

With Juliet Prowse *(left)*

161

party given by Philippe. Still undaunted, Philippe insists that the marriage take place, whereupon François is forced to propose to Simone—and the can-can gets legal clearance after a specially staged performance before the Parisian court.

REVIEWS

"Being condemned by Khrushchev may be an even bigger commercial asset than being banned in Boston, for *Can-Can*, whose dancing the Russian Premier pronounced 'immoral' when he saw it on the Hollywood set last fall, opened last week with an advance sale reportedly bigger than the supercolossal *Ben Hur*'s. The show itself, in color and Todd-AO, turns out to be lavish, easy to look at, and—Mr. K notwithstanding—the sort of sophisticated mediocrity not likely to excite anybody at all. . . . Chevalier and Sinatra are entertaining with their individual, off-hand brands of charm, while the erratic Miss MacLaine acts as though she had a patent on personality, and clearly needs a hard-hearted director who would dare to disillusion her now and then."

Newsweek

"Miss MacLaine—grisette, gamine and cocotte rolled into one continuous explosion—comes off more spectacularly than Sinatra. But then Frankie, after all, defies classification; he remains simply, or not so simply, Sinatra, a 20-year phenomenon."

Philip K. Scheuer, *Los Angeles Times*

"Perhaps because his role was written specifically for him, Sinatra is Sinatra, ring-a-ding-ding and all. His naturalness makes him all the more effective, and his charm and self-assuredness ably complement a vocal style which fits hand in glove with the Porter tunes, particularly *It's All Right with Me*."

Ron, *Variety*

With Maurice Chevalier

OCEAN'S ELEVEN · 1960

With Peter Lawford

With Dean Martin, Peter Lawford and Akim Tamiroff

With Peter Lawford

A Dorchester Production. Released by Warner Bros. Technicolor; Panavision. Produced and directed by Lewis Milestone. Screenplay by Harry Brown and Charles Lederer. Based on an original story by George Clayton Johnson and Jack Golden Russell. Music composed and conducted by Nelson Riddle. Orchestrations by Arthur Morton. Director of photography, William H. Daniels. Film editor, Philip W. Anderson. Art director, Nicolai Remisoff. Set decorator, Howard Bristol. Costumes by Howard Shoup. Makeup supervisor, Gordon Bau. Sound recorder, M.A. Merrick. Associate producers, Henry W. Sanicola and Milton Ebbins. Assistant to the producer, Richard Benedict. Assistant director, Ray Gosnell, Jr. Production manager, Jack R. Berne. Songs "Ain't That a Kick in the Head" and "Eee-o Eleven" by James Van Heusen and Sammy Cahn. Running time, 127 minutes.

164

Listening to mastermind Akim Tamiroff are "Ocean's Eleven": Richard Conte, Buddy Lester, Joey Bishop, Sammy Davis, Jr., Frank Sinatra, Peter Lawford, Dean Martin, Henry Silva, Richard Benedict, Norman Fell, and Clem Harvey.

CAST

Danny Ocean, FRANK SINATRA; *Sam Harmon*, DEAN MARTIN; *Josh Howard*, SAMMY DAVIS, JR.; *Jimmy Foster*, PETER LAWFORD; *Beatrice Ocean*, ANGIE DICKINSON; *Anthony Bergdorf*, RICHARD CONTE; *Duke Santos*, CESAR ROMERO; *Adele Ekstrom*, PATRICE WYMORE; *"Mushy" O'Conners*, JOEY BISHOP; *Spyros Acebos*, AKIM TAMIROFF; *Roger Corneal*, HENRY SILVA; *Mrs. Restes*, ILKA CHASE; *Vincent Massler*, BUDDY LESTER; *George "Curly" Steffens*, RICHARD BENEDICT; *Grace Bergdorf*, JEAN WILLES; *Peter Rheimer*, NORMAN FELL; *Louis Jackson*, CLEM HARVEY; *Mr. Kelly*, HANK HENRY; *Young Man*, LEW GALLO; *Sheriff Wimmer*, ROBERT FOULK; *Mr. Cohen*, CHARLES MEREDITH; *Timmy Bergdorf*, RONNIE DAPO; *Store Proprietor*, GEORGE E. STONE; *De Wolfe*, LOUIS QUINN; *Texan*, JOHN INDRISANO; *Hungry Girl*, CARMEN PHILLIPS; *Deputy*, MURRAY ALPER; *Road Block Deputy*, HOOT GIBSON; *Freeman*, GREGORY GAY; *McCoy*, DON "RED" BARRY; *Client at Casino*, RED SKELTON; *Jack Strager*, GEORGE RAFT; *Tipsy Girl*, SHIRLEY MacLAINE.

With Angie Dickinson

STORY

During the week before Chirstmas, ten oddly assorted men arrive in Las Vegas. They have been called together by Danny Ocean, who is carrying out a plan originated by racketeer Spyros Acebos whereby five gambling casinos will be robbed simultaneously at midnight on New Year's Eve. Danny has picked his ten cohorts from members of the commandos in the 82nd Airborne Division in which he was a sergeant during the war. The scheme of the robbery is ingenious, requiring military precision and perfect timing. An electrical tower will be blown up to black out the city. The emergency light circuits in the casinos will be short-circuited so that the doors to the money vaults will open when the switches are thrown. The loot will be deposited in garbage cans outside the casinos, and the cans will be collected by Josh Howard in his disposal truck. There will be no gunplay.

While waiting for New Year's Eve, Danny, yearning for his estranged wife Beatrice, sends her a wire saying he is seriously ill, and she comes to see him. One of Danny's old flames, Adele Ekstrom, however, shows up, accusing Danny of having run out on her. Beatrice demands that Danny return to New York with her, but naturally he can't, and she leaves him. On New Year's Eve, the holdup goes off beautifully, exactly as planned. But one of the men, Bergdorf, has a heart attack on the street and dies. The gang cannot get the loot out of Las Vegas, but they manage to hide it in Bergdorf's coffin. Unbeknownst to them, however, Bergdorf's widow arranges to have her husband cremated—and Danny and his friends can only look on helplessly as the loot is consumed in flames.

REVIEWS

"Frank! Dean! Sammy! Peter! Angie! Who else could make such terrific excitement and have such fun doing it!" As the ad suggests, *Ocean's Eleven* is a genial group effort by a bunch of real-life pals. First Peter found the property, a story. Frank then formed a producing company, and sold shares in it to Peter and Dean. Then they all went out to Las Vegas and filmed it, while entertaining the night-club customers at night.

"Unfortunately, it is all so genial that the major suspense lies in whether Frank, Dean, *et al.*, will get their hands out of their pockets long enough to pull the robbery which the movie is all about."

Newsweek

"It also ends on much the same note as John Huston's great *Treasure of the Sierra Madre*. However, the difference between Walter Huston's reaction to fate (a classic demonstration of the quintessence of laughter) and that of the prinicipals of *Ocean's Eleven* is highly instructive. The most striking thing about the present cast is its collective slimness; if Mr. Sinatra, Mr. Davis, and Mr. Bishop were to turn sidewise, as the saying goes, they'd disappear."

The New Yorker

"*Ocean's Eleven* figures to be a moneymaker in spite of itself. Although basically a no-nonsense piece about the efforts of eleven ex-war buddies to make off with a multi-million dollar loot from five Vegas hotels, the film is frequently one resonant wisecrack away from turning into a musical comedy. Laboring under the handicaps of a contrived script, an uncertain approach, and personalities in essence playing themselves, the Lewis Milestone production never quite makes its point, but romps along merrily unconcerned that it doesn't."

Tube, *Variety*

"*Ocean's Eleven* fields a cast almost as gaudy as the advertising it freely hands Las Vegas. Frank Sinatra heads the list of big names in the line-up, followed by Clan regulars Dean Martin, Peter Lawford, and Sammy Davis Jr., not to mention Shirley MacLaine, who does an unbilled bit as an inebriated New Year's Eve celebrant. . . . Sinatra plays it cool as though there was nothing much in the script to get worked up about and Martin ambles in and around his role as a cocktail lounge entertainer, comforted throughout by a drink in his hand and a bottle on the table."

Margaret Harford, *Los Angeles Mirror*

With Richard Conte, Buddy Lester, Joey Bishop, Sammy Davis, Jr., Dean Martin, Peter Lawford, Akim Tamiroff, Henry Silva, Richard Benedict, Norman Fell and Clem Harvey.

Frank Sinatra

PEPE · 1960

A G.S.-Posa Films International Production. A Columbia Release. Print by Technicolor; photographic lenses by Panavision; special sequences photographed in Cinema-Scope. Produced and directed by George Sidney. Screenplay by Dorothy Kingsley and Claude Binyon. From a story by Leonard Spigelgass and Sonya Levien. Based on the play Broadway Magic by Ladislas Bush-Fekete. Music supervision and background score by Johnny Green. Associate producer, Jacques Gelman. Director of photography, Joe MacDonald. Film editors, Viola Lawrence and Al Clark. Art director, Ted Haworth; associate, Gunther Gerszo. Set decorator, William Kiernan. Gowns by Edith Head. Makeup supervisor, Ben Lane. Hair stylist, Larry Germaine. Sound by James Z. Flaster. Recording supervisor, Charles J. Rice. Music editor, Maury Winetrobe. Assistant director, David Silver, Script supervisor, Marshall Wolins. "Hooray for Hollywood" special material by Sammy Cahn. "Pepe" and "Mimi" special material and routines by Roger Edens. "The Rumble" instrumental by Andre Previn. Songs: "The Faraway Part of Town" and "That's How It Went, All Right" by Andre Previn and Dory Langdon; "Pepe" by Hans Wittstatt and Dory Langdon; "Lovely Day" ("Concha Nacar") by Augustin Lara and Maria Teresa Lara, English lyrics by Dory Langdon. Choreography for "The Rumble" and "The Faraway Part of Town" by Eugene Loring; choreography for "Tequila" by Alex Romero. Running time, 195 minutes.

CAST

Pepe, CANTINFLAS; Ted Holt, DAN DAILEY; Suzie Murphy, SHIRLEY JONES; Auctioneer, CARLOS MONTALBAN; Lupita, VICKIE TRICKETT; Dancer, MATT MATTOX; Manager, HANK HENRY; Carmen, SUZANNE LLOYD; Jewelry Salesman, STEPHEN BEKASSY; Waitress, CAROL DOUGLAS; Priest, FRANCISCO REGUERRA; Charro, JOE HYAMS; Dancer, MICHAEL CALLAN; Schultzy, ANN B. DAVIS; Studio Gateman, WILLIAM DEMAREST; Immigration Inspector, ERNIE KOVACS; Dennis the Menace, JAY NORTH; Bunny, BUNNY WATERS; and the voice of JUDY GARLAND,

Guest Stars (as themselves)

JOEY BISHOP, BILLIE BURKE, MAURICE CHEVALIER, CHARLES COBURN, RICHARD CONTE, BING CROSBY, TONY CURTIS, BOBBY DARIN, SAMMY DAVIS, JR., JIMMY DURANTE, JACK ENTRATTER, COL. E. E. FOGELSON, ZSA ZSA GABOR, GREER GARSON, HEDDA HOPPER, PETER LAWFORD, JANET LEIGH, JACK LEMMON, DEAN MARTIN, KIM NOVAK, ANDRE PREVIN, DONNA REED, DEBBIE REYNOLDS, CARLOS RIVAS, EDWARD G. ROBINSON, CESAR ROMERO, FRANK SINATRA.

STORY

Pepe, a peon ranch foreman, has raised the beautiful white stallion "Don Juan" from a colt, and in his whimsical mind Don Juan is a son. He has scrimped and saved to buy Don Juan at an auction, but is outbid by a Hollywood director on the skids, Ted Holt, who hopes to use Don Juan as his bid for re-entry in the Hollywood production circles. Pepe sets out to follow Ted Holt and Don Juan to Hollywood, and once in the film capital he has many amusing encounters with filmdom's leading personalities. Pepe finds Don Juan, who has been languishing since being taken from Mexico, but the stallion perks up the instant Pepe appears, and Holt offers Pepe a job to stay with the horse. Holt is unable to make a deal with a producer, and goes to Las Vegas, where he has no better luck, and so gets drunk. Pepe, not knowing anything about gambling, is advised by Frank Sinatra, Cesar Romero, and Joey Bishop, and wins so much money that he can produce the picture himself. Holt has faith in a newcomer, Suzie, and eventually the picture is completed. Holt's faith in Suzie is justified when she is acknowledged to be a hit, and Pepe, who has lost Don Juan to producer Edward G. Robinson, regains the horse as his own "son" again, plus all the colts and the one newborn jackass Don Juan has fathered.

REVIEWS

"Of all the big pictures being offered in this season of big pictures, Pepe, directed and produced by George Sidney, is far and away the best entertainment. Any exhibitor can be proud to play it. . . . Starring the great Mexican comic Cantinflas, Pepe may best be described as the equal of the finest of the old time Charlie Chaplin comedies given super brilliant production. . . . As for the guest appearances, they are all well integrated vignettes whether they concern Crosby autographing a tortilla, Chevalier giving advice about women, Durante outsmarting himself with a cold deck or Sinatra and his 'clan' being taken for a ride at Las Vegas."

Limelight

"It may come as something of a shock to their fans, however, to see Bing Crosby, Frank Sinatra, Peter Lawford without makeup and playing themselves. But perhaps sheer devotion will soften the blow."

Constance Littlefield, *Los Angeles Examiner*

"I cannot remember another film aimed at children that depended for its humor and pathos upon such an unattractive worldly knowingness in its audience. We are tempted to laugh at the peasant as he stands wide-eyed and uncomprehending before the smiling great only because *we* know their names, *we* know the gossip, *we* know the cost of their presence. Dino drinks, Bing has trouble with his sons, Frankie plays the tables at Vegas—everybody knows that except Pepe, the sweet dope, and if we take joy when his innocence triumphs, it is because we ourselves are not innocent."

The New Yorker

THE DEVIL AT 4 O'CLOCK · 1961

A Columbia Picture. Eastman Color. Directed by Mervyn LeRoy. Produced by Fred Kohlmar. Screenplay by Liam O'Brien. Based on the novel by Max Catto. Music by George Duning; orchestrated by Arthur Morton. Director of photography, Joseph Biroc. Film editor, Charles Nelson. Art director, John Beckman. Set decorator, Louis Diage. Makeup supervisor, Ben Lane. Special effects by Willis Cook. Sound supervisor, Charles J. Rice. Sound by Josh Westmoreland. Production assistant, Milton Feldman. Assistant directors, Carter DeHaven, Jr. and Floyd Joyer. Running time, 126 minutes.

With Barbara Luna

CAST

Father Matthew Doonan, SPENCER TRACY; *Harry,* FRANK SINATRA; *Father Joseph Perreau,* KERWIN MATHEWS; *Jacques,* JEAN PIERRE AUMONT; *Marcel,* GREGOIRE ASLAN; *The Governor,* ALEXANDER SCOURBY; *Camille,* BARBARA LUNA; *Matron,* CATHY LEWIS; *Charlie,* BERNIE HAMILTON; *Dr. Wexler,* MARTIN BRANDT; *Aristide,* LOU MERRILL; *Gaston,* MARCEL DALIO; *Paul,* TOM MIDDLETON; *Clarisse,* ANN DUGGAN; *Corporal,* LOUIS MERCIER; *Margot,* MICHELE MONTAU; *Fleur,* NANETTE TANAKA; *Antoine,* TONY MAXWELL; *Louis,* JEAN DEL VAL; *Sonia,* MOKI HANA; *Napoleon,* WARREN HSIEH; *Constable,* WILLIAM KEAULANI; *Captain Olsen,* "LUCKY" LUCK; *Fouquette,* NORMAN JOSEF WRIGHT; *Marianne,* ROBIN SHIMATSU.

STORY

A plane bound for Tahiti stops for the night at the small French island of Kalua, where the Governor is notifying the authorities of a disturbance at the mouth of the island volcano. The passengers are three chained convicts—Harry, Marcel, and Charlie—and Father Perreau, who has come to replace Father Doonan, who is to leave the next day with the pilot, Jacques. The Governor releases the three convicts into Father Doonan's charge, and they are sent to repair the chapel at a children's leper hospital. Harry falls in love with the children's nurse, a lovely blind girl named Camille.

The next day, as Father Doonan prepares to leave Kalua, the volcano erupts and an earthquake rocks the island. Doonan enlists the convicts' aid, promising to speak up for commuting their sentences if they will help him evacuate the hospital and rescue the children. A schooner will wait until the outgoing tide at four o'clock the following afternoon. Hampered by rain, winds, and recurring earthquakes, the procession slowly makes its long way from the hospital to the sea. In a hillside cave where they have taken nighttime refuge, Father Doonan marries Harry and Camille. The next day they lose

Marcel when he falls into a bog and drowns. Father Doonan and Charlie support a weakened bridge as Harry leads the others across, but the bridge collapses, crushing Charlie and stranding Doonan. Harry brings the children safely to the waiting schooner, bids his new bride farewell, and returns to help the trapped men. He finds Charlie dying, Father Doonan praying over him. As Harry crosses himself, the vocano erupts once again, and the entire island explodes and disappears into the sea.

REVIEWS

"In case you're wondering about the title, it stems from a proverb: 'It is hard for a man to be brave when he knows he is going to meet the devil at 4 o'clock.'...Tracy's strong performance, which includes some humor, is another is his long list. Sinatra gives an honest portrayal of the convict who first opposes, then co-operates."

John L. Scott, *Los Angeles Times*

"This zig-zagging spectacular starts out as a South Seas version of *The Power and the Glory*, careens into regions traveled by *My Three Angels*, then suddenly veers into dramatic country vaguely resembling *Inn of the Sixth Happiness*.... Tracy's acting and some of the best character players in the business turn it into the best of all possible hokum. Sinatra, unfortunately, has been tethered to a part stuffed with patented hipsterisms. Believable and touching as he often is, it is still hard to believe that if he really wanted those manacles off he couldn't get the president of MCA over to *Four O'Clock* in five minutes."

Show Business Illustrated

With Bernie Hamilton, Gregoire Aslan   and Spencer Tracy

With Bernie Hamilton and Gregoire Aslan

"In *The Devil at 4 O'Clock*, Spencer Tracy says to Frank Sinatra, 'When I was a kid in Hell's Kitchen, we used to eat punks like you.' And Sinatra replies: 'That was when you had your teeth.' These, sad to say, are the best lines in the film."

Playboy

"Place Spencer Tracy and Frank Sinatra in the middle of action and violence, and you've got a picture worth seeing. . . . Tracy comes through with a strong performance and Frank, in a less showy role, is not far behind him. Sinatra is good, very good."

Sara Hamilton, *Los Angeles Examiner*

With Barbara Luna

With Spencer Tracy, Bernie Hamilton and Gregoire Aslan

With Dean Martin and Peter Lawford

SERGEANTS 3 · 1962

An Essex-Claude Production. Released by United Artists. Technicolor; Panavision. Directed by John Sturges. Produced by Frank Sinatra. Executive producer, Howard W. Koch. Original screenplay by W. R. Burnett. Music by Billy May. Director of photography, Winton C. Hoch. Film editor, Ferris Webster. Art director, Frank Hotaling. Set decorator, Victor Gangelin. Wardrobe by Wesley V. Jefferies and Angela Alexander. Makeup by Bernard Ponedel. Hair stylist, Mary Westmoreland. Sound recorder, Harold Lewis. Assistant director, Jack Reddish. Second unit director, Al Wyatt. Second unit photography, Carl Guthrie. Special effects by Paul Pollard. Song "And the Night Wind Sang," by Johnny Rotella and Franz Steininger. Running time, 112 minutes.

CAST

1st Sgt. Mike Merry, FRANK SINATRA; *Sgt. Chip Deal,* DEAN MARTIN; *Jonah Williams,* SAMMY DAVIS, JR.; *Sgt. Larry Barrett,* PETER LAWFORD; *Sgt. Major Roger Boswell,* JOEY BISHOP; *Mountain Hawk,* HENRY SILVA; *Amelia Parent,* RUTA LEE; *Willie Sharpknife,* BUDDY LESTER; *Corporal Ellis,* PHILLIP CROSBY; *Private Page,* DENNIS CROSBY; *Private Wills,* LINDSAY CROSBY; *Blacksmith,* HANK HENRY; *Colonel Collingwood,* RICHARD SIMMONS; *Watanka,* MICHAEL PATE; *Caleb,* ARMAND ALZAMORA; *White Eagle,* RICHARD HALE; *Morton,* MICKEY FINN; *Corporal,* SONNY KING; *Ghost Dancer,* EDDIE LITTLESKY; *Herself,* "CEFFIE"; *Irregular,* RODD REDWING; *Colonel's Aide,* JAMES WATERS; *Mrs. Parent,* MADGE BLAKE; *Mrs. Collingwood,* DOROTHY ABBOTT; *Telegrapher,* WALTER MERRILL.

STORY

Sergeants Mike Merry, Chip Deal, and Larry Barrett are inseparable U.S. Army men in Indian territory in 1870. During a barroom brawl, a recently freed slave, Jonah Williams, attaches himself to them, and follows the three men when they are ordered to track a tribe of fanatical Sioux Indians to their hideout. Sergeant Barrett is planning to marry Amelia Parent when his enlistment is up, and this expedition is to be his last assignment; his buddies, however, trick him into signing a re-enlistment. Sergeant Deal is captured by the Indians and tortured, but his two buddies and Jonah Williams manage to rescue him, and outwit the planned Indian massacre when Jonah blows a bugle warning the approaching U.S. Cavalry of the thousand Indians waiting to attack. The three sergeants are decorated for bravery, and as Sergent Barrett rides off to claim his bride, Sergeant Merry turns in Barrett's re-enlistment papers, telling the Army that Barrett is a deserter.

REVIEWS

"*Sergeants 3* may have seemed like a natural for the Rat Pack—*Gunga Din* done as a western. After all, hadn't George Stevens made a rootin', tootin' epic of it, with a starry cast, in 1939? ... The trouble with Kipling's poem, however, is that it is based on a single situation—and even W. R. Burnett, who adapted it and transposed it to the Dakota Badlands in the 1870s, hasn't been able to do much more than rough in the preliminaries."

Philip K. Scheuer, *Los Angeles Times*

"The 'Big Three' of Sinatra, Dean Martin and Peter Lawford reenact the parts played in the original by Cary Grant, Victor McLaglen and Douglas Fairbanks, Jr. Of the three, Martin seems by far the most animated and comfortable, Sinatra and Lawford coming off a trifle too businesslike for the irreverent, look-ma-we're-cavalrymen approach."

Tube, *Variety*

With Peter Lawford, Dean Martin and Sammy Davis

With Dean Martin

With Peter Lawford and Dean Martin

"Somewhere east of Suez the ghost of Rudyard Kipling must be whirling like a dervish in its grave.

"Reason is that Frank Sinatra has taken 'that lazeration ragged Gunga Din,' put him in a U.S. Cavalry uniform (Locale Kanab, Utah, circa 1873), given him another kind of Indian as the enemy and made of all this literary emasculation a movie mish-mash.

"It's more din than Gunga, believe me, starting with a barroom brawl and ending with a howling massacre.

"Frankie's film is just unbelievable from start to finish. It's downright amateurish and the technical boys evidently took everybody for a ride with sets that shake, wrong props and other things that will make you say, 'Oh no, it's just not possible!' "

Hazel Flynn, The Hollywood *Citizen-News*

"No, Virginia, *Sergeants 3* is not a sequel to *Butterfield 8*. It's the Rat Pack reprise of *Gunga Din*, transposed from the Queen's Own in Inja to the American West, with the U.S. Cavalry riding to a great many rescues. And away we go with Fisty Frank Sinatra, Dashing Dean Martin, Pistol Pete Lawford—and Sammy Davis, Jr., tailing along via white mule (the real thing, not the firewater)."

Playboy

With Dean Martin and Joey Bishop

With Bob Hope, Bing Crosby, Joan Collins and Dean Martin

THE ROAD TO HONG KONG · 1962

A Melnor Films production. Released by United Artists. Directed by Norman Panama. Produced by Melvin Frank. Original screenplay by Norman Panama and Melvin Frank. Music composed and conducted by Robert Farnon. Musical associates, Douglas Gamley and Bill McGuffie. Musical numbers staged by Jack Baker and Sheila Meyers. Songs by James Van Heusen and Sammy Cahn. Director of photography, Jack Hildyard. Film editor, John Smith. Production designer, Roger Furse. Art directors, Sydney Cain and Bill Hitchinson. Set decorator, Maurice Fowler. Costumes by Anthony Mendleson. Makeup by Dave Aylott. Hair stylist, Joan White. Special effects by Wally Veevers and Ted Samuels. Sound by A.G. Ambler and Red Law. Assistant director, Bluey Hill. Production supervisor, Bill Kirby. Running time, 91 minutes.

CAST

Harry Turner, BING CROSBY; Chester Babcock, BOB HOPE; Diane, JOAN COLLINS; Herself, DOROTHY LAMOUR; The Leader, ROBERT MORLEY; Dr. Zorbb, WALTER GOTELL; Jhinnah, ROGER DELGARDO; Grand Lama, FELIX AYLMER; Lama, PETER MADDEN; Doctor, JULIAN SHERRIER; Agent, BILL NAGY; Photographer, GUY STANDEVEN; Messenger, JOHN MC CARTHY; Servant, SIMON LEVY; Lady at Airport, JACQUELINE JONES; Chinese Girl, MEI LING; Receptionist, KATYA DOUGLAS; Unbilled guest stars: JERRY COLONNA, DEAN MARTIN, DAVID NIVEN, PETER SELLERS, FRANK SINATRA.

STORY

Harry Turner and Chester Babcock are in India, hawking an "Interplanetary Fly-It-Yourself Space Kit," and while attempting to prove to the police that the apparatus really works, Chester is injured. At the Calcutta hospital, Harry is informed that Chester is suffering from amnesia, and Harry is convinced of that when he finds out that Chester cannot remember what girls are. Harry is told about a drug which will cure Chester, and they go to the Tibetan Lamasery, where the Grand Lama restores Chester's memory and gives him a drug enabling him to remember everything he sees.

182

With Bob Hope, Bing Crosby,
Joan Collins and Dean Martin

The duo plan to use this newly acquired ability in a vaudeville memory act, but they are plunged into a wild espionage chase concerning The Third Echelon, a private group determined to conquer space, and Chester finds a very practical use for his memory. Diane, a beautiful secret service agent, mistakes Chester for an agent, and gets into various scrapes with the pair from which she helps them escape. Finally, the three are transported inside a rocket to a distant planet called Plutonius. Chester, who now remembers perfectly what girls are, makes plans to share Diane with Harry, but Diane tells them sweetly that she already has a boy friend on Plutonius. The boy friend turns out to be Frank Sinatra.

REVIEWS

"The boys caper through a series of cockeyed situations. They're chased through Hong Kong's street bazaars, duped by Miss Collins, find themselves in a Tibetan Lamasery, get a hand from their former partner Dorothy Lamour, wisecrack their way through space, land on a distant planet and run smack into 'spacemen' Frank Sinatra and Dean Martin."

John L. Scott, *Los Angeles Times*

"Most of the humor is founded on the over-explored 'inside' joke of stars having a lark by kidding the story,

ad-libbing conversation or coming out of character to give witty directions to a prop man. It is fitting that in almost the last frame, Frank Sinatra and Dean Martin, past masters of this new form of un-comedy, drop in to nudge each other in the ribs and smirk."

Show

"Nor do all the laughs proceed from Bob and Bing's rapid fire lines. Peter Sellers does a delicious scene as an Indian psychiatrist trying to restore Hope's memory, and Frank Sinatra, Dean Martin, and Jerry Colonna appear in surprise bits."

James D. Ivers, *Motion Picture Herald*

"As guest artists Frank Sinatra and Dean Martin help to round off the film, David Niven appears for no good reason and the best interlude is that of Peter Sellers."

Rich, *Variety*

"Bing, who appears on Frank Sinatra's show sometimes as a favor, telephoned Frank and Dean Martin to stop off en route to Monte Carlo and they appeared in the film as spacemen with little toy propellers on their hats as a gag for an ending."

Philip K. Scheuer, *Los Angeles Times*

THE MANCHURIAN
CANDIDATE · 1962

An M. C. Production. Released by United Artists. Directed by John Frankenheimer. Produced by George Axelrod and John Frankenheimer. Executive producer, Howard W. Koch. Screenplay by George Axelrod. Based on the novel by Richard Condon. Music composed and conducted by David Amram. Director of photography, Lionel Lindon. Film editor, Ferris Webster. Art director, Richard Sylbert. Set decorator, George R. Nelson. Costumes by Moss Mabry. Makeup by Bernard Ponedel, Jack Freeman, and Ron Berkeley. Hair stylist, Mary West-moreland; Janet Leigh's hair styles by Gene Shacove. Sound mixer, Joe Edmondson. Special effects by Paul Pollard. Assistant director, Joseph Behm. Dialogue coach, Thom Conroy. Assistant art director, Philip J. Jefferies. Running time, 126 minutes.

CAST

Bennett Marco, FRANK SINATRA; *Raymond Shaw,* LAURENCE HARVEY; *Rosie,* JANET LEIGH; *Raymond's Mother,* ANGELA LANSBURY; *Chunjin,* HENRY SILVA; *Senator John Iselin,* JAMES GREGORY; *Jocie Jordan,* LESLIE PARRISH; *Senator Thomas Jordan,* JOHN MC GIVER; *Yen Lo,* KHIGH DHIEGH; *Corporal Melvin,* JAMES EDWARDS; *Colonel,* DOUGLAS HENDERSON; *Zilkov,* ALBERT PAULSEN; *Berezovo's Lady Counterpart,* MADAME SPIVY; *Secretary of Defense,* BARRY KELLEY; *Psychiatrist,* JOE ADAMS; *Mr. Gaines,* LLOYD CORRIGAN; *Medical Officer,* WHIT BISSELL; *Melvin's Wife,* MIMI DILLARD; *Officer,* ANTON VAN STRALEN; *Gossfeld,* JOHN LAURENCE; *Lembeck,* TOM LOWELL; *Mavole,* RICHARD LA PORE; *Berezovo,* NICK BOLIN; *Silvers,* NICKY BLAIR; *Little,* WILLIAM THOURLBY; *Freeman,* IRVING STEINBERG; *Haiken,* JOHN FRANCIS; *Nominee,* ROBERT RIORDON; *Gomel,* REGGIE NALDER; *Miss Gertrude,* MIYOSHI JINGU; *Korean Girl,* ANNA SHIN; *Gomel's Lady Counterpart,* BESS FLOWERS.

STORY

During the Korean War, an American Army patrol led by Bennett Marco and Raymond Shaw is captured by Chinese Communists and taken to Manchuria, where they are brainwashed into believing that Shaw led a successful action against the Reds and is a hero. Actually he is a subconscious puppet of the Communists who at the sight of a Queen of Diamonds is triggered into obeying instructions without remembering his actions. Back in America, Marco, now a major in Army intelligence, has recurrent nightmares in which he vaguely recalls what really happened, but he is adjudged overwrought and is given sick leave. Still suspicious, Marco goes to New York to see Shaw, and on the train

meets a sympathetic girl named Rosie who tries to get him to date her. At Shaw's apartment, Marco is attacked on sight by Shaw's houseboy, whom Marco recognizes as Chunjin, the "Korean guide" who betrayed the patrol to the Communists. After a karate fight which sends Chunjin to the hospital and Marco to jail, Marco calls Rosie to bail him out, and a romance develops.

Marco meets with Shaw, who has received letters from another patrol member, Corporal Melvin, who has had nightmares similar to Marco's. Shaw also reveals that he hates his mother and his stepfather, Senator John Iselin, for their right-wing political attacks. Marco convinces the Army that Shaw's mind has been "set" to explode at a momentous time, and takes charge of an intelligence unit to work on the mystery. With the help of a psychiatrist, Marco discovers the Queen of Diamonds "key" to controlling Shaw, and attempts to learn who his American agent is and what job he is intended for. Unknown to even Shaw, the agent is his own mother, who plans to have her son shoot the presidential nominee during a rally at Madison Square Garden so that her husband, the vice presidential nominee, can take control of the government. As part of her plan, she uses Shaw to kill her foremost political foe, Senator Thomas Jordan, and his daughter Jocie, Shaw's wife. On the night of the rally, Marco confronts Shaw with the Queen of Diamonds and tries to convince him that he has no control of his own mind. But Shaw follows his mother's instructions and takes a high-powered rifle to a deserted projection booth in the Garden. At the last moment, however, he shifts his sight, kills both his mother and stepfather, and then takes his own life.

With Laurence Harvey

With Janet Leigh

With Laurence Harvey

With Janet Leigh

With Janet Leigh

REVIEWS

"Many loud hurrahs for *The Manchurian Candidate*, a thriller guaranteed to raise all but the limpest hair. It comes to us from a little, half-abandoned western village called Hollywood and shines with the characteristics—energy, pell-mell pace, a smooth, hard, bright surface—for which that village grew world-famous and which we keep hearing, and fearing, it has lost forever. . . . The acting is all of a high order, and Sinatra, in his usual uncanny fashion, is simply terrific."

The New Yorker

"The picture is really fascinating despite its rather far-fetched premise and wholesale slaughter during later passages, and if you're looking for a wild-and-woolly horror film fare—with psychological sidelights and political background—this is it. . . . The cast is uniformly excellent, with Sinatra providing one of his strongest portrayals, and Miss Lansbury scoring in a most bizarre role."

John L. Scott, *Los Angeles Times*

"Sinatra gives a seasoned and in many ways more mature performance than he has ever done before."

James Powers, *The Hollywood Reporter*

"Less showy, but no less effective, is Sinatra, who, after several pix in which he appeared to be sleep-walking, is again a wide-awake pro creating a straight, quietly humorous character of some sensitivity."

Anby, *Variety*

With Leslie Parrish

With Tony Bill

COME BLOW YOUR HORN · 1963

An Essex-Tandem Production. A Paramount Release. Technicolor; Panavision. Directed by Bud Yorkin. Produced by Norman Lear and Bud Yorkin. Executive producer, Howard W. Koch. Screenplay by Norman Lear. Based on the play by Neil Simon. Music composed and conducted by Nelson Riddle. Orchestrations by Gil Grau. Director of photography, William H. Daniels. Film editor, Frank P. Keller. Art directors, Hal Pereira and Roland Anderson. Set decorators, Sam Comer and James Payne. Gowns by Edith Head. Makeup by Wally Westmore. Hair stylists, Christine Widmeyer, Gene Shacove and Frederic Jones. Sound recorders, John Carter and John Wilkinson. Special photographic effects by Paul K. Lerpae. Assistant director, Daniel J. McCauley. Running time, 112 minutes.

Alan Baker, FRANK SINATRA; *Papa Baker*, LEE J. COBB; *Mama Baker*, MOLLY PICON; *Connie*, BABRARA RUSH; *Peggy*, JILL ST. JOHN; *Buddy Baker*, TONY BILL; *Mr. Eckman*, DAN BLOCKER; *Mrs. Eckman*, PHYLLIS MC GUIRE; *Waiter*, HERBIE FAYE; *Barber*, ROMO VINCENT; *Manicurist*, CHARLOTTE FLETCHER; *Tall Girl*, GRETA RANDALL; *Max*, VINNIE DE CARLO; *Desk Clerk*, JACK NESTLE; *Elevator Operator*, EDDIE QUILLAN; *Manager*, GRADY SUTTON; *Snow Eskanazi*, JOYCE NIZZARI; *Eunice*, CAROLE WELLS; *Cab Driver*, JOHN INDRISANO; *Wino*, DEAN MARTIN.

Sinatra's song: "Come Blow Your Horn" by James Van Heusen and Sammy Cahn.

STORY

Bored with living at home with his staid, old-country parents, young Buddy Baker packs his bags and arrives unannounced at the luxurious Manhattan apartment of his elder brother Alan, a hard-drinking, girl-chasing bachelor who never lets his duties at his father's artificial fruit factory interfere with his pleasures. Their parents are shocked, but Alan, delighted at the boy's show of independence, buys Buddy a new wardrobe and introduces him to New York night life. Buddy is such an apt pupil, however, that he soon is taking over his brother's private stock of booze and girls. Alan loses his upstairs girl friend Peggy to Buddy, is beaten up by Mr. Eckman, the husband of another girl friend, and is even jilted by his favorite date, Connie. Frantic, Alan urges Buddy to end his carousing and settle down, but the boy is having too good a time and tells Alan to mind his own business. The argument so jolts Alan that he proposes to Connie, marries her, patches up a marital spiff between his parents, and bequeathes his bachelor pad to the delighted Buddy.

With Dan Blocker

With Tony Bill

With Jill St. John and Lee J. Cobb

189

With Jill St. John

REVIEWS

"Comedy goes well at the Radio City Music Hall. So does Frank Sinatra, there or any place. *Come Blow Your Horn* is destined to regale the Hall's patrons and the star's fans through the Fourth of July holiday. Perhaps longer."

Wanda Hale, New York *Daily News*

"The main thing they have done is to throw the play out the window—all but the bones and central situation. (After all, you have to start *somewhere*.) By shifting the focus from the younger to the older brother, they have strengthened what remains a feeble and familiar story line. But they have also opened it out with gay and inventive business, and paced it with breakneck speed. ... Frank Sinatra, fugitive from a domineering father and the family's artificial-fruit business."

Arthur Knight, *The Saturday Review*

"Sinatra's jaunty performance is his best in some time. The role is perfectly suited to his rakish image. It also affords him an opportunity to manifest his most consumate talent—that of singer. He warbles the lilting title tune, which has been cleverly integrated into the story fabric in accompaniment of a traditional series of fast cuts."

Tube, *Variety*

"If anything, *Come Blow Your Horn* improves on the stage version, which was a hit. ... Frankie tries harder this time not just to do his usual walk-through, and in general succeeds."

Philip K. Scheuer, *Los Angeles Times*

"Sinatra is fine in *Horn*. He is given some good material to work with, and he handles it dexterously and engagingly. Actually, he plays straight man to most of the characters around him, but it doesn't swamp him; he comes off better because of it."

James Powers, *The Hollywood Reporter*

With Barbara Rush

With Molly Picon,
Lee J. Cobb and Tony Bill

THE LIST OF
ADRIAN MESSENGER · 1963

A *Joel Production. A Universal Release. Directed by John Huston. Produced by Edward Lewis. Screenplay by Anthony Veiller. Based on the novel by Philip Mac-Donald. Music by Jerry Goldsmith. Director of photography, Joe MacDonald. Film editor, Terry Morse. Art directors, Alexander Golitzen, Stephen Grimes and George Webb. Set decorator, Oliver Emert. Makeup artist, Bud Westmore. Hair stylist, Larry Germain. Sound recorders, Waldon O. Watson and Frank H. Wilkinson. European photography, Ted Scaife. Assistant director, Tom Shaw. Music supervision, Joseph Gershenson. Unit production manager, Richard McWhorter. Running time, 98 minutes.*

CAST

Anthony Gethryn, GEORGE C. SCOTT; *Lady Jocelyn Bruttenholm,* DANA WYNTER; *Marquis of Gleneyre,* CLIVE BROOK; *Mrs. Karoudjian,* GLADYS COOPER; *Sir Wilfred Lucas,* HERBERT MARSHALL; *Raoul Le Borg,* JACQUES ROUX; *Adrian Messenger,* JOHN MERIVALE; *Anton Karoudjian,* MARCEL DALIO; *Inspector Pike,* BERNARD ARCHARD; *Derek,* WALTER ANTHONY HUSTON; *Carstairs,* ROLAND D. LONG; *Mrs. Slattery,* ANITA SHARP-BOLSTER; *Inspector Seymour,* ALAN CAILLOU; *Lord Ashton,* JOHN HUSTON; *Countryman,* NOEL PURCELL; *Sergeant Flood,* RICHARD PEEL; *Lynch,* BERNARD FOX; *White,* NELSON WELCH; *Hunt Secretary,* TIM DURANT; *Nurse,* BARBARA MORRISON; *Student Nurse,* JENNIFER RAINE; *Maid,* CONSTANCE CAVENDISH; *Orderly,* ERIC HEATH; *Stewardess,* ANNA VAN DER HEIDE; *Airport Stewardess,* DELPHI LAWRENCE; *Whip Man,* STACY MORGAN; *Cyclist,* JOE LYNCH; *Proprietress,* MONA LILIAN; and *Italian,* TONY CURTIS; *George Brougham,* KIRK DOUGLAS; *Woman,* BURT LANCASTER; *Jim Slattery,* ROBERT MITCHUM; *Gypsy Stableman,* FRANK SINATRA.

STORY

Anthony Gethryn, a retired British intelligence officer, is given a list of eleven names by Adrian Messenger and asked to check the whereabouts of the people listed. During the investigation Messenger is killed in a mid-air plane explosion, and Gethryn finds that all of those on the list have also met with seemingly accidental deaths. With the aid of Scotland Yard, Gethryn learns that the victims were former prisoners of war whose escape plan was disclosed to the Nazis by an informer who now has plans for prominence and is removing those who know of his former treachery. To complicate matters, the killer is a master of disguises who changes his identity for each murder. Gethryn discovers that the killer is one of the heirs to the Gleneyre estate and that only a small boy,

Derek, stands in his way of becoming sole owner. The killer plans to eliminate Derek during a fox hunt, but Gethryn moves in and the villain—George Brougham—dies in one of his own traps while attempting to escape.

REVIEWS

"Philip MacDonald's British murder mystery, *The List of Adrian Messenger,* is a genteel whodunit, and the new film version now screening citywide follows the same pattern. It's a leisurely, underplayed thriller with some good performances and a gimmick that turns the feature into a sort of guessing contest.

"The novelty: Five well-known stars—Tony Curtis, Kirk Douglas, Burt Lancaster, Robert Mitchum, and Frank Sinatra—participate in the production wearing disguises. At the conclusion they unmask. I guessed three of the five correctly; the other two are bafflers."

John L. Scott, *Los Angeles Times*

"Since the audience is aware that, besides Kirk Douglas, who appears as himself on the screen, Robert Mitchum, Burt Lancaster, Tony Curtis, and Frank Sinatra are in the cast, heavily disguised, it becomes an accompanying guessing game to the solution of 'who done it' fitting the guest stars to the characters they portray on the screen."

Kate Cameron, the New York *Daily News*

"The novelty devices designed to ignite *The List of Adrian Messenger* commercially backfire against it artistically. The result is a bizarre, but curiously irritating film experience. Discerning picturegoers will be annoyed to see distracting casting excesses mar a basically enthralling murder mystery otherwise executed with considerable cinematic vitality by director John Huston and staff. ... Of the five stars who 'guest,' Kirk Douglas has the major assignment and carries it off colorfully and credibly. The others are Tony Curtis, Burt Lancaster, Robert Mitchum, and Frank Sinatra. Only Mitchum is easily recognizable beneath the facial stickum."

Tube, *Variety*

"Here indeed is a mystery which is by turns fascinating, intriguing, exciting, and at all times wholly satisfying. It has that further patron-stimulating ingredient, an element of surprise, which can be the subject of intense word-of-mouth promotion, since the audience is especially enjoined (as are reviewers) not to reveal the identities of five well-known performers, who appear in the film in disguise. So effective are the disguises, as a matter of fact, that until each reveals his identity at the conclusion of the film, in an epilogue, it is impossible for even the most knowledgeable film fan to do more than guess at the identities. It is easily understood, indeed, that makeup preparations for each of these actors required no less than three and one-half hours each morning. It must be recorded that Bud Westmore was in charge of makeup."

Charles S. Aaronson, *Motion Picture Herald*

After the killer has been hooked and *The End* comes on the screen, a voice shouts: "Hold it! Stop! That's the end of the picture—but it's not the end of the mystery." And for what seems like ten minutes of the most crashing anticlimax to ever climax an anticlimax, the incognito cameo players peel off their makeup. Shucks, with those ears for clues, anybody could have guessed which one was Sinatra all the time.

Time

George C. Scott and Kirk Douglas

4 FOR TEXAS · 1964

With Dean Martin

With Anita Ekberg

With Dean Martin, Anita Ekberg,
Ursula Andress and Marjorie Bennett

A Sam Company Production. Released by Warner Bros. Technicolor. Produced and directed by Robert Aldrich. Executive producer, Howard W. Koch. Original screenplay by Teddi Sherman and Robert Aldrich. Music composed and conducted by Nelson Riddle. Orchestrations by Gil Grau. Director of photography, Ernest Laszlo. Second unit photography by Joseph Biroc, Carl Guthrie, and Burnett Guffey. Film editor, Michael Luciano. Art director, William Glasgow. Set decorator, Raphael Bretton. Costumes by Norma Koch. Makeup by Robert Schiffer. Sound mixer, Jack Solomon. Associate producer, Walter Blake. Second unit director, Oscar Rudolph. Assistant directors, Tom Connors and David Salven. Dialogue supervisor, Robert Sherman. Stunt supervisor, John Indrisano. Production supervisor, Jack R. Berne. Title song by James Van Heusen and Sammy Cahn. Running time, 124 minutes.

CAST

Zack Thomas, FRANK SINATRA; *Joe Jarrett,* DEAN MARTIN; *Elya Carlson,* ANITA EKBERG; *Maxine Richter,* URSULA ANDRESS; *Matson,* CHARLES BRONSON; *Harvey Burden,* VICTOR BUONO; *Prince George,* EDRIC CONNOR; *Angel,* NICK DENNIS; *Mancini,* RICHARD JAECKEL; *Chad,* MIKE MAZURKI; *Trowbridge,* WESLEY ADDY; *Miss Ermaline,* MARJORIE BENNETT; *Brunhilde,* VIRGINIA CHRISTINE; *Widow,* ELLEN CORBY; *Dobie,* JACK ELAM; *Widow,* JESSLYN FAX; *Maitre D',* FRITZ FELD; *Ansel,* PERCY HELTON; *Renee,* JONATHAN HOLE; *Monk,* JACK LAMBERT; *Beauregard,* PAUL LANGTON; *Sweeney,* KEITH MC CONNELL; *Helaine,* MICHEL MONTAU; *Maid,* MAIDIE NORMAN; *Customer,* BOB STEELE; *Bedoni,* MARIO SILETTI; *Mrs. Burden,* EVA SIX; *Pulaski,* ABRAHAM SOFAER; *Williams,* MICHAEL ST. ANGEL; *Secretary,* GRADY SUTTON; *Bartender,* RALPH VOLKIE; *Bartender,* MAX WAGNER; *Doorman,* WILLIAM WASHINGTON; *Alfred,* DAVE WILLOCK; *Croupier,* ARTHUR GODFREY; *Special Guest Stars:* THE THREE STOOGES; TEDDY BUCKNER AND HIS ALL-STARS.

STORY

Zack Thomas and Joe Jarrett are on their way to Galveston in 1870 when their stagecoach is attacked by a gang led by Matson. After repulsing the bandits, Zack discloses a bag containing $100,000, and Joe abruptly relieves him of the money at gunpoint. In Galveston, Joe deposits the loot in a bank run by Harvey Burden, a crook who has supported Zack's efforts to become the town's gambling king. When Zack arrives in town, Matson tries to kill him, but Joe wounds the bandit, saving Zack's life. Then Zack learns that Joe intends to compete with him by converting a derelict riverboat into a gambling saloon. Outraged, Zack raises a gang, planning to take over the boat on opening night. But Burden has plans of his own: to let Zack's and Joe's gang destroy each other and then move in with Matson's bandits and take control himself. On opening night, Zack and Joe decide to wage single combat, but during the fight they discover evidence of Burden's duplicity and join forces. Matson's gang is defeated, Burden is arrested, and Zack and Joe marry their girl friends, Elya and Maxine, in a double wedding.

REVIEWS

"*4 for Texas*, in which Martin shares star billing with Sinatra, is one of those pictures that are known in Hollywood as Clanbakes. They are made by Frankie and his friends, a collection of show business characters who are pleased to call themselves The Clan, and if showbizz-buzz can be believed really are a lot of fun to film. Unfortunately, they are not much fun to see. . . . What's mainly wrong with *Texas*, though, is what's wrong with all Clan pictures: the attitude of the people on the screen. They constitute an in-group, and they seem bored with the outside world. Sometimes, perish the thought, they even are obviously bored with each other. They scratch, they mumble, they hack around. They appear less concerned to entertain the public than to indulge their private fantasies. Maybe they ought to call their next picture *30*."

Time

"The film begins with the brilliant, bombastic, brutal cutting that is the cinematic mark of Aldrich. Loaded with double charges, the humor explodes with gut shots that rock with belly laughter. This beginning has action, humor, fun and it is good cinema.

"Aldrich should have been able to stop there. He may have won enough of the fight with his cast to conquer a few box-office prizes, but his opening is the only good shot he gets at intelligent viewers. Frank Sinatra and Anita Ekberg deflate the film despite the talents of his inflated ego and her ballooning bust. Sinatra worked so little that Aldrich has more shots of the back of the head of Sinatra's double than he has of Sinatra."

J.S., *Cinema*

"It seems that when two or more of the 'Clan' get together, the last thing one should expect is a serious attempt at film-making. *4 for Texas* is a western of sorts, where one suspects the most amusing antics were those that went on off-screen. Probably a good time was had by them all during production: unfortunately there is not very much on screen which will entertain the audi-ence. It remains a slap-happy attempt to guy the Western, sex, and whatever else was in mind at the time."

Films and Filming

"Frank Sinatra and Dean Martin are playing with guns again, and in this giggling galloper they chew sand, spit rust, act tough, and double-cross each other and banker Victor Buono in an effort to get away with $100,000 loot from a stage holdup. . . . Robert Aldrich (*What Ever Happened to Baby Jane?*) directed, and his script was showing."

Cue

With Dean Martin and Victor Buono

With Anita Ekberg

With Dean Martin and Mike Mazurki

With Bing Crosby and Dean Martin

ROBIN AND THE 7 HOODS · 1964

A P-C Productions Picture. Released by Warner Bros. Technicolor; Panavision. Directed by Gordon Douglas. Produced by Frank Sinatra. Executive producer, Howard W. Koch. Original screenplay by David R. Schwartz. Music composed and conducted by Nelson Riddle. Orchestrations by Gil Grau. Associate producer and director of photography, William H. Daniels. Film editor, Sam O'Steen. Art director, LeRoy Deane. Set decorator, Raphael Bretton. Costumes by Don Feld. Makeup supervisor, Gordon Bau. Hair stylist, Jean Burt Reilly. Sound by Everett Hughes and Vinton Vernon. Choreographer for dances, Jack Baker. Assistant directors, David Salven and Lee White. Dialogue supervisor, Thom Conroy. Running time, 123 minutes.

CAST

Robbo, FRANK SINATRA; *John*, DEAN MARTIN; *Will*, SAMMY DAVIS, JR.; *Guy Gisborne*, PETER FALK; *Marian*, BARBARA RUSH; *Sheriff Potts*, VICTOR BUONO; *Six Seconds*, HANK HENRY; *Vermin*, ALLEN JENKINS; *Tomatoes*, JACK LA RUE; *Sheriff Glick*, ROBERT FOULK; *Robbo's Hood*, PHILLIP CROSBY; *Blue Jaw*, ROBERT CARRICART; *Hatrack*, PHIL ARNOLD; *Robbo's Hood*, SONNY KING; *Prosecutor*, RICHARD SIMMONS; *Soupmeat*, HARRY SWOGER; *Gisborne's Hood*, HARRY WILSON; *Robbo's Hood*, RICHARD BAKALYAN; *Charlie Bananas*, BERNARD FEIN; *Cocktail Waitress*, CAROL HILL; *Twitch*, JOSEPH RUSKIN; *Hammacher*, SIG RUMAN; *Police Chief*, BARRY KELLEY; *Mr. Ricks*, HANS CONRIED; *Big Jim*, EDWARD G. ROBINSON; and *Allen A. Dale*, BING CROSBY.

Sinatra's songs (by James Van Heusen and Sammy Cahn): "My Kind of Town," "Style," "Mr. Booze," and "Don't Be a Do-Badder."

STORY

In 1928, Chicago's number one gangster, Big Jim, is shot dead at his own birthday party. Guy Gisborne takes over the mob, but Robbo, a rival gangster, warns Gisborne to stay out of the North Side. Little John, a minor hood from Indiana, joins Robbo's gang just before Robbo and Gisborne wreck each other's nightclubs. Robbo rebuilds, outfitting his new club so that it becomes a revival hall at the flick of a button, and when Gisborne instigates a police raid, the law finds only a group of religious singers. Marian, Big Jim's daughter, gives Robbo $50,000 to kill her father's murderers, but he orders Will, his aide, to dump the money. Will gives it to an orphanage, and Allen A. Dale, an orphanage official, causes the press to hail Robbo as a modern-day Robin Hood. Robbo hires Dale to supervise all his charitable activities.

Robbo falls for the beautiful and educated Marian, and is shocked to find she is just another crook when he discovers that she, with John as her partner, runs a counterfeiting ring using Robbo's charity organization as a front. He fires John and orders Marian out of town. Marian hires Gisborne to kill both Robbo and John, but Gisborne fails and ends up in the foundation of a new pretzel factory. Marian then organizes a women's reform movement, and they wreck Robbo's organization. Penniless, Robbo, Will, and John are reduced to begging in the streets, when a limousine drives up and Marian and Allen A. Dale step out. Dropping money into the trio's hands, Allen and Marian enter her reform club together.

REVIEWS

"The show takes after *Guys and Dolls*. But it is no closer to a classic floating crap game in the Biltmore Garage than it is to Sherwood Forest. Damon Runyon would have winced at some of the lines ('I never asked the boys to work on holidays,' rasps Robinson, 'except once—on St. Valentine's Day'). Still the scenery is opulent and the color appropriately gaudy. Each star takes his turn at the singing and dancing, like bullets blasting from the chambers of a revolver. The songs are unmemorable, yet all fit the occasion like diamond cuff links on a white-on-white shirt. . . . With this off-gait, off-beat film, Sinatra and the Clan have finally made their point. I sincerely hope that they will stop, now that they're ahead. As any seasoned crap player can tell them, the odds against making a point twice in a row are 12 to 7."

Richard Oulahan, *Life*

With Hank Henry, Dean Martin, Sammy Davis Jr., Richard Bakalyan, Bing Crosby and Phillip Crosby

With Sammy Davis Jr. and Dean Martin

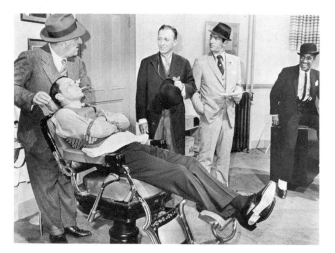

With Hank Henry, Bing Crosby, Dean Martin and Sammy Davis Jr.

With Dean Martin and Barbara Rush

"All the more credit is due to Frankie and his merrie men in view of the incredible twists of fate that plagued the shooting. At the Rosedale cemetery, for instance, they were filming the comical burial of Robinson's remains, and somebody found a gravestone for a John F. Kennedy 1802–1884. It was an occasion for jokes until the news came over a car radio that afternoon, from Dallas. Then a few weeks later, after Sinatra had rehearsed a kidnaping scene, the word came from Lake Tahoe about Frank Sinatra Jr. The kidnaping was deleted from the picture. To get the film done would have been laudable; to get it funny was heroic."

Newsweek

"*Robin and the 7 Hoods* is better than its predecessors because there are not so many inside jokes, because there is more story and, with it, new jokes, and because the stars work harder. One fault of these star-studded enterprises has been that the stars frequently gave the impression that they could give only a small part of their attention and talent to the work at hand. *Robin* has more going for it in Schwartz's script, and Douglas' direction gets more out of the players."

James Powers, *The Hollywood Reporter*

With Barbara Rush

NONE BUT THE BRAVE · 1965

An Artanis Production. Released by Warner Bros. Technicolor; Panavision. Produced and directed by Frank Sinatra. Executive producer, Howard W. Koch. Associate producer, William H. Daniels. Producer for Tokyo Eiga Company and original story by Kikumaru Okuda. Screenplay by John Twist and Katsuya Susaki. Music composed by Johnny Williams. Music supervised and conducted by Morris Stoloff. Japanese music advisor, K. Hirose. Director of photography, Harold Lipstein. Film editor, Sam O'Steen. Art director, LeRoy Deane. Art advisor, Haruyoshi Oshita. Set decorator, George James Hopkins. Makeup supervisors, Gordon Bau and Shu Uemura. Sound by Stanley Jones. Special effects director, Eiji Tsuburaya. Assistant directors, David Salven and M. Tsurushima. Dialogue coaches, Thom Conroy and S. Nakamura. Technical advisor, Kazuo Inoue. Running time, 105 minutes.

CAST

Chief Pharmacist Mate Maloney, FRANK SINATRA; Captain Dennis Bourke, CLINT WALKER; 2nd Lieutenant Blair, TOMMY SANDS; Sergeant Bleeker, BRAD DEXTER; Air Crewman Keller, TONY BILL; Lieutenant Kuroki, TATSUYA MIHASHI; Sergeant Tamura, TAKESHI KATO; Corporal Craddock, SAMMY JACKSON; Corporal Ruffino, RICHARD BAKALYAN; Private Johnson, RAFER JOHNSON; Private Dexter, JIMMY GRIFFIN; Private Searcy, CHRISTOPHER DARK; Private Hoxie, DON DORRELL; Private Magee, PHILLIP CROSBY; Private Waller, JOHN H. YOUNG; Private Swensholm, ROGER EWING; Lance Corporal Hirano, HOMARE SUGURO; Corporal Fujimoto, KENJI SAHARA; Lead Private Ando, MASAHIKO TANIMURA; Private Tokumaru, HISAO DAZAI; Private Goro, SUSUMU KUROBE; Private Ishii, TAKASHI INAGAKI; Private Sato, KENICHI HATA; Private Arikawa, TORU IBUKI; Private Okuda, RYUCHO SHUNPUTEI; Lorie, LARAINE STEPHENS.

STORY

The setting is a small Pacific island, which the war has long ago passed by. Here a small company of Japanese soldiers, under Lieutenant Kuroki, maintain discipline and daily drill, while they slowly build a small ship which they hope will carry them to occupied territory. An American plane, damaged by a Japanese fighter, makes a crash landing on the island. There is a skirmish at first between the two forces, but then a truce is arranged by the Japanese commander and Captain Bourke, the American pilot and senior officer. Chief Pharmacist Mate Maloney successfully amputates the leg of one of the Japanese

soldiers who has been wounded in the skirmish. Neither side has radio communication, but their truce carries the stipulation, insisted upon by the Japanese, that should either side again become part of the war, fighting is to resume at once. The American forces are able to repair their damaged radio, and a destroyer comes to their aid. Fighting is resumed between the two sides, who had become friendly, and the entire Japanese company is wiped out to a man, and only five Americans survive.

REVIEWS

"Sinatra, who also stars with Clint Walker and produces, makes his directorial bow in this story by Kikumaru Okuda and is responsible for some good effects in maintaining a suspenseful pace. . . . Sinatra, although topbilled, plays second fiddle in footage to Walker, who with Mihashi are the dominating figures. Sinatra appears only intermittently, his character only important in the operation scene which he enacts dramatically. Walker gives a lusty performance as the flier, a professional soldier who knows war and how to approach it."

Whit, *Variety*

"As actor, Frank Sinatra takes a secondary role, playing a whisky-swigging Chief Pharmacist's mate. He has one important scene in which, as the medic, he is called upon to save the life of a wounded Japanese soldier.

"As director, Sinatra proves to be most impressive with his handling of the frequent action sequences which keep the film moving at a fairly rapid pace. The director is least experienced when dealing with scenes which should inspire boldness of purpose. More psychological, intellectual, and sociological probing into the private thoughts and acts of the opposing characters would seem to be called for."

Dale Munroe, Hollywood *Citizen-News*

"As producer, director and star of this World War II melodrama, Frank Sinatra is triply committed to a piece of flip moral hindsight. War is archaic, he says. It is also rough on brotherhood. But he cannot conceal his boyish enthusiasm for any activity that brings together a swell bunch of guys. . . . The idea holds some promise, except that Director Sinatra and his scriptwriters goof away tension at every turn. A truce seems inevitable, since both camps are rent by internal strife and riddled with cliches."

Time

"For a non-American, it is hard to see why the film was made. It says nothing new about the effect of war,

With Clint Walker

With Tommy Sands and Clint Walker

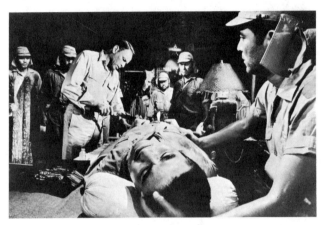

With Susumu Kurobe (*prone*) and Tatsuya Mihashi (*right*)

and what it does concern itself with was better expressed in films of ten years ago. It tries to keep pace with the popular vogue of having the Japanese speak in their own language so for a good third of the film we have the same viewpoints being put over in sub-title form as in the American dialogue. Two thirds through the film we are even given flashbacks to show that both the Japanese and American commanders have similar human problems (which shows that Sinatra can have had little faith in his actors' ability to convey it just with dialogue—so we have both flashback *and* dialogue). Sinatra himself plays the medical officer who uses Scotch for pleasure and work, and has some faint attempts at humour."

Robin Bean, *Films and Filming*

"Provocative and engrossing, the color film is novel for two other reasons: It marks Frank Sinatra's debut as a director, and it is the first co-production between Japanese and American companies to be made in the United States (Kauai Island, Hawaii). . . . Sinatra's style as a director is straightforward and understated. It is to his credit that he tackled a serious subject on his first try when he could have taken the easy way out with still another gathering of The Clan. . . . In front of the camera Sinatra is in top form as a pharmacist's mate with a Rye wit and gets good performances from Clint Walker as the American commander, a solemn giant who offers a fine contrast to Sinatra, and Tatsuya Mihashi as the very likeable Japanese leader."

Kevin Thomas, *Los Angeles Times*

With Clint Walker, Brad Dexter and Tommy Sands

With Jimmy Griffin and Tommy Sands

VON RYAN'S EXPRESS · 1965

A P-R Productions Picture. Released by 20th Century-Fox. Color by DeLuxe; CinemaScope. Directed by Mark Robson. Produced by Saul David. Screenplay by Wendell Mayes and Joseph Landon. Based on the novel by David Westheimer. Music by Jerry Goldsmith. Orchestrations by Arthur Morton. Director of photography, William H. Daniels. Film editor, Dorothy Spencer. Art directors, Jack Martin Smith and Hilyard Brown. Assistant art directors, Ed Graves and Lou Korn. Set decorators, Walter M. Scott and Raphael Bretton. Makeup by Ben Nye. Hair stylist, Margaret Donovan. Sound by Carlton W. Faulkner and Elmer Raguse. Special photographic effects by L. B. Abbott and Emil Kosa, Jr. Second unit photography, Harold Lipstein. Second unit director, William Kaplan. Assistant director, Eli Dunn. Unit production manager, Harry A. Caplan. Running time, 117 minutes.

With Sergio Fantoni and Adolfo Celi

CAST

Colonel Joseph L. Ryan, FRANK SINATRA; Major Eric Fincham, TREVOR HOWARD; Gabriella, RAFFAELLA CARRÀ; Sergeant Bostick, BRAD DEXTER; Captain Oriani, SERGIO FANTONI; Lieutenant Orde, JOHN LEYTON; Chaplain Costanzo, EDWARD MULHARE; Major Von Klemment, WOLFGANG PREISS; Private Ames, JAMES BROLIN; Colonel Gortz, JOHN VAN DREELEN; Major Battaglia, ADOLFO CELI; Italian Train Engineer, VITO SCOTTI; Corporal Giannini, RICHARD BAKALYAN; Captain Stein, MICHAEL GOODLIFFE; Sergeant Dunbar, MICHAEL ST. CLAIR; Von Kleist, IVAN TRIESAULT; Gestapo Agent, WILLIAM BERGER; Italian Nobleman, MIKE ROMANOFF; American Soldier, BUZZ HENRY.

With Sergio Fantoni, Edward Mulhare and Trevor Howard

STORY

The setting is a prisoner of war camp in Italy during those frantic days of change in 1943, when the Allies were landing in Southern Italy, the Italians were trying to get out of the war, and the Nazis were trying to keep the Allies out and the Italians in. A Fascist bully has ruled the POW camp, but with the collapse of Italian rule, he has been thrown out. The British prisoners, headed by Major Fincham, are not in agreement with the lone American, Colonel Joseph Ryan; they think him insufficiently hostile to the Italians and have given a "von" to his name. The British get along with Ryan, however, when the escape is engineered. They seize a German train, and, impersonating German troops even as they evade German pursuers, try to make a run for it to the Swiss border. The train is within sight of the border when it is halted by the Germans. They fight it out, and

206

With Trevor Howard

most of them get across the Swiss border. But "Von" Ryan is one of those who meets a spectacular death.

REVIEWS

"Frank Sinatra fans will be pleased to learn that at last he has made a good picture—*Von Ryan's Express*, based on David Westheimer's thriller about—you guessed it—World War Two. . . . Sinatra isn't an actor in this one, he's a behaver, but at least here he behaves himself well."

Playboy

"Sinatra's expertly done Von Ryan is a harsh character. He sees that he has made a mistake, tries to correct it and even learns a little about compassion in a scene with an Italian girl who has sold out to the Nazis. When she tries to escape, he is forced to shoot her in the back—a scene that will bring gasps because movie heroes, especially Frank Sinatra are not supposed to kill ladies that way. It is a role that calls for nuances that Sinatra has rarely had to express before. Perhaps he found them because of the competition—Trevor Howard is along this time, and he can make a shift of the shoulders as eloquent as a soliloquy."

Thomas Thompson, *Life*

"Under Mark Robson's spirited direction even Sinatra lays off the goldbricking and pitches in as if he almost means it. In fact, he wins admiration so effortlessly that it comes as a shock when he turns his machine pistol on the girl (sympathetically portrayed by Raffaella Carra) as she attempts a dash to freedom."

Philip K. Scheuer, *Los Angeles Times*

"A train-chase that goes on for an hour is the big attraction here, along with a comic conflict between Trevor Howard as a heated Englishman and Frank Sinatra as a cool American, which is such inspired casting that I could wish the dialogue they have been given were more worthy of the occasion. Both actors show the strain a bit. . . ."

Gordon Gow, *Films and Filming*

"As the steely-eyed, curt American officer who takes command as an unpopular chief, Frank Sinatra underplays his role neatly and purposefully where it might easily lead him into an overdramatic trap. . . . It's a tough assignment, but he makes it believable, even at the finale where he is unwittingly sacrificed in staving off a final Nazi assault on the escape train. . . . This is Sinatra at his best as an actor, and far removed from his image as a rollicking, elbow-bending song stylist."

Abe Greenberg, Hollywood *Citizen-News*

With Raffaella Carra

With Edward Mulhare

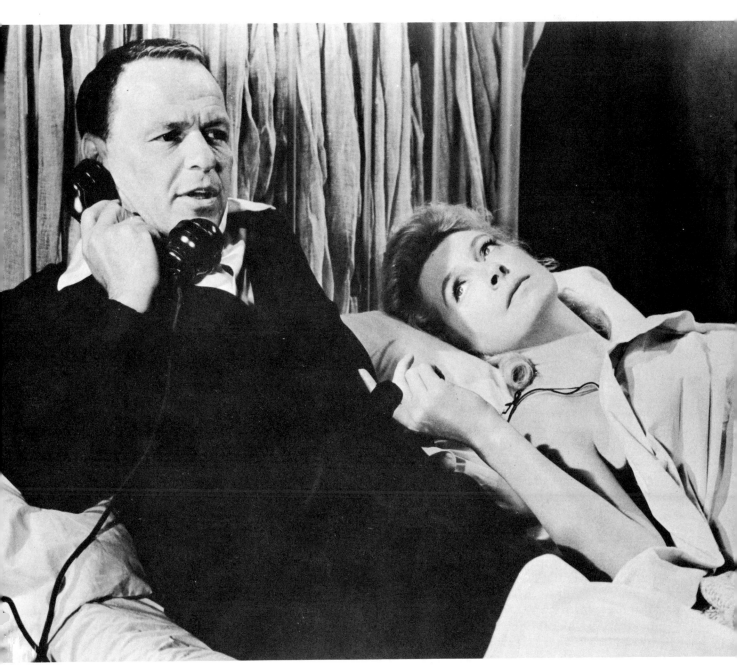

With Deborah Kerr

MARRIAGE ON THE ROCKS · 1965

With Dean Martin

With Dean Martin and Joi Lansing

An A-C Productions Picture. Released by Warner Bros. Technicolor; Panavision. Directed by Jack Donohue. Producer and director of photography, William H. Daniels. Original screenplay by Cy Howard. Music composed and conducted by Nelson Riddle. Film editor, Sam O'Steen. Art director, LeRoy Deane. Set decorators, Arthur A. Krams and William L. Kuehl. Costume designer, Walter Plunkett. Makeup supervisor, Gordon Bau. Hair stylist, Jean Burt Reilly. Choreographer, Jonathan Lucas. Sound recorder, Francis E. Stahl. Production supervisor, Joseph Behm. Assistant director, Richard Lang. Dialogue supervisor, Thom Conroy. Song "Sinner Man" by Trini Lopez, Bobby Weinstein, Bobby Hart, Billy Barberis, and Teddy Randazzo. Running time, 109 minutes.

CAST

Dan Edwards, FRANK SINATRA; *Valerie Edwards*, DEBORAH KERR; *Ernie Brewer*, DEAN MARTIN; *Miguel Santos*, CESAR ROMERO; *Jeannie MacPherson*, HERMIONE BADDELEY; *Jim Blake*, TONY BILL; *Shad Nathan*, JOHN McGIVER; *Tracy Edwards*, NANCY SINATRA; *Lisa Sterling*, DAVEY DAVIDSON; *David Edwards*, MICHEL PETIT; *Lola*, JOI LANSING; *Bunny*, TARA ASHTON; *Miss Blight*, KATHLEEN FREEMAN; *Rollo*, FLIP MARK; *Mr. Turner*, DE FOREST KELLEY; *Kitty*, SIGRID VALDIS; *Mr. Bruno*, BYRON FOULGER; *Dr. Newman*, PARLEY BAER; *Saleslady at Saks*, RETA SHAW; *Mayor*, NACHO GALINDO; *Mr. Smythe*, HEDLEY MATTINGLY; *Guest Star*, TRINI LOPEZ.

STORY

Dan Edwards, president of an advertising agency, has been happily married—he thinks—for 19 years. But even as he and his best friend Ernie Brewer wait for Dan's wife to show so they can celebrate their 19th anniversary, Valerie Edwards is with the family lawyer, telling him she wants a divorce on the grounds that she is bored and Dan is dull. The lawyer suggests that she buy a black lace negligee and go on a second honeymoon with her husband. Ernie Brewer suggests much the same thing; he had proposed to and been rejected by Valerie before she married Dan. So Valerie and Dan go to Mexico on their anniversary. By error they are divorced by an ambulance-chasing attorney; they arrange for a colorful re-marriage ceremony. Dan has to fly home on business, and the crisis also makes him go on to Detroit. Dan arranges with Ernie to go down to Puerta Villa in Mexico to explain the delay to Valerie. Again, the over-anxious attorney makes a mistake, and marries Valerie and Ernie. Valerie tries to use her marriage to Ernie as a means of getting Dan back, but Dan is now having a ball, living a bachelor's life in Malibu. But he isn't really happy, and Valerie discovers that she's pregnant by Dan because of their Mexican second honeymoon. Dan and Valerie are reunited out of loneliness on Thanksgiving Day, and make plans for a church wedding as soon as she can get properly divorced from Ernie.

REVIEWS

"If the laughs are 'fast, furious and felicitous' in *Marriage on the Rocks*, as a Warner blurb claims, I missed most of them. This is the newest comedy from what is more or less the Sinatra clan. . . . I will say that everybody plays with spirit, even if Sinatra does have a way of telegraphing a potentially funny line before he speaks it so that it doesn't live up to its potential."

Philip K. Scheuer, *Los Angeles Times*

With Dean Martin and Hermione Baddeley

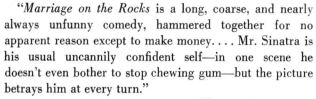

With Cesar Romero and Deborah Kerr

"*Marriage on the Rocks* is a long, coarse, and nearly always unfunny comedy, hammered together for no apparent reason except to make money.... Mr. Sinatra is his usual uncannily confident self—in one scene he doesn't even bother to stop chewing gum—but the picture betrays him at every turn."

The New Yorker

"*Marriage on the Rocks* is the most recent effort to capture for posterity the fanny-pinching sophistication of Dean Martin and Frank Sinatra. In a coy casting switch, Sinatra plays a bored, busy advertising brain who has spent 19 years with his own wife (Deborah Kerr). 'What a swinger he was in the old days,' moons Deborah.... [The film's] least comfortable performer is Actress Kerr, whose fans may well wonder what a nice girl like Deborah is doing in a play like this. Wasted on farce, she sidles from gag to gag with the faintly startled air of a very proper matron who somehow finds herself pouring tea at a disreputable party."

Time

With Cesar Romero and Deborah Kerr

With Deborah Kerr

211

CAST A GIANT SHADOW · 1966

A Mirisch-Llenroc-Batjac Production. Released by United Artists. Color by DeLuxe; Panavision. Produced and directed by Melville Shavelson. Co-producer, Michael Wayne. Screenplay by Melville Shavelson. Based on the book by Ted Berkman. Music composed and conducted by Elmer Bernstein. Orchestrations by Leo Shuken and Jack Hayes. Director of photography, Aldo Tonti. Film editors, Bert Bates and Gene Ruggiero. Production designer, Michael Stringer. Art director, Arrigo Equini. Costume designer, Margaret Furse. Makeup by David Grayson and Euclide Santoli. Hair stylist, Vasco Regianni. Sound recorder, David Bowen. Special effects, Sass Bedig. Production supervisor, Allen K. Wood. Production manager, Nate Edwards. Assistant directors, Jack Reddish, Charles Scott, Jr. and Tim Zinnemann. Music for "Next Year in Jerusalem" by Dov Seltzer. Running time, 139 minutes.

CAST

Col. David "Mickey" Marcus, KIRK DOUGLAS; Magda Simon, SENTA BERGER; Emma Marcus, ANGIE DICKINSON; Major Safir, JAMES DONALD; Ram Oren, STATHIS GIALLELIS; Jacob Zion, LUTHER ADLER; Pentagon Chief of Staff, GARY MERRILL; Abou Ibn Kader, HAYM TOPOL; Mrs. Chaison, RUTH WHITE; James MacAfee, GORDON JACKSON; British Ambassador, MICHAEL HORDERN; British Immigration Officer, ALLAN CUTHBERTSON; Senior British Officer, JEREMY KEMP; Junior British Officer, SEAN BARRETT; Andre Simon, MICHAEL SHILLO; Rona, RINA GANOR; Bert Harrison, ROLAND BARTHROP; Mrs. Martinson, VERA DOLEN; General Walsh, ROBERT GARDETT; First Sentry, MICHAEL BALSTON; Second Sentry, CLAUDE ALIOTTI; Belly Dancer, SAMRA DEDES; Truck Driver, MICHAEL SHAGRIR; First U. N. Officer, FRANK LATTIMORE; Second U. N. Officer, KEN BUCKLE; Aide to General Randolph, RODD DANA; Aide to Chief of Staff, ROBERT ROSS; Pentagon Officer, ARTHUR HANSELL; Parachute Jump Sergeant, DON STURKIE; Yaakov, HILLEL RAVE; Yussuff, SHLOMO HERMON; and Vince, FRANK SINATRA; Asher Gonen, YUL BRYNNER; General Mike Randolph, JOHN WAYNE.

STORY

In late 1949 the British are planning to withdraw from Palestine and the Arabs are openly ignoring the announced formation of the new state of Israel. Colonel David "Mickey" Marcus, West Point graduate, military adviser to F.D.R. and D-Day veteran, is approached by Major Safir to whip the ragged Israeli army into a fighting machine that can face the Arabs when the British

With Kirk Douglas and Yul Brynner

Mandate is lifted. Despite the objections of his wife Emma and General Randolph of the Pentagon, Marcus accepts, and leaves for the Holy Land to work with Jacob Zion, Premier of Israel, and Asher Gonen, leader of the underground army. He is quartered in the home of a beautiful female fighter, Magda Simon, and they fall in love.

The United States recognizes the new state of Israel, and the U.N. calls for a cease-fire between the Arab and Israeli forces. Marcus is ordered to break through to Jerusalem before the truce goes into effect. The Israeli army is so short of ammunition that when an airman, Vince, runs out of bombs, he continues fighting with empty bottles and goes valiantly to his death. The reorganized Israelis are victorious over the powerful Arab host, and Marcus, realizing he still loves his wife, bids Magda farewell. As he walks into a monastery courtyard he is challenged in Hebrew by a sentry, but he has never learned the language of Israel and cannot respond. When he keeps on walking he is shot and killed—only a few hours before the truce takes effect.

REVIEWS

"As a biopic of the late David Marcus, a West Point graduate who was NYC's Commissioner of Correction under Mayor La Guardia, and who died fighting on the side of the Jews in the imbroglios before and immediately after the creation of Israel by the United Nations, *Cast a Giant Shadow* is almost a travesty. As propaganda for Israel it is of dubious value. . . . As for the 'guest' bits played by John Wayne, Yul Brynner, Angie Dickinson, and Frank Sinatra, Shavelson took them so much for granted he didn't even bother to provide intelligent dialogue for them."

Wilfred Mifflin, *Films in Review*

"In 'special guest star' appearances are John Wayne and Frank Sinatra, both playing their usual roles with typical aplomb. . . . Sinatra plays a New Jersey pilot-of-fortune who, for lack of bombs, drops bottles of seltzer water on Arab strongholds. These two Christian personages help project the hoped-for, moral universality of the issues at stake, at the same time offering the moviegoer that comfortable feeling of international brotherhood—corny, superficially stated, but undeniably heartwarming."

Daniel Davis, *Cinema*

"*Cast a Giant Shadow* is an embarrassing movie. . . . Melville Shavelson has provided the picture with a screenplay of flawless vulgarity and has directed it in an appropriate fashion. . . . Fugitively on hand in *Cast a*

214

Giant Shadow are Frank Sinatra and John Wayne—dead ringers for Frank Sinatra and John Wayne. Why no Dean Martin? In such company, he is bound to be looked for, if not missed."

Brendan Gill, The New Yorker

"*Cast a Giant Shadow*, another exercise in movie biography, may be filed as a case of mistaken identity: any resemblance to persons living or dead is sacrificed to make elbowroom for Hero Kirk Douglas. . . . To top the evidence that *Shadow* should not be taken seriously, if at all, Frank Sinatra pops in as a soldier-of-fortune pilot who quips, 'Hey, don't leave me here alone, I'm anti-Semitic.' Musical-comedy exuberance dominates a battle scene that has Sinatra aloft in a Piper Cub, bombing Egyptian tanks with Seltzer bottles and spraying soda at their planes. By then, the movie has trimmed its theme to fit the formula of any Clannish catered affair."

Time

"Frank Sinatra, looking all of 28 years old, lights up the screen as a soldier-of-fortune flier who loses his life bombing Egyptian tanks with seltzer bottles because he had nothing stronger."

Clyde Leech, Los Angeles Herald-Examiner

THE OSCAR · 1966

A Greene-Rouse Production. An Embassy Pictures Release. Pathé Color. Directed by Russel Rouse. Produced by Clarence Greene. Executive producer, Joseph E. Levine. Screenplay by Harlan Ellison, Russell Rouse, and Clarence Greene. Based on the novel by Richard Sale. Music by Percy Faith. Orchestrations by Leo Shuken and Jack Hayes. Director of photography, Joseph Ruttenberg. Film editor, Chester W. Schaeffer. Art directors, Hal Pereira and Arthur Lonergan. Set decorators, Robert Benton and James Payne. Gowns by Edith Head. Makeup by Wally Westmore. Hair stylist, Nellie Manley. Choreographer, Steven Peck. Sound recorders, Harry Lindgren and John Wilkinson. Special photographic effects, Paul K. Lerpae. Process photography, Farciot Edouart. Assistant director, Dick Moder. Dialogue coach, Leon Charles. Production manager, Frank Caffey. Unit production manager, Maurie M. Suess. Music supervisor, Irving Friedman. Songs: "Thanks for the Memory" by Ralph Rainger and Leo Robin; "All the Way" by James Van Heusen and Sammy Cahn. Running time, 119 minutes.

CAST

Frank Fane, STEPHEN BOYD; Kay Bergdahl, ELKE SOMMER; Kappy Kapstetter, MILTON BERLE; Sophie Cantaro, ELEANOR PARKER; Kenneth H. Regan, JOSEPH COTTEN; Laurel Scott, JILL ST. JOHN; Hymie Kelly, TONY BENNETT; Trina Yale, EDIE ADAMS; Barney Yale, ERNEST BORGNINE; Grobard, ED BEGLEY; Orrin C. Quentin, WALTER BRENNAN; Sheriff, BRODERICK CRAWFORD; Network Executive, JAMES DUNN; Herself, EDITH HEAD; Herself, HEDDA HOPPER; Steve Marks, PETER LAWFORD; Herself, MERLE OBERON; Herself, NANCY SINATRA; Sam, JACK SOO; Cheryl Barker, JEAN HALE; Marriage Broker, EDDIE RYDER; Ledbetter, CHRIS ALCAIDE; Sid, JOHN DENNIS; Bert, PETER LEEDS; Stevens, JOHN HOLLAND; Secretary, JEAN BARTEL; Wally, JOHN CROWTHER; Lochner, ROSS FORD; Pereira, WALTER REED; Himself, BOB HOPE; Himself, FRANK SINATRA.

STORY

It is Oscar night in Hollywood, and one of the five nominees for Best Performance by an Actor is Frankie Fane. By flashback we see how Frankie got to the top. When his best friend, Hymie Kelly, met up with him, Frankie was a spieler in a strip joint, and both of them have a hard time of it when they are run out of town by the local sheriff. A drama coach, Sophie Cantaro, likes Frankie in more ways than one and gets him a film job.

Frankie makes it, but he is ruthless and completely selfish. He steps on all women, and even discards Sophie when he no longer has any use for her. He marries Kay Bergdahl, but then misuses her, too. He and his best friend quarrel, and his agent Kappy Kapstetter is given the bum's rush when Frankie wins an Oscar nomination just as he is in despair because of his slipping career. Frankie pull every stunt to get the Oscar, even to exposing unfavorable headlines about his past, knowing that Hollywood will sympathize with him and possibly be on his side if he is being crucified. When the actress giving the Oscar opens the envelope and reads, "The winner is..." Frankie Fane automatically rises like a sleepwalker. Others, seeing him standing, also rise to give a standing ovation to the winner—Frank Sinatra. Frankie Fane, crushed and dejected, falls back into his seat, while Sinatra claims the prized award.

Elke Sommer and Tony Bennett

REVIEWS

"In words that the scriptwriters themselves might have used, this film deserves to stand as a classic: a classic to all that is shoddy and second rate and cliché-ridden, a grim warning to directors and writers on how not to make a film."

Richard Davis, *Films and Filming*

"But this is that true movie rarity—a picture that attains a perfection of ineptitude quite beyond the power of words to describe. You have to see it to disbelieve it and still you will come away wondering what possible excuse there is for it—beyond obvious commercialism."

Richard Schickel, *Life*

"What makes *The Oscar* most distressing is that it boldly equates at just this time a sleazy fiction of attempted engineering of the Academy voting and the bestowal of Academy awards. In support of a squalid story of a downgraded 'oscar' nominee pulling a vicious finagle in hopes of gaining a sympathy vote, Joseph E. Levine has persuaded Frank Sinatra, Merle Oberon, and Bob Hope to give a convincing simulation of the ceremonies on Academy night. With as much *joi de vivre* as they might muster on the Academy stage, these people lend credence to a fable that befouls their community. The injudiciousness of their appearance makes one wonder how wise they are—how actually cheap and degraded have become the sensibilities of the people in Hollywood."

Bosley Crowther, *The New York Times*

ASSAULT ON A QUEEN · 1966

With Tony Franciosa, Virna Lisi and Errol John

A Sinatra Enterprises-Seven Arts Production. A Paramount Release. Technicolor; Panavision. Directed by Jack Donohue. Produced by William Goetz. Screenplay by Rod Serling. Based on the novel by Jack Finney. Music by Duke Ellington. Orchestral arrangements by Van Cleave and Frank Comstock. Associate producer and director of photography, William H. Daniels. Film editor, Archie Marshek. Art director, Paul Groesse. Set decorator, John P. Austin. Miss Lisi's costumes by Edith Head. Makeup by Wally Westmore. Hair stylist, Nellie Manley. Sound by Stanley Jones and Charles Grenzbach. Special effects, Lee Vasque. Special photographic effects, Lawrence Butler and Paul K. Lerpae. Process photography, Farciot Edouart. Assistant director, Richard Lang. Second unit director, Robert D. Webb. Production manager, Gerald D. Wineman. Production supervisor, Joseph C. Behm. Unit production manager, Al Silvani. Technical advisor, Captain Charles Wilbur. Running time, 106 minutes.

CAST

Mark Brittain, FRANK SINATRA; Rosa Lucchesi, VIRNA LISI; Vic Rossiter, TONY FRANCIOSA; Tony Moreno, RICHARD CONTE; Eric Lauffnauer, ALF KJELLIN; Linc Langley, ERROL JOHN; Captain, Queen Mary, MURRAY MATHESON; Master-at-Arms, REGINALD DENNY; Bank Manager, JOHN WARBURTON; Doctor, LESTER MATTHEWS; Trench, VAL AVERY; First Officer, GILCHRIST STUART; Second Officer, RONALD LONG; Third Officer, LESLIE BRADLEY; Fourth Officer, ARTHUR E. GOULD-PORTER; Junior Officer, LAURENCE CONROY; Crewman, ALAN BAXTER; Bartender, JACK RAINE; Assistant Purser, DOUGLAS DEANE; Elevator Operator, NOEL DRAYTON; Chief Radio Operator, DONALD LAWTON; Chief Radio Operator, ROBERT C. SHAWLEY; Lady with the Diamond, BARBARA MORRISON; Executive Officer, ROBERT HOY; Coast Guard Skipper, RAY KELLOGG; Chief, WALT DAVIS.

With Errol John and Virna Lisi

220

With Virna Lisi

A rich Italian girl, Rosa Lucchesi, and her partners, Vic Rossiter and Eric Lauffnauer, interest an ex-submarine officer, Mark Brittain, in diving for lost treasure off the Florida coast. They don't find any treasure, but they do come upon a small sunken German submarine. Lauffnauer, a former U-boat commander, persuades the group to salvage the sub in order to pull off a fantastic scheme—to hijack the *Queen Mary*. The idea of modern piracy sparks the group, and they bring in a top mechanic, Tony Moreno, to put the sub in working order. Rossiter resents the presence of Mark's Negro buddy, Linc Langley, and also finds that in Mark he has a strong rival for the attentions of Rosa.

After reconditioning the sub, the group proceed with their plans to intercept the *Queen Mary*. Posing as British officers, Mark, Rossiter, and Lauffnauer are allowed to board, threatening to torpedo the ship unless the purser's safe is opened to them. As they leave, Rossiter stops to take a diamond ring from a passenger and is killed by the Master-at-Arms. Reaching their sub, Mark and Lauffnauer sight an approaching Coast Guard cutter, and Lauffnauer quickly dives the sub, leaving the loot in the dinghy. Becoming a Prussian U-boat commander again, Lauffnauer at gunpoint announces that he will torpedo the cutter. Rosa grabs his arm and Mark flattens him, but his gun discharges, killing Moreno. Mark surfaces the sub and escapes with Rosa and Linc in a rubber raft. The cutter rams the sub, Lauffnauer goes down with his ship, and the trio are left drifting toward the coast of South America.

REVIEWS

"After *Ocean's 11*, it isn't surprising that Frank Sinatra would have welcomed another property that offered the same elements of suspense, action, and free-wheeling acting and dialogue. If *Assault on a Queen*, despite the tender, loving care applied to its production, doesn't match up to the earlier film, it still makes its mark as solid entertainment.... Sinatra and Miss Lisi are very good in roles that make few demands on their acting ability."

Robe, *Variety*

"For a while the characters swop wisecracks and insults in quite a lively fashion. But the film runs aground with the long, ponderous scenes of making the submarine fit for use. As there are obviously going to be no insurmountable difficulties, these scenes lack tension from that point of view, and about here Rod Serling's dialogue loses all sparkle while Jack Donohue's merely competent direction plays it out faithfully, even that old favourite between hero and heroine, 'we'll be hiding and running for the rest of our lives.'...There's a certain barnacled charm to the whole wildly improbable escapade. It could go straight into TV's Vintage Years of Hollywood."

Allen Eyles, Films and Filming

"Certainly neither Rod Serling, with his screenplay, nor Frank Sinatra and Tony Franciosa, with their respective underacting and overacting, make any constructive contribution to a monotonously inadequate movie about robbing the 'Queen Mary' called *Assault on a Queen*. Sinatra is a tough guy with soft heart and a red plaid lining in his jacket, and gets to say things like 'She's in my gut so deep we breathe together ...'"

The New Yorker

"Sinatra is excellent as the mainspring of the plot. It is the kind of role he does best, sardonic, masculine, sympathetic. He handles the romantic scenes with Miss Lisi with conviction, and he is eminently conceivable as a soft-spoken tough guy."

James Powers, The Hollywood Reporter

With Tony Franciosa and Errol John

With Virna Lisi and Alf Kjellin

With Alf Kjellin

222

With Toby Robins

THE NAKED RUNNER · 1967

With Peter Vaughan

With Inger Stratton

With Derren Nesbitt

With Peter Vaughan

224

A Sinatra Enterprises Production. Released by Warner Bros. Technicolor; Techniscope. Directed by Sidney J. Furie. Produced by Brad Dexter. Screenplay by Stanley Mann. Based on the novel by Francis Clifford. Music by Harry Sukman. Orchestrations by Herbert Spencer. Director of photography, Otto Heller. Film editor, Barry Vince. Art director, Peter Proud. Assistant art director, Bill Alexander. Continuity, Pat Moon. Production manager, Fred Slark. Sound recorders, Maurice Askew and Peter Davies. Sound editors, Arthur Ridot and Alan Bell. Camera operator, Godfrey Godar. Hair dresser, Barbara Ritchie. Assistant director, Michael Dryhurst. Running time, 103 minutes.

CAST

Sam Laker, FRANK SINATRA; Slattery, PETER VAUGHAN; Colonel Hartmann, DERREN NESBITT; Karen, NADIA GRAY; Ruth, TOBY ROBINS; Anna, INGER STRATTON; Cabinet Minister, CYRIL LUCKHAM; Ritchie Jackson, EDWARD FOX; Joseph, J. A. B. DUBIN-BEHRMANN; Patrick Laker, MICHAEL NEWPORT.

STORY

Sam Laker, an American business man, is a widower living in London with his 14-year-old son, Patrick. He is planning to take Patrick with him on a business trip to the Leipzig Fair when he is contacted by a wartime buddy, Martin Slattery, now with British Intelligence. Slattery tells him that a British spy has defected to the Communists and must be killed, and asks Sam, a wartime marksman, to do the job. Sam refuses. Slattery then asks him to at least deliver a message in Leipzig, and Sam reluctantly agrees when he learns that it will help Karen Gisevius, an underground worker who had helped him during the war. Sam delivers the message, but upon returning to his hotel finds that Patrick has been kidnapped. A Colonel Hartmann informs him that his son is being held hostage until he completes a mission for East Germany—the assassination of a man in Copenhagen. For his son's safety, Sam agrees, but the victim fails to appear. Returning to Leipzig, Sam is told that Patrick has been killed by Hartmann because the assignment wasn't carried out. Determined to avenge his son's murder, Sam studies Hartmann's movements and sights his telescopic rifle on a highway Hartmann is scheduled to travel. As the car passes, Sam fires and kills the occupant. As Sam makes his getaway, he is met by Slattery and Hartmann and told that Patrick is safe, that he has been the pawn in an elaborate plan, and that the man he killed was the defector-spy.

225

With Derren Nesbitt

REVIEWS

"It's a Frank Sinatra production, starring Sinatra. Which raises the question: why has Sinatra not developed the professional pride in his movies that he takes in his recordings? *The Naked Runner* might be a good movie to read by if there were light in the theatre. Did Sinatra read the Stanley Mann script? An implausible, unconvincing spy story without a single witty idea, and the star's role that of an anxious lifeless mouse. Sinatra wouldn't come on that way to the television audience; why does he have so little regard for the movie audience?"

Pauline Kael, *The New Republic*

"Of Sinatra, it must be said that even in this undemonstrative rendition of undistinguished material, he commands the screen. Given the plot, there must have been a temptation to shout, moan and chew the scenery. He put the temptation down, way down, and understates the histrionics. The result is a sense of power held in check, of power wasted."

Charles Champlin, Los Angeles *Times*

"Sinatra performs well enough. The only further interest is yet another variation on the mind-bending theme so much in vogue these days. 'It's a question of motivation and response,' intones a gimlet-eyed psychiatrist, preparing Sinatra by proxy for his part as a homicidal puppet. Just as the record industry owes so much to RCA Victor and His Master's Voice, the movie business seems indebted to Pavlov and His Subject's Slobber."

Joseph Morgenstern, *Newsweek*

"The story is full of opportunities for drama, but the audience has only the script's word that *The Naked Runner* is a suspense film. Other than swiveling a pair of nervous ferret eyes, Sinatra shows no hint of emotion.... As in many another amateurish spy film, Sinatra and company have forgotten to look for the enemy within—a soggy scenario that gummed up the caper from the start."

Time

"Sinatra conveys very well, by quiet and interior acting, the demeanour of a man who doesn't much like himself....What the film discloses at the beginning is that the psychological hoax is not being perpetrated by communists, but by British Intelligence, in order to eliminate a defector who is in transit from west to east with a headful of secrets. Laker will be ideal for the job, because all the regular secret agents are known on the other side and are unable to function as nimbly. All that is necessary is to have Laker in the right place at the right time, itching for the kill."

Gordon Gow, *Films and Filming*

"It is curious how Frank Sinatra repeatedly gets himself involved in films about fellows who do violent things with guns—gangsters, soldiers or assassins. He seems intensely attracted to stories in which he as the leading character is called upon to kill."

Bosley Crowther, *The New York Times*

TONY ROME · 1967

With Sue Lyon

With Richard Conte

With Jill St. John

An Arcola-Millfield Production. Released by 20th Century-Fox. Color by DeLuxe; Panavision. Directed by Gordon Douglas. Produced by Aaron Rosenberg. Screenplay by Richard L. Breen. Based on the novel Miami Mayhem *by Marvin H. Albert. Music by Billy May. Director of photography, Joseph Biroc. Film editor, Robert Simpson. Art directors, Jack Martin Smith and James Roth. Set decorators, Walter M. Scott and Warren Welch. Costumes by Moss Mabry. Makeup by Ben Nye; Mr. Sinatra's makeup by Layne Britton. Hair stylist, Edith Lindon. Sound by Howard Warren and David Dockendorf. Assistant to the producer, Michael Romanoff. Assistant director, Richard Lang. Action scenes directed by Buzz Henry. Unit production manager, David Silver. Title song by Lee Hazlewood, sung by Nancy Sinatra. Song "Something Here Inside of Me" by Billy May and Randy Newman. Running time, 110 minutes.*

With Jill St. John

CAST

Tony Rome, FRANK SINATRA; *Ann Archer,* JILL ST. JOHN; *Lieutenant Santini,* RICHARD CONTE; *Rita Kosterman,* GENA ROWLANDS; *Rudolph Kosterman,* SIMON OAKLAND; *Adam Boyd,* JEFFREY LYNN; *Vic Rood,* LLOYD BOCHNER; *Ralph Turpin,* ROBERT J. WILKE; *Sally Bullock,* VIRGINIA VINCENT; *Fat Candy,* JOAN SHAWLEE; *Donald Pines,* RICHARD KRISHER; *Jules Langley,* LLOYD GOUGH; *Oscar,* BABE HART; *Mrs. Schuyler,* TEMPLETON FOX; *Packy,* ROCKY GRAZIANO; *Irma,* ELISABETH FRASER; *Catleg,* SHECKY GREENE; *Lorna Boyd,* JEANNE COOPER; *Henrik Ruyter,* HARRY DAVIS; *Sam Boyd,* STANLEY ROSS; *Georgia McKay,* DEANNA LUND; *Nimmo,* BUZZ HENRY; *Bartender,* JOE E. ROSS; *Maitre D',* MICHAEL ROMANOFF; *Photo Girl,* TIFFANY BOLLING; and DIANA PINES; SUE LYON.

STORY

Tony Rome is a Miami private eye who lives on his boat, the *Straight Pass*. Summoned by his ex-partner, Ralph Turpin, who runs a motel, Tony removes a drunken socialite, Diana Pines, and takes her home to her rich father, Rudolph Kosterman, and her stepmother, Rita. Kosterman hires Tony to discover what troubles Diana. Tony learns that a diamond pin of Diana's is lost and that a lot of people are looking for it, including a man called Nimmo and a gunman, Catleg. It develops that the pin is fake, as, indeed, are all the Kosterman jewels. Turpin is murdered, and Tony thinks the death is connected with Diana's trouble. Aided in his sleuthing by Ann Archer, a predatory divorcee, Tony finds that Diana has been giving money to her alcoholic mother, Lorna, now married to Adam Boyd.

After an attempt by Catleg on Kosterman's life and an attempt by Rita on his own life, Tony learns that Nimmo is Rita's ex-husband and has been blackmailing her because she never got a valid divorce to marry Kosterman. Nimmo took Rita's jewels and replaced them with fakes, and when Diana lost her pin Nimmo tried to retrieve it, killing Turpin and being mortally wounded by him. Tony goes to the Boyd place and finds Boyd and Catleg about to bury Nimmo. Boyd confesses he tried to have Kosterman killed so he could get the family fortune through his stepdaughter, Diana. Lieutenant Santini, called by Tony, arrests Boyd and Catleg, and the Kostermans promise to care for Lorna after they are properly remarried. Tony decides it is time to take a vacation with Ann, but she thinks life with him would be too hazardous and returns to her estranged husband. Tony sets sail alone on the *Straight Pass*.

REVIEWS

"What gives the movie its strength and interest is that in Tony Rome Sinatra is able to play a character much like himself, or part of himself: wisecracking, tough, mobile, romantic, world-bruised but idealistic. Sinatra plays the part, or himself, to the hilt, and while this may not convert any Sinatraphobes to the fold it is likely to delight everybody else."

Charles Champlin, *Los Angeles Times*

"In *Tony Rome*, Frank Sinatra appears as a private eye for the first time. That fact may be of some interest to members of his immediate family.... Others are likely to find the movie nothing more than a blatantly inept, uncredited remake of Humphrey Bogart's 1946 *The Big Sleep*. That Sinatra is no Bogart is hardly news. What is more to the point is that neither Screen Writer Richard Breen nor Director Gordon Douglas affords him much opportunity to be Sinatra, an attractive enough role under proper auspices.... It remains one of Hollywood's major mysteries why a performer who puts so much style into his records so often sabotages his genuine talents in shoddy and ill-chosen movie vehicles."

Time

"It has not escaped the attention of a few hundred million persons in the land that a gentleman named Frank Sinatra is one of the phenomena of our age. Certainly his range and vitality as an entertainer are phenomenal, and his extracurricular reputation is awesome, to say the least. That's why it is provoking—nay, disturbing and depressing beyond belief—to see this acute and awesome figure turning up time and again in strangely tricky and trashy motion pictures. . . His *Von Ryan's Express* was an outrageous and totally disgusting display of romantic exhibitionism in a pseudo-wartime environment. *Marriage on the Rocks* was a tawdry and witless trifle about a bored married man, and *Assault on a Queen* was another of Sinatra's projections of himself as the altogether knowledgeable leader of a gang of thieves.

Now comes the latest selection, *Tony Rome*, which has the master of several realms of contemporary enterprise being cynical but sincere and valiant as a beat-up Miami Beach private eye. The role is strictly one of noncommitment—a lone detective out for himself—and it simply exposes its rugged protagonist in an assortment of corrupt and sleazy environments and incidents. . . . This sort of business is familiar, and if Sinatra chooses to go in for it in a style that emulates Humphrey Bogart's to a certain extent, that's his affair. Although he quite clearly endeavors in this film, as he has done before, to galvanize the character of a me-first loner as Bogart so frequently and effectively did, he comes up with a callous, cool-cat character somewhat short of old Bogey's.

The clue to Sinatra's sad shortcoming is that he willfully or carelessly allows his film—and his film it is, beyond question—to be sprinkled with many globs of sheer bad taste that manifest a calculated pandering to those who are easily and crudely amused. What grieves a long-time moviegoer is to remember how bright and promising he used to be, beginning with his charming performance in *Anchors Aweigh* and moving on into his poignant performance in *From Here to Eternity*."

Bosley Crowther, *The New York Times*

"Frank Sinatra has been a talent in search of a role ever since *The Manchurian Candidate*, and at last, in *Tony Rome*, he has found himself one. Ironically, though, he has had to fit himself into a type molded long before by Humphrey Bogart and, before him, by Dashiell Hammett. Sinatra, now in his middle years, baggy under the eyes, is nicely suited for playing the hardbitten, cynical private eye of Marvin Albert's novel.

Formerly a member of the Miami police force, he works out of an office modeled on Bogey's in *The Maltese Falcon*, lives in a cabin cruiser docked at a Miami marina, checks out a dozen or more oddball characters, flouts the usual police procedures, stumbles over the usual quota of corpses, contributes to the quota himself, gets himself beaten up and knocked out, and finds time during his investigations for some amorous dalliance with one of the females he encounters. If it all sounds highly unoriginal, indeed it is, and I, for one, kept waiting for Mary Astor to show up. Yet *Tony Rome* is lively and entertaining, and for this we must thank both the capable Mr. Sinatra and the persistent ghost of Mr. Bogart. In fact, the film makes no bones about its purpose—that of updating the Bogart 'Shamus' formula, which still can cast its spell."

Hollis Alpert, *The Saturday Review*

With Gena Rowlands

THE DETECTIVE · 1968

An Arcola-Millfield Production. Released by 20th Century Fox. Color by Deluxe; Panavision. Directed by Gordon Douglas. Produced by Aaron Rosenberg. Screenplay by Abby Mann. Based on the novel by Roderick Thorp. Music by Jerry Goldsmith. Orchestration by Warren Barker. Director of photography, Joseph Biroc. Film editor, Robert Simpson, Art directors, Jack Martin Smith and William Creber. Set decorators, Walter M. Scott and Jerry Wunderlich. Costumes by Moss Mabry. Makeup by Dan Striepeke; Mr. Sinatra's makeup by Layne Britton. Hair stylist, Edith Lindon. Special photographic effects by L. B. Abbott and Art Cruickshank. Sound by Harry M. Lindgren and David Dockendorf. Assistant director, Richard Lang. Unit production manager, David Silver. Technical adviser, Lt. Arthur E. Schultheiss, N.Y.P.D. Running time, 114 minutes.

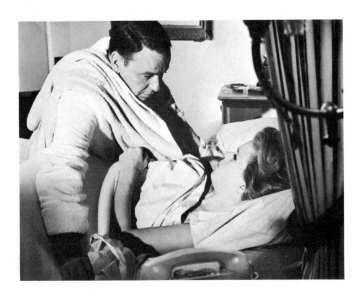

With Lee Remick

CAST

Joe Leland, FRANK SINATRA; *Karen Leland*, LEE REMICK; *Lt. Curran*, RALPH MEEKER; *Lt. Dave Schoenstein*, JACK KLUGMAN; *Chief Tom Farrell*, HORACE McMAHON; *Dr. Wendell Roberts*, LLOYD BOCHNER; *Colin MacIver*, WILLIAM WINDOM; *Felix Tesla*, TONY MUSANTE; *Det. Robbie Loughren*, AL FREEMAN, JR.; *Det. Mickey Nestor*, ROBERT DUVALL; *Mercidis*, PAT HENRY; *Officer Tanner*, PATRICK MC VEY; *Carol Linjack*, DIXIE MARQUIS; *Officer Kelly*, SUGAR RAY ROBINSON; *Rachel Schoenstein*, RENEE TAYLOR; *Teddy Leikman*, JAMES INMAN; *Harmon*, TOM ATKINS; and *Norma MacIver*, JACQUELINE BISSET.

With Tony Musante

STORY

Detective Joe Leland arrives at the scene of a brutal mutilation murder of a homosexual. With the reputation of the hottest homicide man in New York, Leland is proud to be a cop, as his father was, and concerned with doing a good, honest job. He makes the rounds of homosexual hangouts, gets a lead, and arrests a suspect, Felix Tesla. When third degree methods fail, Leland takes over, gains Tesla's confidence, and persuavively extracts a confession. Tesla is electrocuted. Although Leland wins a coveted promotion, he has reservations because he recognized that Tesla was psychotic.

At home, Leland has another problem: his wife, Karen, has become a nymphomaniac. They separate, but Leland, still in love, can't bring himself to divorce her.

Then Norma MacIver approaches Leland, asking him to investigate the death of her husband, Colin, listed by the police as a suicide. Among MacIver's papers Leland finds evidence of an organization involving city officials

With Horace McMahon

With Ralph Meeker

With Lee Remick

With Jacqueline Bisset

who buy ghetto property for public purposes but for private profit. When Curran, a fellow detective, suggests Leland drop the case and hints at a pay-off, Leland belts him. An attempt to kill Leland fails when he kills his two assailants. A psychiatrist friend of Norma's, Dr. Roberts, also tries to halt the investigation. In Roberts' office Leland finds tapes made by MacIver and forces the doctor to play them. The tapes reveal that it was MacIver, tortured by the discovery of his own bisexuality, who killed the homosexual for whose murder Tesla died.

Appalled that he has sent an innocent man to the chair, knowing that he is ruined as a cop, and deeply bitter that so much of his community, and much of his own department, is crooked, Leland decides to make the full story public. He leaves the force to push for reform in new ways, and to rebuild his life, perhaps with Norma, after twenty years as a detective.

REVIEWS

"As for Sinatra, this is his most effective performance in a long time; he acts many scenes with a sharp emotional edge that has been missing in his recent work."

Richard Gertner, *Motion Picture Herald*

"Sinatra has honed his laconic, hep veneer to the point of maximum credibility, and his detective Joe Leland is his best performance and role since *The Manchurian Candidate*."

Ray Loynd, *The Hollywood Reporter*

"The lurid plot line is boldly enlivened, if that is the word, by dialogue that still seems new to the recently liberalized screen. Someone who happens to wander into a showing of *The Detective* after a movie absence of, say, three years, may well doubt what he sees and hears. Abby Mann, adept as he is at finding vulgarities for Sinatra to enunciate, tops himself with the crude moral homilies he inserts, presumably to demonstrate the film's crusading spirit. . . . Yet, teeth-grating, eye-offending as *The Detective* is for much of its length, it must be admitted that Gordon Douglas does have something of a flair for catching the more raffish aspects of city life, the look of a precinct station, routine details of crime detection. And he sees to it that Sinatra emerges as a solid actor as well as solid citizen."

Hollis Alpert, *Saturday Review*

With Al Freeman, Jr.

234

LADY IN CEMENT · 1968

An Arcola-Millfield Production. Released by 20th Century-Fox. Color by DeLuxe; Panavision. Directed by Gordon Douglas. Produced by Aaron Rosenberg. Screenplay by Marvin H. Albert and Jack Guss. Based on the novel by Marvin H. Albert. Music composed and conducted by Hugo Montenegro. Orchestration by Billy May. Director of photography, Joseph Biroc. Film editor, Robert Simpson. Art director, LeRoy Deane. Set decorators, Walter M. Scott and Jerry Wunderlich. Costumes by Moss Mabry. Makeup by Dan Striepeke; Mr. Sinatra's makeup by Layne Britton. Hair stylist, Edith Linton. Sound by Howard Warren and David Dockendorf. Special photographic effects by L. B. Abbott and Art Cruickshank. Assistant to the producer, Michael Romanoff. Assistant director, Richard Lang. Underwater sequence staged by Riccou Browning. Unit production manager, David Silver. Running time, 93 minutes.

With Richard Conte

CAST

Tony Rome, FRANK SINATRA; *Kit Forrest*, RAQUEL WELCH; *Earl Gronsky*, DAN BLOCKER; *Lieutenant Santini*, RICHARD CONTE; *Al Mungar*, MARTIN GABEL; *Maria Baretto*, LAINIE KAZAN; *Hal Rubin*, PAT HENRY; *Paul Mungar*, STEVE PECK; *Audrey*, VIRGINIA WOOD; *Arnie Sherwin*, RICHARD DEACON; *Danny Yale*, FRANK RAITER; *Frenchy*, PETER HOCK; *Shev*, ALEX STEVENS; *Sandra Lomax*, CHRISTINE TODD; *Sidney, the Organizer*, MAC ROBBINS; *The Kid, Tighe Santini*, TOMMY UHLAR; *Paco*, RAY BAUMEL; *McComb*, PAULY DASH; *The Pool Boy*, ANDY JARRELL.

With Pat Henry

STORY

Scouting for buried treasure off the Florida coast near Miami, Tony Rome finds a dead, naked girl, her feet encased in cement. Attempting to discover her identity, Tony meets a huge ex-convict named Gronsky, a former boy friend of the "lady in cement," who hires Tony to confirm the nude's identity. Tony soon becomes involved with Kit Forrest, a shapely heiress, and Al Mungar, a former racket chief. Kit, an alcoholic, has been led by Mungar to believe that she is the dead girl's murderer. With occasional help—and hindrance—from his detective friend, Lieutenant Santini, Tony solves the mystery of the water-logged lady, and hies himself off to the Bahamas with Kit.

REVIEWS

"To follow the success of last year's *Tony Rome*, 20th-Fox has put together a similar package about the

Miami-based detective, re-teamed star Frank Sinatra with producer Aaron Rosenberg and director Gordon Douglas, and added the double-barreled charms of Raquel Welch to flesh out the proceedings. The result is a brittle, gutsy drama spiked with some hard-hitting dialog and a healthy amount of exposed flesh that should appeal to all but the discerning and the squeamish."

Box Office

"*Lady in Cement* follows in the gumshoe ruttings of *Tony Rome* but has the better fortune to follow Frank Sinatra's hit, *The Detective*. The sequel to Sinatra's original Miami Beach lounge act is better on several counts. It manages to have fun at its own expense rather than relying wholly on leering bad taste. While it continues Fox's recent breakthrough in nipple exposure and again drags on the fags, broads and hoods who people the world of small time private eye Tony Rome, the film has a fresher script, lighter hands playing, and the same sharp direction and cinematography. Sinatra has refined the characterization to a sort of resort-Leo Gorcey . . . "

John Mahoney, *The Hollywood Reporter*

"Tony Rome is back and, as before, Frank Sinatra has got him down perfectly. Sinatra projects this ex-cop-turned-private-shamus with a time-tested fictional blend of insouciance, cynicism, battered but surviving idealism, wisecrackery, courage, libido, thirst and all the more interesting hungers. He clearly enjoys the role and it is this evident pleasure which carbonates the thin material with lively amusement."

Charles Champlin, *Los Angeles Times*

"The sum total of this mass of pseudo-reality will be titillation in part for some, repulsion for those looking for the slightest relationship to the human condition."

Edward Lipton, *Film and Television Daily*

With Raquel Welch

With Dan Blocker

With Alex Stevens and Dan Blocker

With Michele Carey

DIRTY DINGUS MAGEE · 1970

Released by Metro-Goldwyn-Mayer. MetroColor; Panavision. Produced and directed by Burt Kennedy. Screenplay by Tom & Frank Waldman and Joseph Heller. Based on the novel The Ballad of Dingus Magee *by David Markson. Music by Jeff Alexander; additional music by Billy Strange. Title song by Mack David, sung by The Mike Curb Congregation. Director of photography, Harry Stradling, Jr. Film editor, William B. Gulick. Art directors, George W. Davis and J. McMillan Johnson. Set decorators, Robert R. Benton and Chuck Pierce. Costumes by Yvonne Wood. Makeup by Shotgun Britton. Hair stylist, Naomi A. Cavin. Sound by Hal Watkins and Bruce Wright. Associate producer, Richard E. Lyons. Assistant director, Al Jennings. Unit production manager, John W. Rogers. Stunt coordinator, Jerry Gatlin. Running time, 91 minutes.*

CAST

Dingus Magee, FRANK SINATRA; *Hoke Birdsill*, GEORGE KENNEDY; *Belle Knops*, ANNE JACKSON; *Prudence Frost*, LOIS NETTLETON; *John Wesley Hardin*, JACK ELAM; *Anna Hotwater*, MICHELE CAREY; *General*, JOHN DEHNER; *Rev. Green*, HENRY JONES; *Stuart*, HARRY CAREY, JR.; *Chief Crazy Blanket*, PAUL FIX; *Shotgun Rider*, DONALD BARRY; *Stagecoach Driver*, MIKE WAGNER.

STORY

During the 1880's near Yerkey's Hole, New Mexico, Hoke Birdsill runs into a larcenous indigent, Dingus Magee, who robs him. Hoke reports the robbery to the local mayor, Belle Knops, who is also the madame of the tiny town's sole industry, a whorehouse supported by cavalrymen from a nearby fort. Appointed sheriff by Belle, Hoke goes after Dingus, finds him in the bushes with Anna Hotwater, a young Indian girl, and locks him in jail. Belle learns that the cavalry is moving out (the General wants to beat Custer to the Little Big Horn) and fears her business will be ruined. When Anna helps Dingus escape, Belle blames the Indians and convinces the cavalry to stay and crush the "uprising."

Everyone else is after Dingus: Hoke is after him for stealing a stagecoach strongbox, the Indians are after him for refusing to trade his carbine for Anna, and *she* is after him to "make bim bam." Dingus, in turn, is after Belle and her money, although he takes time to dally with the local school teacher, Prudence Frost, whose amorousness belies her name. After repeated chases, captures, and escapes, Dingus finally flees from Yerkey's Hole with Belle's money and the buxom Anna.

REVIEWS

"Burt Kennedy is one of the best directors working in westerns today. He's equally at home with comedy (*The Rounders, Support Your Local Sheriff*) and with grim allegory (*Welcome to Hard Times*). But with *Dirty Dingus Magee* he has come a cropper—and how! Kennedy puts his cast through a series of shenanigans of description-defying silliness. In the title role is Frank Sinatra as a frontier rascal. George Kennedy is his equally unscrupulous pal. The crude double entendres and sexy romping these middle-agers go through are enough to make you cringe with embarrassment for them. In its absence of wit, furthermore, the chiseling and double-crossing the stars indulge in and the burlesquing of Indians and their ways that we're supposed to find so funny is merely disgusting. A lot of talent is wasted in *Dirty Dingus Magee*. So is our time in watching it."

Kevin Thomas, Los Angeles *Times*

"The wonder is that it took three writers to fashion the screenplay for *Dirty Dingus Magee*, because this MGM release has to be the most tasteless, witless and fatuous spoof on Western conventions yet to have been filmed."

Craig Fisher, *The Hollywood Reporter*

"The laughs are cheap and very scarce and the corruption of values is total in *Dirty Dingus Magee*, a Western spoof that carried several gifted people a bit too far along the low road. Joseph Heller is credited as one of the screenplay's three authors, believe it or not. . . . Director Burt Kennedy, heretofore the creator of a few better-than-average Westerns, settles for stock commercial japes. His idea of a sight gag is a dog lifting its leg in front of a burning brothel."

Playboy

"Sinatra, who proved his acting abilities in such pictures as *From Here to Eternity* and *Man with the Golden Arm*, merely lends his presence to *Dirty Dingus*—and not too much of that. . . . He seems neffably bored and totally uncommitted to the whole project—as well he might be."

Arthur Knight, *Saturday Review*

With Michele Carey

With Michele Carey and Paul Fix

240

Released by Metro-Goldwyn-Mayer. Metrocolor; 70mm. Executive producer, Daniel Melnick. Produced, directed and written by Jack Haley, Jr. Photography by Gene Polito, Ernest Laszlo, Russell Metty, Ennio Guarnieri, Allan Green; Music adapted by Henry Mancini. Music Supervision by Jesse Kaye. Editors: Bud Friedgen, David W. Blewitt. Running time: 137 minutes.

CAST

Narrator-Hosts: FRED ASTAIRE, BING CROSBY, GENE KELLY, PETER LAWFORD, LIZA MINNELLI, DONALD O'CONNOR, DEBBIE REYNOLDS, MICKEY ROONEY, FRANK SINATRA, JAMES STEWART, ELIZABETH TAYLOR

STORY

Lengthy extracts from the memorable musicals from MGM's Golden Years—one hundred of them from 1929's *The Hollywood Revue* to 1958's *Gigi*—made up this unique, critically acclaimed and hugely popular nostalgia extravaganza. Cherished moments from these musicals were hosted, in various segments, by (mainly) MGM stars—Crosby had done only three pictures for the studio, O'Connor two, Minnelli just one (as a toddler) but was there to reminisce about mom and dad. Each wandered about the soon-to-be-no-more MGM lot, with Sinatra opening and closing the film and commenting, sometimes flippantly, about singers such as Charles King (from *Broadway Melody of 1929*), Nelson Eddy and Jeanette MacDonald, and others. *Variety* seemed to take to *That's Entertainment!* calling it "outstanding, stunning, sentimental, exciting, colorful, enjoyable, spirit-lifting, tuneful, youthful, invigorating, zesty, respectful, heart-warming, awesome, cheerful, dazzling and richly satisfying." The success of this box office smash prompted MGM to put together *That's Entertainment, Part 2* in 1976 (directed by Gene Kelly) and then *That's Dancing!* in 1985—neither of which had the cohesion of the original which, it was agreed, used up all the prime clips.

REVIEWS

"When Grahame Greene was a movie critic in the 1930s, he detested close-ups of the open mouths of singers; his reviews complained steadily of teeth and tonsils. He would be miserable at *That's Entertainment!* ... but those who don't

share his phobia will hugely enjoy this movie...The pleasures are abundant...This isn't nostalgia, it's history."

Nora Sayre, *The New York Times*

"Jack Haley, Jr. wrote, produced and directed the sensational panorama, which should appeal to nostalgia fans of any age...*That's Entertainment!* is not about what people were, but what they did. And what they did, they did right...There's no point in enumerating all the clips, nor any particular favorites, since at this particular film feast, there are special memories for anyone over 30 and a whole lot of new experiences for younger patrons. Sinatra's closing comments note that the era of these films will never return—costs alone would be prohibitive, not counting contemporary attitudes of what constitutes class and chic."

Murf., *Variety*

THAT'S ENTERTAINMENT! • 1974

CONTRACT ON CHERRY STREET · 1977

An Artanis Production for Columbia Pictures Television. Metrocolor. Executive producer, Renée Valente. Produced by Hugh Benson. Directed by William A. Graham. Written by Edward Anhalt. Based on the book by Philip Rosenberg. Music by Jerry Goldsmith. Photography by Jack Priestley. Film editor, Eric Albertson. Art director, Robert Gundlach. Set decorator, Leslie S. Bloom. Costume designer, John Boxer. Makeup, Michael Maggi. Technical advisor, Sonny Grosso. Running time: 155 minutes.

CAST

Deputy Inspector Frank Hovannes, FRANK SINATRA; *Tommy Sinardos,* JAY BLACK; *Emily Hovannes,* VERNA BLOOM; *Capt. Ernie Weinberg,* MARTIN BALSAM; *Vincenzo Seruto,* JOE DE-SANTIS; *Baruch Waldman,* MARTIN GABEL; *Ron Polito,* HARRY GUARDINO; *Al Palmini,* JAMES LUISI; *Lou Savage,* MICHAEL NOURI; *Eddie Manzaro,* MARCO ST. JOHN; *Robert Obregon,* HENRY SILVA *Jack Kittens,* RICHARD WARD; *Bob Halloran,* ADDISON POWELL; *Fran Marks,* STEVE INWOOD; *Otis Washington,* JOHNNY BARNES; *Phil Lombardi,* LENNY MONTANA; *Richie Saint,* MURRAY MOSTON; *Mickey Sinardos,* ROBERT DAVI; *Jeff Diamond,* NICKY BLAIR; *Flo Weinberg,* ESTELLE OMENS; *Jimmy Monks,* RAY SERRA; *Himself,* BILL JORGENSON; *Rhodes,* SONNY GROSSO; *Al Jenner,* RANDY JURGENSON; *Admissions nurse,* LOUISE CAMPBELL; *Silvera,* JILLY RIZZO

STORY

In his television movie debut, Frank Sinatra is Frank Hovannes, a hard-driven New York deputy police inspector who heads up the elite Office of Crime Control. He is under increasing pressure from department brass to clean up a numbers racket, and goes over the edge when his close friend and team partner, Ernie Weinberg, is killed in a shoot-out. With members of his squad, and unauthorized, he goes after key underworld leaders, but it isn't long before his men have taken the law into their own hands. A mobster not on his hit list is slain, and he despairs that his plan to nab the city's top gangsters has gotten out of control and utimately will lead to an atrocious bloodbath.

REVIEWS

"*Contract on Cherry Street* stars Frank Sinatra in the first film he made for television. With a script by Edward Anhalt,

the project begins promisingly with some crisp dialogue and crisp location shots reminiscent of the best of *Kojak* or a previous Sinatra film called *The Detective*...Frank and his fellow cops want desperately to succeed, but, as someone hysterically notes, 'everybody is one somebody's payroll'...They set out to kill the killers, triggering a chain of events that ends in disaster for just about everybody, including the creators of this fascist fantasy...From Mr. Sinatra on down, there are a number of quite good performances wasted in this curious exercise...the birdbrained plot of *Contract on Cherry Street* proves fatal to all concerned.

John J. O'Connor, *The New York Times*

With Johnny Barnes

THE FIRST DEADLY SIN · 1980

An Artanis/Cinema Seven production. A Filmways release. TVC Color, prints by Movielab. Executive producers, Frank Sinatra and Elliott Kastner. Produced by George Pappas and Mark Shanker. Directed by Brian G. Hutton. Screenplay by Mann Rubin. Based on the novel by Lawrence Sanders. Music by Gordon Jenkins. Director of photography, Jack Priestley. Film editor, Eric Albertson. Art director, Woody Mackintosh. Set decorator, Robert Drumheller. Costume designer, Gary Jones. Costumes for Faye Dunaway, Theoni V. Aldredge. Makeup, Mike Maggi. Stunt coordinator, Stefanie Brooks. Running time: 112 minutes.

CAST

Lt. Edward Delaney, FRANK SINATRA; *Barbara Delaney*, FAYE DUNAWAY; *Daniel Blank*, DAVID DUKES; *Dr. Bernardi*, GEORGE COE; *Monica Gilbert*, BRENDA VACCARO; *Christopher Langley*, MARTIN GABEL; *Capt. Broughton*, ANTHONY ZERBE; *Dr. Sanford Ferguson*, JAMES WHITMORE; *Charles Lipsky*, JOE SPINELL; *Sonny Jordeen*, ANNA NAVARRO; *Sgt. Corelli*, JEFFREY DE MUNN; *John Rogers*, JOHN DEVANEY; *Calvin Sawtell*, JON DE VRIES; *Ben Johnson*, HUGH HURD; *Officer Curdy*, EDDIE JONES; *Officer Kendall*, VICTOR ARNOLD; *Carl Braggs*, TOM SIGNORELLI; *Delivery man*, FRED FUSTER; *Bill Garvin*, REUBEN GREEN; *Walt Ashman*, RICHARD BACKUS

STORY

Edward Delaney, a dedicated New York police lieutenant preparing to call it a career, finds himself immersed in cracking a particularly grisly murder, caring for a wife who's growing weaker in the hospital after a possibly bungled kidney operation, and breaking in a new by-the-book precinct commander. With the help of Dr. Sanford Ferguson, the police mortician, and Christopher Langley, an expert on weapons at the Metropolitan Museum, Delaney tracks down the murder implement—a climber's icepick—and determines he's on the trail of a psychopath, finally whittling down the list of suspects to one Daniel Blank (the name Delaney assigns to this "cipher"). Delaney proceeds to relentlessly harass Blank, who claims to have powerful friends in high places. Blank goads Delaney into shooting him, sinking his own career.

With Faye Dunaway

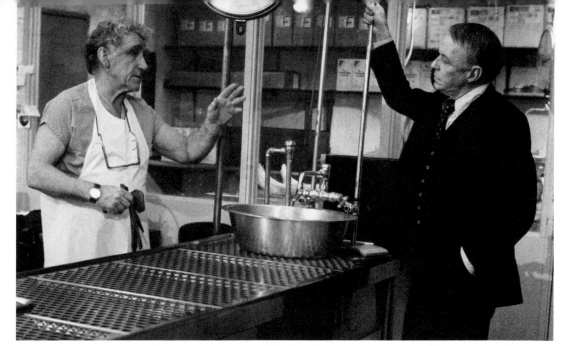

With James Whitmore

REVIEWS

"*The First Deadly Sin* worked better as a novel than it does as a film, since the devices that made the book eerie are confusing on the screen...[it] becomes a meandering tale, slowed down by tangential subplots and never as sharply honed as it might be. The mood is glum but never effectively bleak, and it's seldom suspenseful...Frank Sinatra plays Delaney as a hard-boiled professional, though the frequent hospital scenes with Faye Dunaway, who plays Mrs. Delaney, are designed to show the detective's softer side. Mr. Sinatra, returning to the screen after a long hiatus, is tough and credible in his role. But he and Miss Dunaway don't make a convincing enough couple to account for the long intervals the camera spends at her bedside."

Janet Maslin, *The New York Times*

"Otherwise a fairly routine and turgid crime meller, *The First Deadly Sin* commands some interest as Frank Sinatra's first film in 10 years and the first one in some time more that he appears to have taken with complete seriousness...he's

serious, direct and not at all the wise guy, amounting to a decent perf, even if the role might have called for a more obsessive and desperate attitude in the face of his career and wife slipping away from him simultaneously. The way he plays it, one can read the underlying feelings into his behavior, which might have worked to greater advantage had the telling of the tale possessed a more compelling edge."

Cart., *Variety*

"A certain gritty realism—in the environs of morgue and hospital—fails to elucidate the allegory which seems to be hovering in the background of this murky thriller. Religious imagery proliferates, and an odd parallel enforced only through the editing between the killer without a motive and the disease without a name. But a coherent theme never materialises and the religious symbols remain perfunctory and strictly exterior, in the end a convenient hook on which to hang the psychology of the rather unconvincing psychopath."

Mark Lefanu, *Monthy Film Bulletin*

With Joe Spinell

With Burt Reynolds and reuning erstwhile "Rat Pack" buddies Dean Martin, Shirley MacLaine and Sammy Davis, Jr. on the set.

CANNONBALL RUN II · 1983

A Golden Harvest Film. Released by Warner Bros. Technicolor. Executive producers, Raymond Chow and Andre Morgan. Produced by Albert S. Ruddy. Directed by Hal Needham. Screenplay by Hal Needham, Albert S. Ruddy and Harvey Miller. Based on characters created by Brock Yates. Music by Al Capps. Music supervisor, Snuff Garrett. Music coordinator, Dave Pell. Director of photography, Nick McLean. Animated sequence, Ralph Bakshi. Film editor, William Grodean. Art director, Tho. E. Azzari. Set decorator, Charles M. Graffo. Special effects, Philip Cory. Costume supervisor, Norman Stalling. Makeup, Tom Ellingwood. Stunt coordinator, Alan R. Gibbs. Running time: 108 minutes.

CAST

J.J. McClure, BURT REYNOLDS; *Victor ("Chaos")*, DOM DeLUISE; *Blake*, DEAN MARTIN; *Fenderbaum*, SAMMY DAVIS, JR.; *Sheik*, JAMIE FARR; *Betty*, MARILU HENNER; *Hymie*, TELLY SAVALAS; *Veronica*, SHIRLEY MACLAINE; *Jill*, SUSAN ANTON; *Marcie*, CATHERINE BACH; *1st fisherman*, FOSTER BROOKS; *2nd fisherman*, SID CAESAR; *Jackie*, JACKIE CHAN; *1st Chip*, TIM CONWAY; *Terry*, TONY DANZA; *Doc*, JACK ELAM; *Sonny*, MICHAEL GAZZO; *Arnold*, RICHARD KIEL; *2nd Chip*, DON KNOTTS; *King*, RICARDO MONTALBAN; *Homer*, JIM NABORS; *3rd fisherman*, LOUIS NYE; *Mrs. Goldfarb*, MOLLY PICON; *Don, Don*, CHARLES NELSON REILLY; *Tony*, ALEX ROCCO; *Slim*, HENRY SILVA; *Mack*, JOE THEISMANN; *Mel*, MEL TILLIS; *Caesar*, ABE VIGODA; *3rd Chip*, FRED DREYER; *Japanese Father*, DALE ISHIMOTO; *Pilots*, ARTE JOHNSON AND FRED S. RONNOW; *Young Cop*, CHRIS LEMMON; *Cal*, GEORGE LINDSAY; *The Slapper*, DOUG McCLURE; *Jilly*, JILLY RIZZO; *Police Officer*, DUB TAYLOR; AND FRANK SINATRA *as The Chairman*

STORY

Stunt racer J.J. McClure and his sidekick "Chaos" join a semi-illegal Trans American Cannonball Run in search of the $1 million prize being offered by the sheik son of a Middle Eastern king, not knowing that the fix is in so that his tribe can win. Among the characters with whom they get involved during the run from California to Connecticut: a couple of con-men pretending to be priests; a pair of brassy golddiggers from the chorus line of *The Sound of Music* passing themselves off as nuns; a metal-toothed giant and a kick-boxing Oriental; two fast-driving, mechanically-inclined bimbos; an inept Mafioso operating out of a ghost town near Las Vegas; a recalcitrant orangutan, and a powerful Vegas figure who looks suspiciously like Frank Sinatra, called on to help the racers abandon their rivalries and attempt to rescue the sheik after he is seized by mobsters. Who wins out of those listed above and gets not only the sheik's million but his undying gratitude should be obvious.

REVIEWS

Directed in slam-bang style by Hal Needham, the film is an endless string of cameo performances from a cast whose funny participants are badly outnumbered and whose television roots are unmistakable...the huge cast ranges from sleazy...to superfluous. Most of the performers who've been absent from the screen for a while look the worse for wear. Dean Martin has a bedroom scene with a woman much, much younger than he, and Frank Sinatra appears briefly, playing a [mob] king...The fact that *Cannonball Run II* isn't much good may not prevent it from becoming this summer's best-loved lowest-common-denominator comedy."

Janet Maslin, *The New York Times*

"While director Hal Needham continues to undermine his well-staged stuntwork with muddy photography and listless slapstick, Albert S. Ruddy must rate some credit for deal-making ability: in addition to winning Frank Sinatra's forgiveness after *The Godfather*, he has managed to reunite the supporting cast for [Francis] Coppola's Mafia epic (Alex Rocco, Michael Gazzo, Abe Vigoda) and the *Ocean's 11* Rat Pack (Sinatra, Davis, Martin) without coming up with so much as a funny line between them."

Kim Newman, *Monthly Film Bullentin*

"This film is so inept that the best actor in it is Jilly Rizzo. But he has a great advantage: he's only on screen five seconds. He doesn't have to talk...A combination of cynicism and arrogance hover over the production. The film plays as if former Cannonball colleagues—producer Albert Ruddy, director Hal Needham and stars Burt Reynolds, Dom DeLuise, Dean Martin and Sammy Davis, Jr.—don't even have to make an effort anymore. It's the good ol' boy network kind of fimmaking, joined this time by Frank Sinatra (playing himself) and Shirley MacLaine, in terms not endearing...If ever there's need of a classic example to show how overcrowding a production with a ton of stars is self-destructive, this is it."

Loyn, *Variety*

A SINATRA MISCELLANY

MAJOR BOWES' AMATEUR THEATRE OF THE AIR (1935)

Produced at Biograph Studios by Biograph Productions, Inc. Released by RKO Radio Pictures. Produced and Directed by John H. Auer. Photographed by Larry Williams and Tommy Hogan.

Major Bowes' Amateur Theatre of the Air was a series of two-reel short subjects, filmed in New York. Sinatra appeared in one of them, though exactly which one is not known. Director John Auer recalls that Sinatra and his instrumental group looked so ill-nourished that, to disguise their appearance, he had them perform a minstrel show in blackface. Sinatra was paid thirty-five dollars.

THE ROAD TO VICTORY (1944)

Produced by Warner Bros. for the U.S. Treasury Department. War Activities Committee release No. 98. Directed by LeRoy Prinz. Executive producer, Jack L. Warner. Produced by Gordon Hollingshead and Arnold Albert. Screenplay by James Bloodworth. Based on an original story by Mannie Manheim. Musical director, Leo F. Forbstein. Title song by Frank Loesser. Running time, 10 minutes.

CAST

OLIVE BLAKENEY, JACK CARSON, BING CROSBY, CARY GRANT, JAMES LYDON, IRENE MANNING, DENNIS MORGAN, CHARLES RUGGLES, FRANK SINATRA.

Sinatra's song: "Hot Time in the Town of Berlin" by Joe Bushkin and John De Vries.

The Road to Victory, distributed in the United States to promote the Fifth War Loan, was an abbreviated version of *The Shining Future*, originally produced by Warner Bros. in two reels for Canada's Sixth Victory Loan. The original cast, in addition to those listed above, included Deanna Durbin, Benny Goodman and his orchestra, Harry James, Herbert Marshall, and Harold Peary, but their footage was cut when *The Shining Future* was reduced to one reel for *The Road to Victory*.

THE ALL-STAR BOND RALLY (1945)

Produced by 20th Century-Fox for the U.S. Treasury Department. War Activities Committee release No. 120. Directed by Michael Audley. Produced by Fanchon. Script by Don Quinn. Music supervised by Alfred Newman. Music conducted by Emil Newman. Incidental score by Cyril J. Mockridge. Orchestrations by Arthur Morton, Maurice de Packh, Herbert Taylor, Herbert Spencer and Gene Rose. Musical arrangements for Frank Sinatra by Axel Stordahl. Director of photography, James Van Trees. Film editor, Stanley Rabjohn. Special photographic effects by Fred Sersen and Rollo Flora. Production supervisors, Ray Klune and Max Golden. Co-ordinator, Tom W. Baily. Assistant director, William Eckhardt. Unit production manager, Nate Watt. Song "Buy, Buy, Buy a Bond" by Jimmy McHugh and Harold Adamson. Running time, 19 minutes.

CAST

VIVIAN BLAINE, JEANNE CRAIN, BING CROSBY, LINDA DARNELL, BETTY GRABLE, JUNE HAVER, BOB HOPE, FAYE MARLOWE, HARPO MARX, FIBBER MC GEE AND MOLLY, CARMEN MIRANDA, FRANK SINATRA, Harry James and his orchestra.

Sinatra's song: "Saturday Night" by Jule Styne and Sammy Cahn.

SPECIAL CHRISTMAS TRAILER (1945)

Produced by Metro-Goldwyn-Mayer. Directed by Harry Loud. Musical directors, Nathaniel Shilkret and Axel Stordahl. Running time, 3 minutes.

Sinatra's song: "Silent Night, Holy Night" by Franz Gruber and Father Joseph Mohr.

This special Christmas short was distributed by MGM during December 1945.

LUCKY STRIKE SALESMAN'S MOVIE 48-A (1948)

Produced by The American Tobacco Co. Running time, 10 minutes.

The film describes the cultivation, harvesting, storing, buying, and manufacture of tobacco, and shows the work of three auctioneers, a warehouseman, and a buyer.

Sinatra appeared on screen with the Lucky Strike Quartette and the Hit Parade Orchestra, conducted by Axel Stordahl.

Sinatra's song: "Embraceable You" by George and Ira Gershwin.

INVITATION TO MONTE CARLO (1959)

A Richmond Film Production. Released by Valiant Films. Technicolor; Cinepanoramic. Written, produced, and directed by Euan Lloyd. Commentary written by Jack Davies; spoken by Leo Genn, Nicole Maurey, and E. V. H. Emmett. Cameramen, John Wilcox, Tony Braun, and Egil Woxholt. Music by William Hill Bowen; played by the George Melachrino Orchestra. Film editor, Terry Trench. Running time, 46 minutes.

CAST

Jacqueline, GERMAINE DAMAR; *Lindy,* GILDA EMMANUELI; *The Matron,* KATHARINE PAGE; *The Postman,* JEFFERSON CLIFFORD; PRINCE RAINIER OF MONACO, PRINCESS GRACE OF MONACO, FRANK SINATRA.

STORY

Lindy, a British orphan child, is picked to take a present to the royal baby of Prince Ranier and Princes Grace in the Principality of Monaco. The present is a kitten named "Tosca," and the slight narrative concerns Lindy's adventures en route from London to Monte Carlo, chaperoned by an air hostess. The film was made as a travel feature with the full cooperation of Monaco. Frank Sinatra is seen in one sequence, probably filmed at the time he was on the Riviera for the premiere of *Kings Go Forth.*

SINATRA IN ISRAEL (1962)

Produced by the Israeli Federation of Histadruth. Narrated by Frank Sinatra. Running time, 22½ minutes.

Sinatra's songs: "In the Still of the Night" by Cole Porter; "Without a Song" by Vincent Youmans.

This short was filmed in 1962 during Sinatra's nine-day tour of Israel, where he performed several concerts.

WILL ROGERS HOSPITAL TRAILER (1965)

Sinatra appeared in and narrated this 2½-minute trailer, describing the work of the Will Rogers Hospital, the O'Donnell Memorial Research Laboratories and the Will Rogers Teaching Institute at Saranac Lake, New York, and appealing for contributions to the Will Rogers Memorial Fund.

THREE "LOST" FILMS

In 1943 Frank Sinatra appeared in The March of Time's film, *Music at War,* singing "The Song Is You" by Jerome Kern and Oscar Hammerstein II, at Hunter College, New York. The March of Time, with the approval of the Navy, had been called in to take shots of the singer's appearance before a group of WAVES. RKO Radio Pictures, to whom Sinatra was then under contract, sued to prevent distribution of the short subject on the grounds that his filmed appearance violated his contract, and an injunction against showing the film was granted. Sinatra's scenes were deleted, and the short, retitled *Upbeat in Music,* was released in December of 1943.

An unrealized Sinatra project much to be regretted is the unfinished *Finian's Rainbow* (1954–1955), produced and directed by John Hubley for release by Distributors Corporation of America. Planned as a full-length animated film, it featured the voices of Frank Sinatra, Ella Logan, Barry Fitzgerald, Ella Fitzgerald, Louis Armstrong, and Jim Backus. Although no animation was done, scoring and recording were completed under musical director Lyn Murray. Sinatra's songs, from the score by Burton Lane and E. Y. Harburg, included "If This Isn't Love," "Necessity," "Old Devil Moon," and "Great Come and Get It Day." After $300,000 had been spent preparing *Finian's Rainbow,* additional financing could not be found and the film was abandoned.

In 1955 Sinatra was signed for the role of Billy Bigelow in 20th Century-Fox's lavish version of Rodgers and Hammerstein's *Carousel.* Fox intended shooting the film both in conventional 35mm. CinemaScope and in its new 55mm. CinemaScope for road showings. Sinatra maintained that one process was enough and that the work of shooting each sequence twice would prevent his fulfilling singing engagements in Las Vegas, but the studio held firm. On the day before production started at Boothbay Harbor, Maine, Sinatra walked out, on the grounds that Fox was in fact asking him to make two movies for the price of one. He was replaced by Gordon MacRae, and the extensive pre-recordings that Sinatra had made went to waste. Ironically, Fox found that it could reduce 55mm. prints to 35mm., and *Carousel* finally was shot only in the larger process.